BASIC
Microcomputer Programs
for
Urban Analysis
and Planning

BASIC
Microcomputer Programs
for
Urban Analysis
and Planning

John R. Ottensmann
Indiana University School of Public and
Environmental Affairs, Indianapolis

Chapman and Hall / New York
Methuen / London

To my parents

First published 1985
by Chapman and Hall
29 West 35th St., New York, N.Y. 10001
Published in Great Britain by Methuen & Co. Ltd.
11 New Fetter Lane, London EC4P 4EE

© 1985 Chapman and Hall

Printed in the United States of America

Library of Congress Cataloging in Publication Data

Ottensmann, John R.
    BASIC microcomputer programs for urban analysis and
planning.

    Bibliography: p.
    Includes index.
    1. Cities and towns—Computer programs. 2. City
planning—Computer programs. 3. Basic (Computer
program language) I. Title. II. Title: B.A.S.I.C.
microcomputer programs for urban analysis and planning.
HT153.O88 1985   307'.12'0285425   84-27514
ISBN 0-412-00741-X
ISBN 0-412-00871-8 (pbk.)

British Library Cataloging in Publication Data

Ottensmann, John R.
    BASIC microcomputer programs for urban
analysis and planning.
    1. City planning—Computer programs 2. Basic
(Computer program language) 3. Microcomputers
I. Title
711'.4'0285424   HT166

ISBN 0-412-00741-X
ISBN 0-412-00871-8 Pbk

Contents

Trademarks

Apple and Applesoft are trademarks of Apple Computer, Inc.
Atari is a trademark of Atari Corporation.
CBASIC is a registered trademark of Compiler Systems, Inc.
CP/M is a registered trademark of Digital Research Corporation.
IBM is a registered trademark of International Business Machines Corporation.
Lotus and 1-2-3 are trademarks of Lotus Development Corporation.
Microsoft is a registered trademark of Microsoft Corporation.
Multiplan is a trademark of Microsoft Corporation.
Osborne 1 is a trademark of Osborne Computer Corporation.
VisiCalc is a registered trademark of VisiCorp, Inc.
Z-80 is a registered trademark of Zilog Corporation, a division of Exxon Corporation.

Preface

The analytical models employed in urban analysis and planning require the power of computers for most practical applications. The development of microcomputers brings this computing power to many prospective users of these models. This book presents a series of BASIC language programs implementing many of the common analytical models—programs that allow the methods to be used on most microcomputers.

Very little specialized computer knowledge is required to use these programs. All of the programs are completely interactive; the user merely enters the required information in response to prompts by the programs. The programs have not been designed for specific machines. Instead, they have been written in a very limited common subset of the BASIC language, in a manner that permits their operation on nearly all computers with BASIC. Thus, the programs should run on most microcomputers. The programs are thoroughly commented and are structured with multiple subroutines. Users fluent in BASIC will be able to follow the operation of these programs and can readily make modifications to meet special needs.

Nine programs are included for population and economic forecasting, for spatial interaction, and for facility location. Programs for the Trend Projection Models and the Population Cohort-Survival Model address the making of population projections. For economic forecasting, three programs are included: Economic Base Model, Shift and Share Model, and Input–Output Model. Single- and Double-Constrained Gravity Model programs meet the needs for the analysis and projection of spatial interactions. For determining locations for public facilities, programs are provided for the Facility Location on a Plane Model and the Facility Location on a Network Model.

The first chapter of this book gives a general description of the programs along with detailed instructions for their operation. The nine programs are presented in separate chapters. Each of these chapters describes the model or models being implemented, including all relevant analytical details. A description of the program, its features, and its operation comes next. A sample problem is presented, accompanied by the record of the actual process of using the program for generating a solution. Finally, each chapter concludes with the full listing of the BASIC program.

The concluding chapter gives a very brief introduction to other applications of microcomputers in urban planning. Additional usable material is provided in the appendices, which include subroutines adding graphics display capabilities to several of the programs. The routines in Appendix A generate fairly crude character graphics displays that will work on virtually any system. The more sophisticated high-resolution graphics routines in Appendix B have been designed to be adapted to those microcomputers with the appropriate graphics capabilities, such as the IBM Personal Computer and the Apple II.

Earlier versions of several of the programs included here were used in the teaching of a graduate course on urban and regional planning methods at the Indiana University School of Public and Environmental Affairs. I wish to thank the students for their ideas and feedback.

Some of the ideas leading to the writing of these programs and this book were presented at the conferences of the Association of Collegiate Schools of Planning in 1981 and 1982. I would like to express my appreciation to the participants for their suggestions and comments.

Jan Neuenschwander, my wife, played a major role in encouraging me to write this book and helped me in innumerable ways. My daughter Sandra deserves thanks just for being such a joy. The dedication of this book to my parents, Walter and Hildegarde Ottensmann, is a small token of thanks for many things done over many years.

Chapter 1

Using BASIC Programs for Urban Analysis

During the past several decades, urban and regional analysts and planners have developed a wide variety of analytical models for use in planning. The importance of the methods—and their general acceptance—is reflected in their being required learning for virtually all students in graduate planning programs and in their inclusion on the examination of the American Institute of Certified Planners. Most of the methods taught are computationally intensive and require computers for all but the simplest of applications. Mainframe computers and the necessary technical support capabilities have long been standard in the larger planning agencies, but access to computing and the expertise required to use the models have not been available to large numbers of planners, especially in the smaller and less sophisticated planning agencies. Because of this, generations of planning students have been taught these methods, and then many have never used them after beginning professional practice.

The development of low-cost microcomputers promises to revolutionize this situation. Considerable computer power—comparable to the large mainframes of only two decades ago— can be placed on a planner's desk at a price affordable to many, if not most, planning agencies. When the current generation of planning students reaches professional practice, they can soon expect to have available the computational resources to apply sophisticated planning models to the problems with which they will deal.

The key to making possible the wider application of analytical planning models is the availability of appropriate software—the computer programs—implementing the models unique to urban and regional planning. Such software is required by the practicing professional desiring to apply the models using the office microcomputer. It is also needed for the training of planning students in the use of microcomputers in the application of planning models.

This book presents nine computer programs written in the BASIC language implementing the major models taught and used in urban and regional planning. The programs are designed for use on most microcomputers (and other computers with BASIC) by planners with a very limited knowledge of computers and programming. The users of these programs need only enter them into the computer and then respond to questions asking for the data and computational options. This is all that would be required to apply some of these rather sophisticated models to urban and regional planning problems. The programs are simple and straightforward, making them especially suitable for planners in smaller agencies and for students learning the methods.

More sophisticated microcomputer software for planning is beginning to become available commercially.[1] Much of this software, however, deals with geographical database management, transportation analysis and modeling, and fiscal impact modeling. It does not address most of the basic planning models implemented by the programs in this book. In addition, the commercial software is usually limited to specific machines and is often very expensive. As with the earlier application of larger computers in planning, the use of this microcomputer software is likely to begin in the larger agencies with greater resources and specialized expertise and only gradually diffuse down to the planners in smaller agencies.

In contrast to this "top down" diffusion, microcomputers open up the possibility of the "grass roots" diffusion of the use of computers and planning methods.[2] Individual planners, without specialized expertise but with an interest in using computers to implement planning models, can begin using these programs with virtually any microcomputer. The applications will be simple, and so should the computer software to support these applications. The BASIC computer programs in this book are specifically intended to support such individual initiative and "grass roots" diffusion.

In addition to their use by practicing planning professionals, these programs can be effectively used in the teaching of urban analysis and planning methods. They provide students with the opportunity to apply easily the models, avoiding both the tedium of hand calculation and the complexity of typical batch programs operating on mainframe computers. The interactive nature of the programs allows experimentation with the models and enhances learning. Indeed, many of the programs included were first written for and used in the teaching of the graduate planning methods course at the Indiana University School of Public and Environmental Affairs.

The learning of planning methods through the use of these programs provides the students with the ability to move directly to the application of the models using any available computer system. This can take place when the student enters professional practice, or even earlier in the context of a workshop course requiring the application of the methods. As part of the planning methods course mentioned above, the students were required to complete a facility location study for the Boy's Club of Bloomington, Indiana, which was contemplating relocation. The assignment involved the application of the program for facility location on a plane. Students worked in teams. Each team made small modifications to the program to better accommodate the tasks at hand and then used the program to conduct the analysis. The availability of the program made possible the application of the planning model to a real problem in a manner that is directly transferable to professional practice.

The relative simplicity of these programs should not lead one to underestimate their power in solving planning problems of significant size. In a study of optimal service locations for the poverty population in Indianapolis, this author used an early version of the public facility location program in Chapter 9.[3] The study utilized data on the poverty populations and the locations of the 179 census tracts in the city in determining locations for up to five centers. An early vintage, inexpensive microcomputer (an Ohio Scientific Challenger 1-P with 8K of RAM) was used to do all of the analyses. A problem that would be considered highly computationally intensive was thus handled with a simple BASIC program and an inexpensive microcomputer. The only limitation was speed; some of the more elaborate analyses did take over 20 minutes to be completed.

The Planning Methods Implemented

The programs in this volume implement the most commonly taught and used analytical models for urban and regional planning. The focus is on those models particular to planning. More general methods, such as statistical analyses, linear programming, and critical path and PERT scheduling techniques, are used by a broader range of professions. Both printed listings of BASIC programs and commercial software for a variety of machines are readily available to planners desiring to use these other methods.[4]

The programs cover many of the models presented in the standard planning methods texts, including *Urban Planning Analysis: Methods and Models* by Krueckeberg and Silvers and *Applied Models in Urban and Regional Analysis* by Oppenheim.[5] Indeed, this volume of programs can be most effectively used in conjunction with such texts, which give more detail on the methods than can be provided here. All of the models implemented by these programs are dealt with in the Krueckeberg and Silvers and Oppenheim texts, with the exception of the public facility location models. A small book by Rushton, *Optimal Location of Facilities*, provides a good introduction in this area.[6]

The first two programs are devoted to the standard population projection models. The Trend Projection Models program provides for simple trend extrapolation using a variety of models. The Population Cohort-Survival Model program implements this more complex method in a flexible manner that allows for easy experimentation.

Three programs are devoted to economic forecasting. The Economic Base Model program provides for estimation of basic activity using either location quotient or minimum requirements approaches. The Shift and Share Model program implements a second commonly used method. The Input–Output Model program does all of the complex calculations required in making projections.

A pair of spatial interaction models is next: The Single-Constrained Gravity Model program and the Double-Constrained Gravity Model program. In each program, the user is given a variety of options regarding the specification of origin and destination zones, the entry of distances, the choice of the functional form, and so on.

The last two programs determine the optimal distance-minimizing locations for public facilities: The Facility Location on a Plane Model and the Facility Location on a Network Model. These methods are taught less frequently in planning programs, but they have many useful applications and are of growing importance.

Each of the programs is presented in a separate chapter, following a common format:

1. Description of the method
2. Description of the program
3. Presentation of a sample problem
4. References to texts
5. Output from a sample run
6. Program listing

The first section provides a concise overview of the model and indicates precisely the technique implemented in the program. All of the relevant equations are presented, using notation similar to that employed within the programs. While all important aspects of the model are discussed, the presentation does not provide extensive detail on all issues relating to the method and its use. To do so would have required the writing of a planning methods text. Instead, references are given in each chapter to the expositions of the model in a number of different works.

The second section of each chapter describes the actual BASIC program. Data requirements are specified and instructions for the operation of the program are given. The various options (provided in each of the programs) are outlined so that the prospective user can understand the capabilities of the program.

A sample problem is then presented to illustrate the application of the program. A list of references provides sources for further information on the model in a variety of texts on planning and urban analysis. A complete printout of the operation of the program in solving the sample problem follows, showing each step of the data input and program output as it would appear to the user. Each chapter concludes with the listing of the program in BASIC. Both the sample output and the program listings are reproduced directly from the printed output from the computer. This ensures that the format will be identical to that produced on the screen and avoids the possibility of errors being introduced in typesetting the material.

Using the Programs

All of the programs have been designed for use by persons with limited knowledge of computers and BASIC programming. Some minimal knowledge of BASIC, gained by writing, entering, and running a few simple BASIC programs, would be required initially to enter, check out, and save the programs.[7] Once this is accomplished, however, a few simple instructions on how to load and execute the programs on the computer being used would enable even a beginning user to utilize these programs successfully.

The programs have been written so they will run successfully on nearly all microcomputers with BASIC. They will also work on larger timesharing systems that have BASIC available. Systems differ in the procedures for getting BASIC started, in saving and loading programs, and in interrupting executing programs. Users will need to consult the documentation for their specific computers and implementations of BASIC to determine the details.

To use a program, begin by entering BASIC on the computer. On some microcomputers, this happens when the machine is turned on; other systems will require one or more commands. Be sure that the memory is cleared of all statements by typing NEW and pressing the "Return" key. (On some systems this is marked "Enter.") Start entering the program by typing in one line at a time, exactly as it is shown in the program listing. Begin with the line number, and conclude by pressing the Return key. If a mistake is discovered in a line that has already been entered, simply retype the line correctly and press Return. The new line will automatically replace the old.

To execute the program, type RUN and press Return. The programs are all completely interactive. The program will present questions asking for data and then stop and wait for a response. Type in the response—the appropriate number—and press Return. At other times, the program may ask for a choice from a menu, or list of options. Again, enter the appropriate option and press Return. When output is being printed to the screen, the message CONTINUE? will appear and output will stop, to keep information from scrolling off the top of the screen. Pressing Return will continue the printing of the output.

A step-by-step example of the process of executing one of the programs should make this clear. Assume that the program Trend Projection Models has been entered or loaded into the computer. To begin, type:

    RUN<Return>

All information which the user enters will be underlined. The symbol <Return> means press the Return key; it will not print out on the screen. The program responds by printing out the following:

    TREND PROJECTION MODELS
    FOR UNIFORMLY-SPACED DATA

    NUMBER OF DATA VALUES (DATA VALUES
    PLUS PERIODS PROJECTED MUST BE LESS
    THAN 18)?

At this point, the program stops, waiting for a response. Assume three population values are to be entered for 1960, 1970, and 1980. Type in:

    3<Return>

This will appear on the same line, after the question mark. The program responds with two more questions, after which the appropriate responses are again typed in:

    FIRST YEAR OF DATA? 1960<Return>
    YEARS BETWEEN DATA VALUES? 10<Return>

Having determined this information, the program can now ask for the actual data values. The responses are made in a similar manner, as indicated here:

    ENTER DATA VALUES FOR EACH YEAR
        1960 ? 6000<Return>
        1970 ? 6600<Return>
        1980 ? 7100<Return>

Now that the data have been entered, the program presents a list of choices concerning the model to be used in the trend projection:

    TREND PROJECTION MODELS:
        1 - LINEAR (DIRECT)
        2 - LINEAR (REGRESSION)

```
3 - EXPONENTIAL (DIRECT)
4 - EXPONENTIAL (REGRESSION)
5 - MODIFIED EXPONENTIAL
```

NUMBER OF MODEL DESIRED?

Each of the models is described and documented in the first section of Chapter 2 on the Trend Projection Models program. To choose the Linear (Direct) model, for example, simply type:

1<Return>

There is one last question, which should be self-explanatory; enter an appropriate choice:

NUMBER OF PERIODS TO BE PROJECTED? 3<Return>

The program now starts to print its output:

```
         LINEAR MODEL (DIRECT) PROJECTIONS

     YEAR      DATA        PROJECTION
     1960      6000
     1970      6600          6550
     1980      7100          7150
     1990                    7650
     2000                    8200
     2010                    8750

         CONTINUE?
```

After finishing the reading of this table, press Return and the remainder of the projection output is printed:

```
MEAN SQUARED ERROR = 2500
CHANGE PER PERIOD B = 550
```

Finally, the program gives the option of repeating the analysis in order to try another model or have more periods projected:

REPEAT WITH SAME DATA (1=YES, 0=NO)?

Since all facets of running one of the programs have been demonstrated, type:

0<Return>

The program will stop execution. With most versions of BASIC, this will be followed by some type of prompt indicating that the program has finished and that the computer is back to the BASIC command level. This might be "OK," "Ready," or some prompt symbol such as "]."

This assumes that everything works according to plan. What if an error message of some sort appears either upon entering the program lines or upon executing the program? (Versions of BASIC differ as to when they make certain kinds of checks.) The most likely problem is that an error was made in entering the line specified. Check this and correct it by retyping the entire line correctly. Occasionally an error is indicated on one line, but the actual mistake is located on another. Or the program runs, but produces incorrect results. Again, errors in program entry are the most likely problems, but they will be harder to find. Every effort has been made to write these programs so they will execute correctly with almost any version of BASIC, and the actual programs listed will produce the sample output shown in each chapter. Nevertheless, problems might occasionally arise. In such cases, a better knowledge of the workings of BASIC on the particular machine may be necessary to uncover the problem. A detailed account of program debugging in BASIC is beyond the scope of this book. More information can be found in texts on BASIC.

One other problem might arise in using these programs. The program works fine, but a discovery is made while running the program of an earlier error in entering information or of an incorrect choice of an option. For one of these reasons—or any other reason—it may be desirable to terminate execution of the program. This may be done in order to start over or to quit altogether. Most computers and versions of BASIC allow the user to interrupt and stop a program. A Control-C is often used; this is obtained by pressing the key labeled CONTROL or CTRL (sort of a special shift key) and then also pressing C. On other systems, separate keys labeled BREAK or STOP may be used. In any case, once the program is stopped, it can be started over at the beginning by once again typing RUN and pressing Return.

After a program has been entered and determined to run correctly, the program should be saved in permanent storage (most often on some type of disk) for future use. Usually this involves the command SAVE, though variations exist on how this is to be used, allowable file names, and so forth. Once the program has been saved, a command to LOAD (or sometimes OLD) with the name of the program will make it again available for use. Consult the documentation for the specific system on how to save and load programs.

The Nature of the Programs

This section provides further details on the BASIC programs included in this book. This information is not needed to use these programs successfully. But it will be of interest to those with some knowledge of BASIC programming interested in the way the programs have been written and why, and perhaps contemplating the making of modifications to the programs to meet special needs. More detail on the subset of BASIC used, program structure, and suggestions for programmers are provided in Appendix C.

The language BASIC was chosen for these programs because of its nearly universal availability on microcomputers. Indeed, many machines have BASIC interpreters "built-in," with the BASIC in ROM (Read Only Memory). Microcomputers without BASIC in ROM usually have versions of BASIC available on disk, and it is now not uncommon for this software to be supplied "bundled" with the machine. Both because of this widespread use of BASIC and because BASIC is easy to learn, far more microcomputer users know something about BASIC than any other programming language.

Furthermore, most versions of BASIC are implemented as interpreters with their own programming environments. Users can enter programs, run them, modify them, rerun them, and save and load them, all by issuing simple commands and without leaving BASIC. The user is not obligated to learn how to use a separate editor, learn a series of commands for compiling and loading programs, learn far more about the operating system, or go through an elaborate and repetitive process of editing, compiling, loading, and executing while debugging programs. This makes interpreted BASIC far easier to use than most compiled languages, which usually have such requirements. The penalty paid is in speed of execution; interpreted languages generally execute far more slowly than compiled languages. This is not likely to be a problem for small applications. If the programs are adapted for much larger problems, speed of execution could become an issue. BASIC compilers are available for many microcomputer systems, however, and the programs in this book should work well with them.

Many might argue that a structured language such as Pascal would have been preferable for writing a series of programs such as these. This would certainly have made the programs easier to understand and modify for special applications. However, BASIC programs can be written clearly and documented in a manner that overcomes some of the weaknesses of the language. BASIC is so much more widely available than Pascal or any other contender that the choice was never really an issue. To make these programs usable by the largest possible number of planners with microcomputers required that they be written in BASIC.

Unfortunately, wide variations exist among the various dialects of BASIC available, both on microcomputers and on larger computer systems. A program written to run correctly with one version of BASIC will not necessarily work with another version. Only the most fundamental elements of the language are relatively uniform from one version to the next. To provide a series of programs that would operate successfully with most versions of

BASIC requires that they be written in a very limited subset of the language common to most implementations. These programs were so written, using only a small portion of the capabilities included in most versions of BASIC. The subset of BASIC employed in these programs is specified in Appendix C. It conforms in all respects to American National Standards Institute Minimal BASIC, a proposed common subset.[8] The limitations on the BASIC used here are in some respects even more restrictive than those specified in the standards. This should ensure that the programs will operate successfully with most versions of BASIC.

The restriction of the programs to such a limited subset of the language produces code that is longer and sometimes more awkward than if other features of many versions of BASIC had been employed. Experienced BASIC programmers will quickly spot sections of the programs that could have been handled far better *in their versions of BASIC*. The desire to write BASIC programs that would be transportable to the greatest number of systems demanded strict adherence to the limited BASIC subset defined in Appendix C.

All of the programs in the book were developed using Microsoft BASIC-80 running under the CP/M operating system on the Osborne 1 computer. As a test of transportability to a very different version of BASIC, all programs were also compiled and executed using CBASIC. Programs were also operated at various stages in their development on an Ohio Scientific Challenger 1-P, an Apple II+, an IBM Personal Computer, and Digital Equipment DEC-10, DEC-20, and VAX-11 computers.

The length of output lines was generally limited to 40 characters so that the programs would work with unenhanced Apple II's and other computers designed for use with television sets and having limited displays. Such output formatting is less than optimal in some cases for systems with full 80-column displays; but, again, the desire to provide for the execution of these programs on the widest range of computers required the compromise. Several of the programs do provide an option for wider output where appropriate. This is specified by setting the value of the variable F (for fields) to indicate the number of fields or columns of output. The programs are also limited in length and variable storage requirements, and most should execute on systems with at least 16K of available RAM (in addition to BASIC). (See Appendix C for more details.)

Efforts have been made to provide programs that are clearly structured and well documented. All of the variables used in the programs are defined in REMark statements at the beginning. The major segments of the program and all subroutines are likewise identified with REMark statements. Data input, model computations, and printing of results are all carried out by separate subroutines. While minimal BASIC lacks the facilities for true structured programming, the code has been written to avoid as much as possible the transfers of control that produce the messy, tangled programs that are all too common in BASIC. Those familiar with BASIC should be able to follow the programs fairly easily.

An important objective in writing these programs was to provide for their easy modification to meet special needs. Especially when using these programs in planning practice, simple modifications might considerably enhance the utility of the programs. The most common changes users will want to make to the programs involve input, output, and program capacity. Users with a moderate knowledge of BASIC should be able to implement such changes without great difficulty.

The amount of data that can be accepted by the programs is limited by the sizes of the arrays, declared in the DIMension statements. The sizes set should be sufficiently large for teaching purposes and for most applications in smaller planning offices. The program capacities are about as large as one would want for the input of data interactively, as the programs provide. Nevertheless, some applications will involve more data and require greater program capacity. This can be increased simply by appropriately increasing the sizes of the arrays in the DIMension statements. Some versions of BASIC allow variables to be used in dimensioning arrays. This could be done, but it would require repositioning the DIMension statements after the point in the program at which the appropriate variable values were first input.

If the capacity of a program is increased, two issues may need to be addressed. First, entering the larger number of data values interactively may become a problem, so alternate means of data input might need to be provided. Second, the larger array sizes may cause the output from the programs to scroll off the screen. The solution would be to build pauses into the output procedures or to direct output to a printer.

If the same data are to be used repeatedly with a program or if a very large volume of data is to be entered, the interactive input provided in the programs may prove cumbersome and inefficient. For repeated use of the same data, which is likely in practical applications, alternate procedures for input might be desired. It would be relatively simple to replace any of the INPUT statements with appropriate READ and DATA statements (also eliminating the prompting PRINT statements). This would allow the data to be saved along with the program. Alternatively, data could be input from files, though this process is more complex and requires greater knowledge of the version of BASIC being used.

The most common output modification would be to direct the output of a program to a printer rather than the video display terminal used with most systems. All of the programs output all of the data that have been entered, so printing the output can provide a complete record of the operation of the program. The option of obtaining printed output could not be provided in a transportable manner, however, since the procedure varies widely from one version of BASIC to another. Methods for printing output can include substituting LPRINT statements for PRINT statements; including additional special commands in BASIC to direct output to the printer, such as LPRINTER or PR#1; using PRINT # to output to a disk file for later printing; or output redirection by the operating system. The user will have to determine the appropriate procedure for the system being used in order to make the appropriate modifications.

Customizing these programs for specific applications will not necessarily require a high degree of BASIC programming sophistication. In the planning methods course during which some of these programs were first used, students were given two weeks of instruction in BASIC and were required to write two simple BASIC programs. They then used some of the programs presented in this volume while learning the planning methods. A final assignment involved the preparation of a facility location study, mentioned earlier. Because the students were doing repeated analyses using the same set of coordinates each time, they modified the program to use READ and DATA statements to input the coordinates. One enterprising student went even further in making program modifications, adding an entire routine to one program so he could use it for research in another course.

The programs include very limited error-trapping and editing facilities. This is difficult to implement in a minimal, transferable BASIC. (String functions vary from one version of BASIC to another.) Attempts to include such capabilities would also have made the programs much longer. This in turn would have discouraged prospective users from entering and using the programs. It was felt that the ease with which a program can be interrupted and run again in interpreted BASIC makes these programs very usable in their current form. Of course, a knowledgeable BASIC programmer could add error-trapping and editing features to these programs for any system.

The set of programs presented in this volume represent a first step in making urban and regional planning models available on microcomputers. These are simple, straightforward BASIC programs usable in planning practice and in the teaching of planning methods. They can be used on most of the wide variety of microcomputers now available and on larger timesharing systems with BASIC. Certainly more sophisticated software for urban and regional planning will be developed in the coming years. These programs offer a point of departure for microcomputer applications in urban analysis and planning that can be used now.

Notes

[1] Advertisements for commercial microcomputer software for urban and regional planning and occasional articles on the subject can be found in *Planning* magazine.

[2] This distinction was originally made in an earlier article. See Ottensmann, J. R., "Microcomputers in Applied Settings: The Example of Urban Planning," *Sociological Methods and Research*, Vol. 9, No. 4 (May 1981), 493–501.

[3] Ottensmann, J. R., "The Spatial Dimension in the Planning of Social Services in Large Cities," *Journal of the American Planning Association*, Vol. 47, No. 2 (April 1981), 167–174.

[4] One good general source of BASIC program listings, which includes simple statistical analysis programs, is Poole, L. and Borchers, M., *Some Common BASIC Programs*, 3rd ed. (Berkeley, Calif.: Osborne/McGraw-Hill, Inc., 1979). A variety of management science techniques of interest to urban and regional planners are included in a book of BASIC programs by Bui, X. T., *Executive Planning with BASIC* (Berkeley, Calif.: SYBEX, Inc., 1982).

[5] Krueckeberg, D. A. and Silvers, A. L., *Urban Planning Analysis: Methods and Models* (New York: John Wiley & Sons, Inc., 1974); Oppenheim, N., *Applied Models in Urban and Regional Analysis* (Englewood Cliffs, N.J.: Prentice-Hall, Inc., 1980).

[6] Rushton, G., *Optimal Location of Facilities* (Wentworth, N.H.: COMPress, Inc., 1979).

[7] There are very many introductory texts on BASIC that can be used to acquire this knowledge. One simple, straightforward volume that the author has used in teaching BASIC programming is Davis, W. S., *BASIC: Getting Started* (Reading, Mass.: Addison-Wesley Publishing Company, 1981).

[8] The programs also conform, with one exception, to the Level Zero (most restrictive) standards for BASIC program interchange recommended by the Conduit program exchange at the University of Iowa. The one exception involves the use in these programs of the implied LET statement, which is almost universally accepted and is normal BASIC programming practice. Users wishing to add the LET in each assignment statement could do so easily. See Frederick, J. R., ed., Furguson, N., Hurst, S., and Trotter, P., *CONDUIT BASIC Guide* (Iowa City: CONDUIT, The University of Iowa, 1979).

Chapter 2

Trend Projection Models

The Models

Perhaps the simplest method for projecting population or other quantities is extrapolation from an existing trend. The pattern existing in a series of values over time is assumed to continue into the future, providing the basis for making the projection. While planning methods texts frequently present trend projection models in the context of making population projections, the models can be used for making projections of other quantities of interest to planners, such as employment or numbers of housing units. Trend projection models are very simple tools, however, and should be used with care because the conditions for making an assumption of a continuing trend are often not met. Nevertheless, these methods may represent the best one can do in certain situations and are important and commonly used in planning. The Trend Projection Models program presented in this chapter allows projections to be made with linear and exponential models (with both direct and regression solutions) and the modified exponential model.[1]

With data on population or other values at uniform intervals (say every 10 years, from the census), a trend is established from the pattern of change from one period to the next. If the absolute amount of the change is constant, when the values are plotted against time, they will lie in a straight line. This is a linear trend, which is illustrated in the first section of Figure 2.1. The linear model can be expressed mathematically as

$$P_t = P_0 + bt$$

where P_t is the population at period t, P_0 is the starting population at period zero, t is the number of periods, and b is the amount of change from one period to the next. The easiest method for determining b (referred to as

LINEAR	EXPONENTIAL	MODIFIED EXPONENTIAL

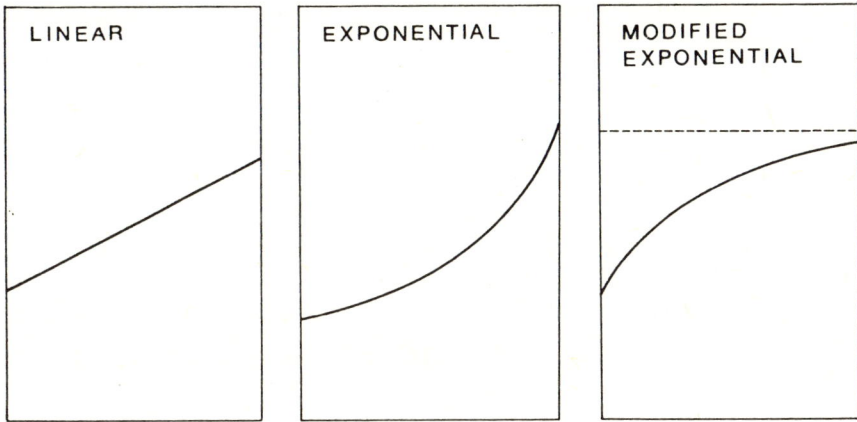

Figure 2.1   Linear, exponential, and modified exponential trends.

the "direct" method in the program) is to take the mean of the changes in the observed intervals. With n observations, the formula is

$$b = \frac{1}{n-1}\sum_{i=2}^{n}(P_i - P_{i-1})$$

remembering that n observations yield $n - 1$ intervals. With such a direct solution, the last available data point is then used as the starting point P_0 in making the projections. As a test of the performance of the model, each existing data point can be projected from its predecessor.

Although slightly more complex, the use of linear regression is often considered to be superior in applying the linear trend model. Linear regression determines the equation of the line minimizing the sum of the squared errors—the distances from the line to the actual data points.[2] For the linear model, the population values are regressed on time to determine the intercept P_0 and the slope of the line b. The equation incorporating these values is used for projection.

An alternative trend would have population changing at a constant proportional (or percentage) rate. Thus, a population growing over time would be increasing by ever greater amounts, and a declining population would decrease by progressively smaller amounts. Such an exponential trend is illustrated in the second portion of Figure 2.1. The mathematical formula for the exponential model is

$$P_t = P_0(1 + r)^t$$

where r is the proportional rate of change from one period to the next. Since the rate of change is assumed constant in the exponential model, a direct solution for r would involve the calculation of the mean rate of change over the observed intervals:

$$r = \frac{1}{n-1} \sum_{i=2}^{n} \frac{P_i - P_{i-1}}{P_{i-1}}$$

As with the direct solution to the linear model, the last available data point would be used as the starting point P_0 in making the projections.

Since the equation for the exponential model is not linear, linear regression methods cannot be applied directly. But a transformation of the exponential model can be performed by taking the logarithms of both sides, yielding

$$\log P_t = \log P_0 + [\log(1 + r)]\, t$$

and this equation is linear with respect to $\log P_t$ and t. Now linear regression can be used, regressing the logarithms of the observed values P_t on t. The intercept of the regression line is equal to $\log P_0$ and the slope is equal to $\log (1 + r)$. The estimates of P_0 and r can then be computed and used in the equation for the exponential model for making projections.

Growth of a population could occur at a decreasing rate, approaching an upper limit. This form of trend might be appropriate, for example, in a community with population growth constrained by a fixed amount of available land, which determines a maximum population capacity. One assumption that yields such a trend is that the amount of growth remaining (the difference between the population and the limit) is a constant ratio from one time period to the next. This is the basis for the modified exponential model, shown in the third section of Figure 2.1, which can be expressed mathematically as

$$P_t = K - (K - P_0)\, v^t$$

where K is the upper limit and v is the proportion of the growth remaining between successive time periods. Given a value for K, a direct solution for v can be obtained by calculating the mean proportion of growth remaining in the observed intervals:

$$v = \frac{1}{n-1} \sum_{i=2}^{n} \frac{K - P_i}{K - P_{i-1}}$$

By taking the last available data point as the starting point P_0, the assumed value of K, and the calculated value of v, the equation for the modified exponential model can be used for projection. Note that since the upper limit K is simply assumed at the start of the computation, one may wish to try several values for K and compare the results with the observed values.

The Program

The Trend Projection Models program provides for the input of uniformly spaced data and the selection of five trend models: (1) linear (direct solution); (2) linear (regression solution); (3) exponential (direct solution); (4) exponential (regression solution); and (5) modified exponential. The program makes projections for any specified number of periods. The output includes the original data, projections for both current and future years, appropriate model parameters, and the mean squared error in the prediction of the observed data values. The program can be repeated as often as desired with any set of data, allowing for the choice of different models, numbers of projection periods, and limit values for the modified exponential model. The program is limited to a maximum of 18 values—initial data points input by the user plus projected values. Results of the projections are rounded to the nearest integer.

The program begins with data input. The user is asked the first year for which the data values are available, the number of years between the data values, and the total number of data points. The program prompts the user for the entry of the individual data values. Then a menu of the five trend projection models available is listed. The user enters the number of the model desired and the number of periods to be projected.

The program output includes a table with the year, the actual data values (for those years input), and the values projected using the model chosen. In addition, the mean squared error in predicting observed data values is given, along with the model parameters that have been computed. The latter include the rates of change for the model and, for regression solutions, the estimate of P_0 and the correlation coefficient. The user is given the option of repeating the analysis using the same data, in which case the menu of the model choices is again displayed.

Differences in the nature of the parameter estimation between the direct and regression solutions leads to variations in the manner in which projections can be made and the mean squared errors calculated. With regression solutions, both parameters of the model equation are calculated, and these are used for making the projections for all years. For example, with the linear model with the regression solution, values for P_0 and b are provided by the regression. The equation $\hat{P}_t = P_0 + bt$ is then used in making the projections, where $\hat{P}_t$ is the projected value of P_t. To determine the mean squared error (MSE), this procedure is followed: The projected values are subtracted from the actual data values to determine the errors, and these quantities are squared, summed, and divided by the number of data values to determine the mean squared error. The formula is

$$MSE = \frac{1}{n} \sum_{i=1}^{n} (P_i - \hat{P}_i)^2$$

where P_i is the observed value and $\hat{P}_i$ is the projected value from the equation.

The direct solutions determine only the change coefficient, b, r, or v, and a previous observed data value must be used in making any projection. For projections beyond the range of the observed values, the last value is used, and the number of periods is counted from that point. With the linear model, for example, $\hat{P}_t = P_n + b\,(t - n)$ would be used for projection. For determining projected values for the years for which observations are available, the preceding period's value is used as the base. So with the linear model, $\hat{P}_t = P_{t-1} + b$. This implies that a projection cannot be made for the first year. Lacking this first-year projection, the mean squared error can be calculated only for the data values 2 to n; the program adjusts accordingly.

BASIC programmers wishing to understand and modify the program will be interested in this brief explanation of its structure: The main routine, lines 10 to 540, controls the flow the the program, provides for the choice of the models, and makes calls to subroutines for data entry, model computation, and output. Initial data entry is carried out by the subroutine at line 4000. After a model has been selected, the program jumps to the appropriate subroutine for computing the results; these begin at lines 1000, 1500, 2000, 2500, and 3000. The subroutines involving regression solutions make a further call to a simple regression subroutine beginning at line 3500. The results are printed out by individual subroutines for each model at lines 7000, 7500, 8000, 8500, and 9000. Each of these subroutines in turn calls a subroutine at line 9500 that handles the printing of the table of actual and projected values.

Sample Problem

The following population data for a small city have been collected from the census:

Year	Population
1940	9,200
1950	10,900
1960	11,700
1970	12,800
1980	13,100

Population projections are to be made up to the year 2030. Given that the city is fixed in area and the available vacant land is gradually being used up, the modified exponential model may be most appropriate, with a maximum limit of 15,000. Because people are more familiar with the idea of constant growth, perhaps a linear trend projection using the regression solution should also be made for comparative purposes.

The sample run illustrates the use of the Trend Projection Models program in conducting the analysis, showing exactly what would appear on the display. The user of the program enters the information following the question marks, each time pressing the Return key. All other information is generated by the program.

In this problem, the modified exponential model did appear to be more appropriate. The projected values were closer to the actual values for the years 1950 to 1980, which is reflected in the lower mean squared error. The user of the program could have continued on to conduct more analyses with the same data if desired, trying different models and different limit values for the modified exponential model.

References

Isard, W., *Methods of Regional Analysis: An Introduction to Regional Science* (Cambridge, Mass.: M.I.T. Press, 1960), Chapter 2, pp. 5–15.

Krueckeberg, D. A. and Silvers, A. L., *Urban Planning Analysis: Methods and Models* (New York: John Wiley & Sons, Inc., 1974), Chapter 8, pp. 259–274.

Oppenheim, N., *Applied Models in Urban and Regional Analysis* (Englewood Cliffs, N. J.: Prentice-Hall, Inc., 1980), Chapter 2, pp. 32–39.

Notes

[1] Other trend models are not included in the program because they are documented less thoroughly for users in the standard texts and they are used less frequently in planning.

[2] Both Krueckeberg and Silvers and Oppenheim include explanations of linear regression. See Krueckeberg, D. A. and Silvers, A. L., *op cit.*, pp. 161-180; and Oppenheim, N., *op cit.*, pp. 277-302. One may also consult virtually any introductory statistics text.

```
      TREND  PROJECTION  MODELS  SAMPLE  RUN


      TREND PROJECTION MODELS
      FOR UNIFORMLY-SPACED DATA

      NUMBER OF DATA VALUES (DATA VALUES
      PLUS PERIODS PROJECTED MUST BE LESS
      THAN 18)? 5

      FIRST YEAR OF DATA? 1940
      YEARS BETWEEN DATA VALUES? 10

      ENTER DATA VALUES FOR EACH YEAR
            1940 ? 9200
            1950 ? 10900
            1960 ? 11700
            1970 ? 12800
            1980 ? 13100


      TREND PROJECTION MODELS:
            1 - LINEAR (DIRECT)
            2 - LINEAR (REGRESSION)
            3 - EXPONENTIAL (DIRECT)
            4 - EXPONENTIAL (REGRESSION)
            5 - MODIFIED EXPONENTIAL

      NUMBER OF MODEL DESIRED? 5
      NUMBER OF PERIODS TO BE PROJECTED? 5
      FINAL (LIMIT) VALUE? 15000


      MODIFIED EXPONENTIAL MODEL PROJECTION

      YEAR           DATA          PROJECTION
       1940          9200
       1950          10900          10589
       1960          11700          11882
       1970          12800          12490
       1980          13100          13327
       1990                         13555
       2000                         13901
       2010                         14164
       2020                         14364
       2030                         14517

      CONTINUE?

      MEAN SQUARED ERROR = 69368.5
      LIMIT K = 15000
      RATE OF CONVERGENCE V = .760519
```

```
REPEAT WITH SAME DATA (1=YES, 0=NO)? 1


TREND PROJECTION MODELS:
    1 - LINEAR (DIRECT)
    2 - LINEAR (REGRESSION)
    3 - EXPONENTIAL (DIRECT)
    4 - EXPONENTIAL (REGRESSION)
    5 - MODIFIED EXPONENTIAL

NUMBER OF MODEL DESIRED? 2
NUMBER OF PERIODS TO BE PROJECTED? 5


LINEAR MODEL (REGRESSION) PROJECTION

YEAR          DATA          PROJECTION
 1940         9200          9600
 1950         10900         10570
 1960         11700         11540
 1970         12800         12510
 1980         13100         13480
 1990                       14450
 2000                       15420
 2010                       16390
 2020                       17360
 2030                       18330

CONTINUE?

MEAN SQUARED ERROR = 104600
INTERCEPT (PERIOD ZERO ESTIMATE) A = 8630
SLOPE (CHANGE PER PERIOD) B = 970
CORRELATION COEFFICIENT = .973346


REPEAT WITH SAME DATA (1=YES, 0=NO)? 0
```

TREND PROJECTION MODELS PROGRAM LISTING

```
10 REM TREND PROJECTION MODELS
20 REM BY JOHN R. OTTENSMANN
30 REM VARIABLES
40 REM    D(I) - DATA VALUES FOR PERIOD I
50 REM    P(I) - PROJECTED VALUES
60 REM    Y(I) - REGRESSION VECTOR
70 REM    A, B, K, R, V - MODEL PARAMETERS
80 REM    C - CHOICE OF MODEL
90 REM    E - MEAN SQUARED ERROR
100 REM    L - FIRST YEAR
110 REM    M - YEARS BETWEEN PERIODS
120 REM    N - NUMBER OF DATA VALUES
130 REM    S - PERIODS TO BE PROJECTED
140 REM    T - FIRST PERIOD PROJECTED
150 REM    X1, X2, Y1, Y2, Z - REGRESSION SUMS
160 DIM D(18), P(18), Y(18)
170 REM READ INPUT DATA
180 PRINT
190 PRINT
200 PRINT "TREND PROJECTION MODELS"
210 PRINT "FOR UNIFORMLY-SPACED DATA"
220 GOSUB 4000
230 REM BEGIN PROJECTION PROCESS
240 PRINT
250 PRINT
260 PRINT "TREND PROJECTION MODELS:"
270 PRINT TAB(5); "1 - LINEAR (DIRECT)"
280 PRINT TAB(5); "2 - LINEAR (REGRESSION)"
290 PRINT TAB(5); "3 - EXPONENTIAL (DIRECT)"
300 PRINT TAB(5); "4 - EXPONENTIAL (REGRESSION)"
310 PRINT TAB(5); "5 - MODIFIED EXPONENTIAL"
320 PRINT
330 PRINT "NUMBER OF MODEL DESIRED";
340 INPUT C
350 PRINT "NUMBER OF PERIODS TO BE PROJECTED";
360 INPUT S
370 REM JUMP TO SUBROUTINES TO CALCULATE AND OUTPUT
380 IF C <> 1 THEN 410
390 GOSUB 1000
400 GOSUB 7000
410 IF C <> 2 THEN 440
420 GOSUB 1500
430 GOSUB 7500
440 IF C <> 3 THEN 470
450 GOSUB 2000
460 GOSUB 8000
470 IF C <> 4 THEN 500
480 GOSUB 2500
490 GOSUB 8500
500 IF C <> 5 THEN 550
```

```
510 PRINT "FINAL (LIMIT) VALUE";
520 INPUT K
530 GOSUB 3000
540 GOSUB 9000
550 PRINT
560 PRINT
570 PRINT "REPEAT WITH SAME DATA (1=YES, 0=NO)";
580 INPUT A
590 IF A = 0 THEN 9999
600 GOTO 240
990 REM LINEAR MODEL (DIRECT) SUBROUTINE ******************
1000 B = 0
1010 FOR I = 2 TO N
1020 B = B + D(I) - D(I-1)
1030 NEXT I
1040 B = B / (N - 1)
1050 REM CALCULATE PREDICTED VALUES
1060 FOR I = 2 TO N
1070 P(I) = INT(D(I-1) + B + .5)
1080 NEXT I
1090 FOR I = 1 TO S
1100 P(N+I) = INT(D(N) + B*I + .5)
1110 NEXT I
1120 T = 2
1130 RETURN
1490 REM LINEAR MODEL (REGRESSION) SUBROUTINE *************
1500 FOR I = 1 TO N
1510 Y(I) = D(I)
1520 NEXT I
1530 GOSUB 3500
1540 REM CALCULATE PREDICTED VALUES
1550 FOR I = 1 TO N+S
1560 P(I) = INT(A + B*I + .5)
1570 NEXT I
1580 T = 1
1590 RETURN
1990 REM EXPONENTIAL MODEL (DIRECT) SUBROUTINE *************
2000 R = 0
2010 FOR I = 2 TO N
2020 R = R + (D(I) - D(I-1)) / D(I-1)
2030 NEXT I
2040 R = R / (N - 1)
2050 REM CALCULATE PREDICTED VALUES
2060 FOR I = 2 TO N
2070 P(I) = INT(D(I-1)*(1+R) + .5)
2080 NEXT I
2090 FOR I = 1 TO S
2100 P(N+I) = INT(D(N)*(1+R)^I + .5)
2110 NEXT I
2120 T = 2
2130 RETURN
2490 REM EXPONENTIAL MODEL (REGRESSION) SUBROUTINE *********
2500 FOR I = 1 TO N
```

```
2510 Y(I) = LOG(D(I))
2520 NEXT I
2530 GOSUB 3500
2540 A = EXP(A)
2550 B = EXP(B) - 1
2560 REM CALCULATE PREDICTED VALUES
2570 FOR I = 1 TO N+S
2580 P(I) = INT(A*(B+1)^I + .5)
2590 NEXT I
2600 T = 1
2610 RETURN
2990 REM MODIFIED EXPONENTIAL MODEL SUBROUTINE *************
3000 V = 0
3010 FOR I = 2 TO N
3020 V = V + (K - D(I)) / (K - D(I-1))
3030 NEXT I
3040 V = V / (N - 1)
3050 REM CALCULATE PREDICTED VALUES
3060 FOR I = 2 TO N
3070 P(I) = INT(K - (K - D(I-1))*V + .5)
3080 NEXT I
3090 FOR I = 1 TO S
3100 P(N+I) = INT(K - (K - D(N))*V^I +.5)
3110 NEXT I
3120 T = 2
3130 RETURN
3490 REM REGRESSION SUBROUTINE ****************************
3500 X1 = 0
3510 X2 = 0
3520 Y1 = 0
3530 Y2 = 0
3540 Z = 0
3550 FOR I = 1 TO N
3560 X1 = X1 + I
3570 X2 = X2 + I^2
3580 Y1 = Y1 + Y(I)
3590 Y2 = Y2 + Y(I)^2
3600 Z = Z + I*Y(I)
3610 NEXT I
3620 B = (N*Z - X1*Y1) / (N*X2 - X1^2)
3630 A = (Y1 - B*X1) / N
3640 R = (N*Z -X1*Y1) / SQR((N*X2 - X1^2)*(N*Y2 - Y1^2))
3650 RETURN
3990 REM DATA INPUT SUBROUTINE ****************************
4000 PRINT
4010 PRINT "NUMBER OF DATA VALUES (DATA VALUES"
4020 PRINT "PLUS PERIODS PROJECTED MUST BE LESS"
4030 PRINT "THAN 18)";
4040 INPUT N
4050 PRINT
4060 PRINT "FIRST YEAR OF DATA";
4070 INPUT L
4080 PRINT "YEARS BETWEEN DATA VALUES";
```

```
4090 INPUT M
4100 PRINT
4110 PRINT "ENTER DATA VALUES FOR EACH YEAR"
4120 FOR I = 1 TO N
4130 PRINT TAB(5); L+M*(I-1);
4140 INPUT D(I)
4150 NEXT I
4160 RETURN
6990 REM LINEAR MODEL (DIRECT) OUTPUT SUBROUTINE ***********
7000 PRINT
7010 PRINT
7020 PRINT "LINEAR MODEL (DIRECT) PROJECTIONS"
7030 GOSUB 9500
7040 PRINT "CHANGE PER PERIOD B ="; B
7050 RETURN
7490 REM LINEAR MODEL (REGRESSION) OUTPUT SUBROUTINE *******
7500 PRINT
7510 PRINT
7520 PRINT "LINEAR MODEL (REGRESSION) PROJECTION"
7530 GOSUB 9500
7540 PRINT "INTERCEPT (PERIOD ZERO ESTIMATE) A ="; A
7550 PRINT "SLOPE (CHANGE PER PERIOD) B ="; B
7560 PRINT "CORRELATION COEFFICIENT ="; R
7570 RETURN
7990 REM EXPONENTIAL MODEL (DIRECT) OUTPUT SUBROUTINE ******
8000 PRINT
8010 PRINT
8020 PRINT "EXPONENTIAL MODEL (DIRECT) PROJECTION"
8030 GOSUB 9500
8040 PRINT "RATE OF CHANGE PER PERIOD R ="; R
8050 RETURN
8490 REM EXPONENTIAL MODEL (REGRESSION) OUTPUT SUBROUTINE **
8500 PRINT
8510 PRINT
8520 PRINT "EXPONENTIAL MODEL (REGRESSION) PROJECTION"
8530 GOSUB 9500
8540 PRINT "PERIOD ZERO ESTIMATE ="; A
8550 PRINT "RATE OF CHANGE PER PERIOD R="; B
8560 PRINT "CORRELATION COEFFICIENT ="; R
8570 RETURN
8990 REM MODIFIED EXPONENTIAL MODEL OUTPUT SUBROUTINE ******
9000 PRINT
9010 PRINT
9020 PRINT "MODIFIED EXPONENTIAL MODEL PROJECTION"
9030 GOSUB 9500
9040 PRINT "LIMIT K ="; K
9050 PRINT "RATE OF CONVERGENCE V ="; V
9060 RETURN
9490 REM PROJECTION OUTPUT SUBROUTINE ********************
9500 PRINT
9510 PRINT "YEAR"; TAB(13); "DATA"; TAB(27); "PROJECTION"
9520 IF T = 1 THEN 9540
9530 PRINT L; TAB(13); D(1)
```

```
9540 FOR I = T TO N
9550 PRINT L+M*(I-1); TAB(13); D(I); TAB(27); P(I)
9560 NEXT I
9570 FOR I = N+1 TO N+S
9580 PRINT L+M*(I-1); TAB(27); P(I)
9590 NEXT I
9600 GOSUB 9900
9610 REM COMPUTE AND PRINT MEAN SQUARED ERROR
9620 E = 0
9630 FOR I = T TO N
9640 E = E + (D(I) - P(I))^2
9650 NEXT I
9660 E = E / (N - T + 1)
9670 PRINT
9680 PRINT "MEAN SQUARED ERROR ="; E
9690 RETURN
9890 REM PAUSE OUTPUT SUBROUTINE ***************************
9900 PRINT
9910 PRINT "CONTINUE";
9920 INPUT A$
9930 RETURN
9999 END
```

Chapter 3

Population Cohort-Survival Model

The Model

The cohort-survival model represents the standard approach for making population projections in urban and regional planning. The model involves the separate treatment of births, deaths, and migration, applied to a population disaggregated by age and sex. The Population Cohort-Survival Model program presented in this chapter provides for any number of cohorts, three choices for the handling of migration, and the option to modify any of the data and rerun the model.

The basic input data for the cohort-survival model include the population broken down by sex and a series of age-specific cohorts. The nature of the standard model requires that these cohorts be the same size (except for the oldest, open-ended interval), and this interval becomes the period for making projections. Thus, if five-year cohorts are selected (0–4 years, 5–9 years, and so forth, up to 85 years and over), projections will be made for five-year intervals. While five- or ten-year cohorts are most often used in planning practice, the program provides for user selection of any cohort size.

During any projection period, the members of any given cohort age and enter the succeeding cohort. Thus the population of any cohort at the end of the period is equal to the population in the next younger cohort at the start of that period, less the number who have died. (This temporarily ignores any migration.) The cohort-survival model uses survivorship rates—the proportion of a cohort surviving from one time period to the next—rather than death rates. This process of aging and survival can then be expressed as

$$P_{i,t+1}^s = S_i^s P_{i,t}^s$$

where $P_{i,t}^s$ is the population of sex s (male or female), at time t, for cohort i (of a total of n cohorts), and S_i^s is the survivorship rate (proportion surviving) of sex s and cohort i. The above expression yields the population of all but the oldest cohort. Surviving members of the oldest cohort remain in that group, so the projection of cohort n is as follows:

$$P_{n,t+1}^s = S_{n-1}^s P_{n-1,t}^s + S_n^s P_{n,t}^s$$

The necessary age- and sex-specific survivorship rates, which tend to be relatively stable, can be computed from published reports.[1]

The population of the youngest cohort consists of children born during (and surviving to the end of) the preceding period. Demographers assume births to be a function of the numbers of women of childbearing age. If $P_{i,t}^f$ is the number of females in cohort i at time t, and B_i is the birth rate (including survival to the next period) for that cohort, then $B_i P_{i,t}^f$ is the number of births to women in that cohort. The total number of births during the period t to $t + 1$, surviving to $t + 1$, is, then,

$$B_{t+1} = \sum_{i=1}^{n} B_i P_{i,t}^f$$

These now must be apportioned among the male and female cohorts. Let f be the proportion born and surviving who are female. Then the projected numbers in the first female and male cohorts at time $t + 1$, ignoring migration, are

$$P_{1,t+1}^f = f\, B_{t+1} = f \sum_{i=1}^{n} B_i P_{i,t}^f$$

$$P_{1,t+1}^m = (1 - f)\, B_{t+1} = (1 - f) \sum_{i=1}^{n} B_i P_{i,t}^f$$

Birth rates are not nearly as stable as survivorship rates, but they too can be estimated from published statistics.

Migration into and out of the region represents the most difficult aspect of population projection. This is especially true for small areas, in which migration is likely to be of relatively greater importance compared with the natural increase associated with births and deaths. For simplicity and because of data limitations, most treatments of migration focus on net migration, the difference between the volume of migration into the region and away from the region. Positive net migration represents a gain for the region; negative net migration represents a loss. Levels of net migration to a region in the past may be determined by examining population changes in a preceding period. The actual population changes by age and sex are compared with those that would have been expected based on processes of natural increase alone. The residual is assumed to represent net migration.[2] Such past migration patterns, however, may or may not be appropriate for use in making population projections. In general, the projection of migration is very complex and involves the making of subjective judgments.

Two standard approaches may be taken in including migration in a cohort-survival model. Absolute levels of net migration may be added to (or subtracted from) the population projected by natural increase in each age-sex cohort, with the assumption being made that these levels remain constant. Alternatively, net migration may be assumed to be proportional to the population in each cohort at the beginning of the period. In this case, the migration rates are assumed to be constant. The program provides for both options, as well as the option of no migration.

Inclusion of absolute levels of net migration requires the numbers of migrants into or out of the region for each cohort. This can be designated by M_i^s, representing the net migration into the region for sex s in age cohort i. With net outmigration in a cohort, M_i^s will have a negative value. If $P_{i,t+1}^{s*}$ is the population projected for period $t + 1$ in sex s, cohort i based only on natural increase (survivorship and births), then the projected population using absolute migration levels will simply be

$$P_{i,t+1}^s = P_{i,t+1}^{s*} + M_i^s$$

The use of migration rates involves an additional step, beginning with the age- and sex-specific rates of migration as a function of the cohort sizes at the beginning of the period. The migration rates m_i^s for sex s and age cohort i represent the ratio of net migration to population at the beginning of a period. With data on net migration in the previous period from $t - 1$ to t, $M_{i,t-1\,\text{to}\,t}^s$, migration rates could be calculated as follows:

$$m_i^s = \frac{M_{i,t-1\,\text{to}\,t}^s}{P_{i,t-1}^s}$$

Net migration is then determined in making a projection by using such migration rates and the current populations:

$$M_{i,t\,\text{to}\,t+1}^s = m_i^s\, P_{i,t}^s$$

The inclusion of the net migration in the cohort-survival model with the migration rates is as follows:

$$P_{i,t+1}^s = P_{i,t+1}^{s*} + m_i^s P_{i,t}^s$$

Once again, the user is cautioned that results are no better than the assumptions made regarding migration. The program provides for the handling of migration, but it cannot ensure meaningful results.

The Program

The Population Cohort-Survival Model program is quite flexible, allowing for any size and number of cohorts, offering three options for the handling of migration, and allowing any of the input data to be changed and new projections to be produced without restarting the program and reentering all of the data. The user of the program is first asked to specify the number and size of cohorts and the starting year. (As written, the program allows for up to 18 cohorts, which is sufficient for handling five-year cohorts.) Using this information, the program prompts the user to enter the beginning population, survivorship rates, and birth rates, by age cohort and, except for birth rates, by sex. Birth rates are requested for all cohorts; for those below and above childbearing age (as determined by the user), zero is to be entered. The proportion of births that are female must also be provided.

A menu of options for the projection of migration is then displayed, offering choices of no migration or of using absolute migration levels or migration rates. After a choice has been made, the user is prompted for the appropriate levels or rates, if required.

The program then begins the output, first displaying tables of survivorship rates, birth rates, and migration levels or rates. Populations are output for each period, beginning with the first. The user is asked after each period whether projections for the next period are desired or not; thus projection can be continued as long as desired.

Upon finishing with the projection, the user can either terminate the program or select the option of changing any data and repeating the analysis. In the latter case, a menu is displayed listing the options for data modification. When a choice has been made to modify either population, survivorship rates, birth rates, or migration, the user will be asked for the new information in exactly the same way as at initial input. After the entry of new values, the program prints back the new values and begins the output of the population projections as before.

The program is more elaborate than the one in the preceding chapter, but BASIC programmers should have no problem following or modifying the program. All populations and rates are stored in arrays, and several additional arrays are used in transferring data to and from subroutines. Three arrays hold population data: The initial data are stored in P, which is not altered unless new data are entered. This is moved to Q, which holds the starting data for the projection period. The projected populations are placed in R. At the conclusion of the projections for one period, the new populations in R are placed in Q for the next projection cycle.

The main routine from lines 10 through 790 controls the flow of the program, calling subroutines for data input, model computation, and output.

Upon starting, subroutines at lines 4000, 4500, 5000, 5500, and 6000 are called for data input of initial cohort information, population, survivorship rates, birth rates, and migration information. The latter subroutine provides for the choice of the migration options as well as for the input of any required data. Survivorship rates, birth rates, and migration values are then printed out by subroutines at 7000, 7500, and 8000. The original population is copied from P to Q and is printed out by the subroutine beginning at line 8500. If the user desires the projection of the next period's population, a call is made to the model computation subroutine at line 1000. The new, projected population is then once again printed out by the subroutine at line 8500. After making the projections, the user can choose to change values and repeat from the options listed in a menu. Depending on the choice selected, calls are made to the appropriate subroutines to input the data and print out the revised values. The program then proceeds with the population output and projection.

Two utility subroutines are used for data entry and output. All of the input subroutines obtain age-specific data by calling the cohort data input routine at line 6500. This returns the information in a vector U, which is then moved by the calling subroutine to the appropriate array. The output subroutines place the data for an age- and sex-specific table into the array V and call the table output subroutine at line 9000, which handles the printing of the table.

Sample Problem

The planner begins with the following data on the population of a city in 1980, survivorship rates, and birth rates. The cohort-survival model requires a large amount of input data; to keep the example reasonable, five 15-year cohorts are being employed:

		Males	Females
Population:	0-14	1760	1740
	15-29	1530	1550
	30-44	1250	1280
	45-59	990	1040
	60 & over	740	810
Survivorship Rates:	0-14	0.91	0.95
	15-29	0.85	0.90
	30-44	0.76	0.82
	45-59	0.67	0.71
	60 & over	0.35	0.41

Birth Rates:	0-14	0.0
	15-29	1.8
	30-44	0.5
	45-59	0.0
	60 & over	0.0

Proportion of Births Female: 0.48

Projections are to be made for 1995, assuming no migration. Owing to the large volume of input data required by the cohort-survival model, the listing of the sample run is longer than for some of the other programs. The initial data entry and the results of the analysis without migration are shown in the first part of the sample run.

Analysis of migration patterns in previous periods and in some similar cities suggests that substantial net inmigration could be expected in the younger cohorts, with some outmigration in the older cohorts. The following set of migration rates are to be employed in making a modified projection:

		Males	Females
Migration Rates:	0-14	0.05	0.05
	15-29	0.10	0.08
	30-44	0.03	0.02
	45-59	−0.02	0.00
	60 & over	−0.06	−0.05

Continuing the program after the first set of population projections, the option of changing migration is selected, the migration rate option is indicated, and the rates are entered. The remaining output from the sample run indicates the revised migration information and shows the projections incorporating the effects of that migration. While the sample run is terminated at this point, as many analyses as desired could be made.

References

Krueckeberg, D. A. and Silvers, A. L., *Urban Planning Analysis: Methods and Models* (New York: John Wiley & Sons, Inc., 1974), Chapter 8, pp. 275–282.

Masser, I., *Analytical Models for Urban and Regional Planning* (Newton Abbot: David & Charles, 1972), Chapter 2, pp. 17–36.

Oppenheim, N., *Applied Models in Urban and Regional Analysis* (Englewood Cliffs, N. J.: Prentice-Hall, Inc., 1980), Chapter 2, pp. 45–62.

Wilson, A. G., *Urban and Regional Models in Geography and Planning* (London: John Wiley & Sons, 1974), Chapter 7, pp. 77–87.

Notes

[1] Information on the computation of the survivorship rates and the other rates required by the cohort-survival model can be found in many of the sources listed in the References at the end of the chapter. Additional information can be found in Shyrock, H. and Siegel, J. *The Methods and Materials of Demography* (Washington, D.C.: U. S. Bureau of the Census, 1971) and Pittenger, D. B., *Projecting State and Local Populations* (Cambridge, Mass.: Ballinger Publishing Company, 1976).

[2] The Cohort-Survival Model program could be used in conducting such an analysis. The population at the beginning of the period could be projected to the end. These projected values by age and sex could be subtracted from the actual population values with the results used as estimates of net migration. The program could be expanded to provide for the input of the previous period's population and then automatically include the previous period's migration in making the projection. However, the process of handling migration in population projection raises too many complex issues, and the inclusion of such an automatic capability could make it seem too simple and would be misleading.

POPULATION COHORT-SURVIVAL MODEL SAMPLE RUN

POPULATION COHORT-SURVIVAL MODEL

NUMBER OF COHORTS (MAXIMUM 18)? 5
YEARS PER COHORT? 15
STARTING YEAR? 1980

ENTER POPULATION IN YEAR 1980

NUMBERS OF MALES
    0 - 14 ? 1760
    15 - 29 ? 1530
    30 - 44 ? 1250
    45 - 59 ? 990
    60 & UP? 740

NUMBERS OF FEMALES
    0 - 14 ? 1740
    15 - 29 ? 1550
    30 - 44 ? 1280
    45 - 59 ? 1040
    60 & UP? 810

ENTER SURVIVORSHIP RATES

RATES FOR MALES
    0 - 14 ? .91
    15 - 29 ? .85
    30 - 44 ? .76
    45 - 59 ? .67
    60 & UP? .35

RATES FOR FEMALES
    0 - 14 ? .95
    15 - 29 ? .90
    30 - 44 ? .82
    45 - 59 ? .71
    60 & UP? .41

ENTER BIRTH RATES
    0 - 14 ? 0
    15 - 29 ? 1.8
    30 - 44 ? .5
    45 - 59 ? 0
    60 & UP? 0

PROPORTION OF BIRTHS FEMALE? .48

```
MIGRATION OPTIONS:
    1 - NO MIGRATION
    2 - ABSOLUTE MIGRATION LEVELS
    3 - MIGRATION RATES

CHOICE OF OPTION? 1


SURVIVORSHIP RATES

AGE            MALES           FEMALES
 0 - 14         .91             .95
15 - 29         .85             .9
30 - 44         .76             .82
45 - 59         .67             .71
60 & UP         .35             .41

CONTINUE?


BIRTH RATES

AGE            MALES           FEMALES
 0 - 14         0               0
15 - 29         0               1.8
30 - 44         0               .5
45 - 59         0               0
60 & UP         0               0

CONTINUE?

PROPORTION OF BIRTHS FEMALE = .48

CONTINUE?


ABSOLUTE MIGRATION LEVELS

AGE            MALES           FEMALES
 0 - 14         0               0
15 - 29         0               0
30 - 44         0               0
45 - 59         0               0
60 & UP         0               0

CONTINUE?
```

```
POPULATION IN YEAR 1980

AGE           MALES          FEMALES
 0 - 14       1760           1740
15 - 29       1530           1550
30 - 44       1250           1280
45 - 59        990           1040
60 & UP        740            810
TOTAL         6270           ᴢ420

NEXT PERIOD (1=YES, 0=NO)? 1


POPULATION IN YEAR 1995

AGE           MALES          FEMALES
 0 - 14       1784           1646
15 - 29       1602           1653
30 - 44       1301           1395
45 - 59        950           1050
60 & UP        922           1071
TOTAL         6559           6815

NEXT PERIOD (1=YES, 0=NO)? 0


REPEAT ANALYSIS WITH OPTION TO
CHANGE DATA (1=YES, 0=NO)? 1

OPTIONS FOR DATA MODIFICATION:
    1 - POPULATION
    2 - SURVIVORSHIP RATES
    3 - BIRTH RATES
    4 - MIGRATION

CHOICE OF OPTION? 4

MIGRATION OPTIONS:
    1 - NO MIGRATION
    2 - ABSOLUTE MIGRATION LEVELS
    3 - MIGRATION RATES

CHOICE OF OPTION? 3

ENTER MIGRATION RATES

MALE MIGRATION
     0 - 14 ? .05
    15 - 29 ? .1
    30 - 44 ? .03
    45 - 59 ? -.02
    60 & UP? -.06
```

```
FEMALE MIGRATION
      0 - 14 ? .05
     15 - 29 ? .08
     30 - 44 ? .02
     45 - 59 ? 0
     60 & UP? -.05
```

MIGRATION RATES

AGE	MALES	FEMALES
0 - 14	.05	.05
15 - 29	.1	.08
30 - 44	.03	.02
45 - 59	-.02	0
60 & UP	-.06	-.05

CONTINUE?

POPULATION IN YEAR 1980

AGE	MALES	FEMALES
0 - 14	1760	1740
15 - 29	1530	1550
30 - 44	1250	1280
45 - 59	990	1040
60 & UP	740	810
TOTAL	6270	6420

NEXT PERIOD (1=YES, 0=NO)? 1

POPULATION IN YEAR 1995

AGE	MALES	FEMALES
0 - 14	1872	1733
15 - 29	1755	1777
30 - 44	1338	1421
45 - 59	930	1050
60 & UP	878	1030
TOTAL	6773	7011

NEXT PERIOD (1=YES, 0=NO)? 0

REPEAT ANALYSIS WITH OPTION TO
CHANGE DATA (1=YES, 0=NO)? 0

POPULATION COHORT-SURVIVAL MODEL PROGRAM LISTING

```
10 REM POPULATION COHORT-SURVIVAL MODEL
20 REM BY JOHN R. OTTENSMANN
30 REM VARIABLES
40 REM     B(I) - BIRTH RATE BY COHORT
50 REM     M(I,J) - MIGRATION VALUES BY COHORT AND SEX
60 REM     P(I,J) - ORIGINAL POPULATION
70 REM     Q(I,J) - CURRENT POPULATION
80 REM     R(I,J) - POPULATION AT END OF PERIOD
90 REM     S(I,J) - SURVIVORSHIP RATES
100 REM     U(I) - COHORT INPUT STORAGE
110 REM     V(I,J) - TABLE PRINT STORAGE
120 REM     C - CHOICE OF MIGRATION OPTION
130 REM     F - PROPORTION OF BIRTHS FEMALE
140 REM     N - NUMBER OF COHORTS
150 REM     W - YEARS PER COHORT
160 REM     Y - STARTING YEAR
170 REM     Z - CURRENT YEAR
180 DIM B(18), M(18,2), P(18,2), Q(19,2), R(18,2), S(18,2)
190 DIM U(18), V(18,2)
200 REM INPUT DATA
210 PRINT
220 PRINT
230 PRINT "POPULATION COHORT-SURVIVAL MODEL"
240 GOSUB 4000
250 GOSUB 4500
260 GOSUB 5000
270 GOSUB 5500
280 GOSUB 6000
290 REM OUTPUT RATES
300 GOSUB 7000
310 GOSUB 7500
320 GOSUB 8000
330 REM PUT ORIGINAL POPULATION IN CURRENT ARRAY
340 FOR I = 1 TO N
350 FOR J = 1 TO 2
360 Q(I,J) = P(I,J)
370 NEXT J
380 NEXT I
390 Z = Y
400 REM OUTPUT CURRENT POPULATION
410 GOSUB 8500
420 PRINT
430 PRINT "NEXT PERIOD (1=YES, 0=NO)";
440 INPUT A
450 IF A = 0 THEN 500
460 REM COMPUTE NEXT PERIOD POPULATION
470 GOSUB 1000
480 GOTO 410
490 REM OPTION TO CHANGE AND REPEAT
500 PRINT
```

```
510 PRINT
520 PRINT "REPEAT ANALYSIS WITH OPTION TO"
530 PRINT "CHANGE DATA (1=YES, 0=NO)";
540 INPUT A
550 IF A = 0 THEN 9999
560 PRINT
570 PRINT "OPTIONS FOR DATA MODIFICATION:"
580 PRINT TAB(5); "1 - POPULATION"
590 PRINT TAB(5); "2 - SURVIVORSHIP RATES"
600 PRINT TAB(5); "3 - BIRTH RATES"
610 PRINT TAB(5); "4 - MIGRATION"
620 PRINT
630 PRINT "CHOICE OF OPTION";
640 INPUT A
650 IF A <> 1 THEN 680
660 GOSUB 4500
670 GOTO 340
680 IF A <> 2 THEN 720
690 GOSUB 5000
700 GOSUB 7000
710 GOTO 340
720 IF A <> 3 THEN 760
730 GOSUB 5500
740 GOSUB 7500
750 GOTO 340
760 IF A <> 4 THEN 560
770 GOSUB 6000
780 GOSUB 8000
790 GOTO 340
990 REM NEW POPULTION COMPUTATION SUBROUTINE **************
1000 Z = Z + W
1010 REM COMPUTE SURVIVORS FOR NEXT PERIOD
1020 FOR J = 1 TO 2
1030 FOR I = 1 TO N - 1
1040 R(I+1,J) = Q(I,J) * S(I,J)
1050 NEXT I
1060 R(N,J) = R(N,J) + Q(N,J) * S(N,J)
1070 NEXT J
1080 REM COMPUTE BIRTHS FOR NEXT PERIOD
1090 R(1,1) = 0
1100 R(1,2) = 0
1110 FOR I = 1 TO N
1120 R(1,1) = R(1,1) + Q(I,2) * B(I) * (1 - F)
1130 R(1,2) = R(1,2) + Q(I,2) * B(I) * F
1140 NEXT I
1150 REM COMPUTE MIGRATION
1160 FOR I = 1 TO N
1170 FOR J = 1 TO 2
1180 IF C = 3 THEN 1210
1190 R(I,J) = R(I,J) + M(I,J)
1200 GOTO 1220
1210 R(I,J) = R(I,J) + M(I,J) * Q(I,J)
1220 NEXT J
```

```
1230 NEXT I
1240 REM PUT NEW POPULATION IN CURRENT ARRAY
1250 FOR I = 1 TO N
1260 FOR J = 1 TO 2
1270 Q(I,J) = INT(R(I,J) + .5)
1280 NEXT J
1290 NEXT I
1300 RETURN
3990 REM INITIAL DATA INPUT SUBROUTINE ********************
4000 PRINT
4010 PRINT "NUMBER OF COHORTS (MAXIMUM 18)";
4020 INPUT N
4030 PRINT "YEARS PER COHORT";
4040 INPUT W
4050 PRINT "STARTING YEAR";
4060 INPUT Y
4070 RETURN
4490 REM POPULATION INPUT SUBROUTINE **********************
4500 PRINT
4510 PRINT "ENTER POPULATION IN YEAR"; Y
4520 PRINT
4530 PRINT "NUMBERS OF MALES"
4540 GOSUB 6500
4550 FOR I = 1 TO N
4560 P(I,1) = U(I)
4570 NEXT I
4580 PRINT
4590 PRINT "NUMBERS OF FEMALES"
4600 GOSUB 6500
4610 FOR I = 1 TO N
4620 P(I,2) = U(I)
4630 NEXT I
4640 RETURN
4990 REM SURVIVORSHIP INPUT SUBROUTINE ********************
5000 PRINT
5010 PRINT "ENTER SURVIVORSHIP RATES"
5020 PRINT
5030 PRINT "RATES FOR MALES"
5040 GOSUB 6500
5050 FOR I = 1 TO N
5060 S(I,1) = U(I)
5070 NEXT I
5080 PRINT
5090 PRINT "RATES FOR FEMALES"
5100 GOSUB 6500
5110 FOR I = 1 TO N
5120 S(I,2) = U(I)
5130 NEXT I
5140 RETURN
5490 REM BIRTH RATE INPUT SUBROUTINE **********************
5500 PRINT
5510 PRINT "ENTER BIRTH RATES"
5520 GOSUB 6500
```

```
5530 FOR I = 1 TO N
5540 B(I) = U(I)
5550 NEXT I
5560 PRINT
5570 PRINT "PROPORTION OF BIRTHS FEMALE";
5580 INPUT F
5590 RETURN
5990 REM MIGRATION DATA INPUT SUBROUTINE ******************
6000 PRINT
6010 PRINT "MIGRATION OPTIONS:"
6020 PRINT TAB(5); "1 - NO MIGRATION"
6030 PRINT TAB(5); "2 - ABSOLUTE MIGRATION LEVELS"
6040 PRINT TAB(5); "3 - MIGRATION RATES"
6050 PRINT
6060 PRINT "CHOICE OF OPTION";
6070 INPUT C
6080 IF C = 1 THEN 6130
6090 IF C = 2 THEN 6200
6100 IF C = 3 THEN 6230
6110 GOTO 6000
6120 REM NO MIGRATION OPTION
6130 FOR I = 1 TO N
6140 FOR J = 1 TO 2
6150 M(I,J) = 0
6160 NEXT J
6170 NEXT I
6180 GOTO 6370
6190 REM LEVEL AND RATE INPUT
6200 PRINT
6210 PRINT "ENTER ABSOLUTE MIGRATION LEVELS"
6220 GOTO 6250
6230 PRINT
6240 PRINT "ENTER MIGRATION RATES"
6250 PRINT
6260 PRINT "MALE MIGRATION"
6270 GOSUB 6500
6280 FOR I = 1 TO N
6290 M(I,1) = U(I)
6300 NEXT I
6310 PRINT
6320 PRINT "FEMALE MIGRATION"
6330 GOSUB 6500
6340 FOR I = 1 TO N
6350 M(I,2) = U(I)
6360 NEXT I
6370 RETURN
6490 REM COHORT DATA INPUT SUBROUTINE ********************
6500 FOR I = 1 TO N - 1
6510 PRINT TAB(5); (I-1)*W; "-"; I*W-1;
6520 INPUT U(I)
6530 NEXT I
6540 PRINT TAB(5); (N-1)*W; "& UP";
6550 INPUT U(N)
```

```
6560 RETURN
6990 REM SURVIVORSHIP RATE OUTPUT SUBROUTINE **************
7000 PRINT
7010 PRINT
7020 PRINT "SURVIVORSHIP RATES"
7030 FOR I = 1 TO N
7040 FOR J = 1 TO 2
7050 V(I,J) = S(I,J)
7060 NEXT J
7070 NEXT I
7080 GOSUB 9000
7090 GOSUB 9900
7100 RETURN
7490 REM BIRTH RATE OUTPUT SUBROUTINE *********************
7500 PRINT
7510 PRINT
7520 PRINT "BIRTH RATES"
7530 FOR I = 1 TO N
7540 V(I,1) = 0
7550 V(I,2) = B(I)
7560 NEXT I
7570 GOSUB 9000
7580 GOSUB 9900
7590 PRINT
7600 PRINT "PROPORTION OF BIRTHS FEMALE ="; F
7610 GOSUB 9900
7620 RETURN
7990 REM MIGRATION DATA OUTPUT SUBROUTINE *****************
8000 PRINT
8010 PRINT
8020 IF C = 3 THEN 8050
8030 PRINT "ABSOLUTE MIGRATION LEVELS"
8040 GOTO 8060
8050 PRINT "MIGRATION RATES"
8060 FOR I = 1 TO N
8070 FOR J = 1 TO 2
8080 V(I,J) = M(I,J)
8090 NEXT J
8100 NEXT I
8110 GOSUB 9000
8120 GOSUB 9900
8130 RETURN
8490 REM CURRENT POPULATION OUTPUT SUBROUTINE **************
8500 PRINT
8510 PRINT
8520 PRINT "POPULATION IN YEAR"; Z
8530 FOR J = 1 TO 2
8540 Q(N+1,J) = 0
8550 FOR I = 1 TO N
8560 Q(N+1,J) = Q(N+1,J) + Q(I,J)
8570 V(I,J) = Q(I,J)
8580 NEXT I
8590 NEXT J
```

```
8600 GOSUB 9000
8610 PRINT "TOTAL"; TAB(13); Q(N+1,1); TAB(27); Q(N+1,2)
8620 RETURN
8990 REM TABLE OUTPUT SUBROUTINE *************************
9000 PRINT
9010 PRINT "AGE"; TAB(13); "MALES"; TAB(27); "FEMALES"
9020 FOR I = 1 TO N - 1
9030 PRINT (I-1)*W; "-"; I*W-1; TAB(13); V(I,1);
9040 PRINT TAB(27); V(I,2)
9050 NEXT I
9060 PRINT (N-1)*W; "& UP"; TAB(13); V(N,1); TAB(27); V(N,2)
9070 RETURN
9890 REM PAUSE OUTPUT SUBROUTINE *************************
9900 PRINT
9910 PRINT "CONTINUE";
9920 INPUT A$
9930 RETURN
9999 END
```

Chapter 4

Economic Base Model

The Model

The economic base model provides one of the simplest approaches for the forecasting of economic activity. The fundamental concept is quite simple: The local economy is divided into two sectors—a basic sector and a nonbasic or service sector. Those economic activities resulting in the export of goods or services from the region, generating income from outside, are viewed as basic. The sale of goods and services to others within the region takes place in the nonbasic or service sector. The basic sector "drives" the local economy, providing the income that fuels activity in the service sector. The level of economic activity in the service sector thus depends on the level of basic activity. The relationship between the basic and service sectors is determined using current data. Then, given a forecast of future levels of basic economic activity, a prediction can be made of future economic activity in the service sector. Alternatively, the economic base model can be used for impact assessment, determining the consequences of a change in basic sector activity (such as a plant opening or closing) for the local economy as a whole.

Formally, the economic base model itself is very simple. Total economic activity is the sum of activity in the basic and nonbasic or service sectors:

$$E = E_B + E_S$$

where E is the total economic activity, E_B is the basic economic activity, and E_S is the service or nonbasic economic activity. Employment is the most often used measure of economic activity because the data are more readily available, though other measures such as regional income might also be used. The current basic and nonbasic activity levels are used to determine an economic base multiplier R:

$$R = \frac{E_S}{E_B}$$

A fundamental assumption is that this basic–nonbasic ratio remains constant and thus can be used for prediction. Given a forecast future value for the level of basic economic activity (or the change in basic activity) E_B', the new level of activity in the nonbasic sector is simply

$$E_S' = RE_B'$$

where E_S' is the predicted level of nonbasic economic activity. It is not unusual in economic base analyses to further assume that the regional population is dependent on the total level of economic activity. Current data can be used to determine a population multiplier,

$$Q = \frac{P}{E}$$

where P is the region's population and Q is the multiplier. If this ratio is also assumed to be constant, then future population levels can in turn be predicted from future levels of economic activity:

$$P' = Q E'$$

where P' is the predicted population and E' is the predicted total economic activity, the sum of the predicted basic and nonbasic levels.

Using the economic base model requires information on the level of current basic economic activity. Surveys of local firms to determine the proportions of sales outside the region represent one possibility for obtaining the required information, but such surveys are very costly. For simple economies, it may be possible to specify a priori some industrial categories as being the export or basic sector of the local economy, with all other categories being nonbasic. This might be reasonable for a mining town, for example. In most situations, however, neither of these approaches for determining the size of the economic base will be satisfactory.

The remaining alternative is to employ published economic statistics on regional and national economic activity to estimate the size of the region's economic base. Two different approaches—the location quotient method and the minimum requirements method—are commonly used for such estimation. Both use data on regional economic activity broken down by industrial sector. Estimates are made of the level of activity needed in each industry to meet local (nonbasic) needs. For sectors with greater levels of economic activity, the excess is assumed to be export or basic activity. The only difference between the two methods is the manner in which the estimate of the economic activity needed to meet local requirements is made.

The location quotient approach assumes that to meet local needs a region requires a level of economic activity in an industry proportional to the level in the nation as a whole. For example, if five percent of national employment is in industry A, that proportion just meets national needs (ignoring international imports and exports). Thus, a region would require five percent of its employment in industry A to meet local needs. Any excess would be production for export from the region and would be basic employment. Analysis begins with the location quotient for each industry:

$$LQ_i = \frac{E_{iR}/E_R}{E_{iN}/E_N}$$

where LQ_i is the location quotient for industry i; E_{iR} is the regional economic activity in industry i; E_R is the total regional economic activity; E_{iN} is the national economic activity in i; and E_N is the total national economic activity. The location quotient is a ratio of the proportion of regional economic activity in i to the proportion of national economic activity in i. If the location quotient for an industry is exactly one, the proportions are identical and the region is just able to meet local needs. Location quotients less than one imply less than proportional activity in the region, forcing the region to import the goods or services produced by the industry. With location quotients greater than one, the region more than meets its needs in industry i and can export to the rest of the nation. Industries with location quotients greater than one contribute to basic economic activity. Since the national proportion in industry i, E_{iN}/E_N, is assumed to be required to meet local needs, the remainder of the region's activity in industry i is then basic:

$$E_{iRB} = E_{iR} - \left[\frac{E_{iN}}{E_N} \right] E_R$$

where E_{iRB} is the estimate of basic economic activity in region R in industry i. The total volume of basic economic activity is then the sum of these estimates for all industries with location quotients greater than one.

The minimum requirements method compares the region under consideration not to the nation but to other similar regions. If, for example, the region under consideration is a small metropolitan area, comparisons would be made with other small metropolitan areas. The smallest proportion of economic activity in industry i for all of the regions is assumed to be sufficient to meet local needs. This is the minimum requirement:

$$MR_i = \min_j \left[\frac{E_{ij}}{E_j} \right], \qquad j = 1,2,\ldots,n$$

where MR_i is the minimum requirement in industry i; E_{ij} is the economic activity in industry i in region j, for regions 1 to n; E_j is the total economic activity in region j; and $\min_j$ is the minimum of the proportions across all n regions. Since this minimum requirement is assumed to be the proportion needed to meet local needs, the amount of basic economic activity in region R for industry i, E_{iRB}, is then:

$$E_{iRB} = E_{iR} - (MR_i)E_R$$

Once again, total basic economic activity in region R is the sum of the basic activity in all industry sectors.

The minimum requirements method produces larger estimates of basic economic activity than the location quotient method. The accuracy of the two methods (and indeed the choice of one over the other) is related to the degree of industrial disaggregation, that is, the number of industry sectors used in the analysis.

The Program

The Economic Base Model program provides for the estimation of basic economic activity using either the location quotient or the minimum requirements method, computes the values for the economic base model, and allows projection of future levels of economic activity given a projection of the new level (or the change in the level) of basic economic activity. Up to 18 industry sectors can be used and data on up to 18 different regions (for the minimum requirements model) can be entered. Computed measures of economic activity are rounded to the nearest integer.

The program first offers the choice of using either the location quotient or the minimum requirements approach. Both require data on levels of economic activity in the region of concern (referred to as the "target" region) disaggregated by industry. The location quotient method requires similar data for the nation as a whole, while the minimum requirements method requires this type of data for a number of comparison regions. The program also asks if population is to be included in the analysis. If it is, the target region population is also required and must be entered.

The program asks for the number of economic sectors into which the data are disaggregated and then prompts the user for the appropriate data. Using the location quotient method, regional and national data by sector are requested. These data are then printed out, along with the location quotients and the estimates of basic economic activity by sector.

When the minimum requirements method is selected, economic activity levels by sector are first entered for the target region. The number of additional comparison regions is requested, and the user is then prompted to enter the data for each of these. Levels of economic activity by region and sector are printed out, followed by the minimum requirements and estimates of basic economic activity by sector.

Following this for both methods is an economic base model summary for the target region, including total, basic, and nonbasic economic activity; the economic base multiplier; and, if population was included, the regional population and population multiplier. The user is then given the option of making a projection. To do so requires entry of a projected value for basic economic activity. The projection is made using the values determined for the economic base model. Printed out are the projected basic, nonbasic, and total economic activity and the projected population (if that option was chosen earlier). Projections for other basic economic activity levels can be repeated as many times as desired.

For more convenient output of the economic activity levels in multiple regions when using the minimum requirements method, the program provides the option of having the tables extend beyond the normal 40 column limit. An 80-column screen can display as many as five columns of data, as opposed to only two on a 40-column screen. The width of the output is specified by assigning the appropriate value for the number of fields of output to the variable F in line 220. For example, with $F = 5$, five columns of output would be displayed, suitable for an 80-column screen.

The main program routine, from lines 10 through 630, controls the flow of the program, giving the options for method, population, and projection, and provides for the input of projected basic economic activity. After the initial question, the main routine calls a subroutine at line 4000 to input the target region economic activity. If the location quotient method has been chosen, the main routine calls subroutines at line 4500 for remaining data entry (of national economic activity), at line 1000 for computation, and at line 7000 for output of the data and results. For the minimum requirements method, comparable subroutines to perform the same functions are used at lines 5000, 1500, and 7500. The subroutine at line 8000 then outputs the summary economic base results for both methods. For projections, after the entry of the projected basic economic activity, the subroutine at line 8500 prints out the final results.

Sample Problem

A planner wishes to ascertain the impact of a new plant about to open in a medium-sized urban region. He or she has assembled the following data on employment in the region for five sectors:

Sector	Regional Employment
1	9,600
2	8,200
3	8,900
4	1,900
5	7,600

The regional population is 215,000. The first estimate uses the location quotient method for estimating employment in the basic sector. This requires comparable employment data for the nation as a whole:

Sector	National Employment
1	6,700,000
2	24,700,000
3	11,200,000
4	4,100,000
5	15,400,000

In the first sample run of the Economic Base Model program, the location quotient option is selected and the regional and national employment values are entered as requested. Location quotients and basic employment by sector are reported, and the summary values for the economic base model are given. Going on to make the projection, the additional basic employment generated by the new plant, 150, is entered. The program then prints out the additional nonbasic employment, the total employment increase, and the population increase projected as a result of the new plant.

For comparison, the minimum requirements method for the estimation of basic sector employment is also tried. This requires data on employment by sector in comparable urban regions. For the example, data for three additional regions are used:

Sector	Region 2 Employment
1	2,900
2	11,800
3	4,800
4	1,200
5	4,900

Sector	Region 3 Employment
1	2,500
2	11,800
3	6,300
4	2,100
5	7,300

Sector	Region 4 Employment
1	4,400
2	15,900
3	7,600
4	7,900
5	14,200

The program is run again, this time selecting the minimum requirements option. The program prompts the user for the required data and reports the minimum requirements, basic employment by sector, and values for the economic base model. This time, estimates of basic employment are greater, and the economic base multiplier is smaller. The new basic employment generated by the plant is entered for the projection, and the somewhat smaller increases in nonbasic employment, total employment, and population are printed out.

References

Isard, W., *Methods of Regional Analysis: An Introduction to Regional Science* (Cambridge, Mass.: M.I.T. Press, 1960), Chapter 5, pp. 123–126 and Chapter 6, pp. 189–213.

Krueckeberg, D. A. and Silvers, A. L., *Urban Planning Analysis: Methods and Models* (New York: John Wiley & Sons, Inc., 1974), Chapter 12, pp. 389–406.

Masser, I., *Analytical Models for Urban and Regional Planning* (Newton Abbot: David & Charles, 1972), Chapter 3, pp. 63–69.

Oppenheim, N., *Applied Models in Urban and Regional Analysis* (Englewood Cliffs, N. J.: Prentice-Hall, Inc., 1980), Chapter 3, pp. 72–77, 90–93.

ECONOMIC BASE MODEL SAMPLE RUN ONE

ECONOMIC BASE MODEL

OPTIONS FOR BASIC SECTOR ESTIMATION:
    1 - LOCATION QUOTIENT
    2 - MINIMUM REQUIREMENTS

CHOICE OF OPTION? 1

DO YOU WISH TO INCLUDE TARGET REGION
POPULATION (1=YES, 0=NO)? 1

TARGET REGION POPULATION? 215000

NUMBER OF ECON SECTORS (18 MAX)? 5

ENTER TARGET REGION (REGION 1) ECONOMIC
ACTIVITY BY SECTOR
    SECTOR 1 ? 9600
    SECTOR 2 ? 8200
    SECTOR 3 ? 8900
    SECTOR 4 ? 1900
    SECTOR 5 ? 7600

ENTER NATIONAL ECONOMIC ACTIVITY
    SECTOR 1 ? 6700000
    SECTOR 2 ? 24700000
    SECTOR 3 ? 11200000
    SECTOR 4 ? 4100000
    SECTOR 5 ? 15400000

SECTOR	TARGET REG ECON ACTIV	NATIONAL ECON ACTIV
1	9600	6.7E+06
2	8200	2.47E+07
3	8900	1.12E+07
4	1900	4.1E+06
5	7600	1.54E+07

CONTINUE?

SECTOR	LOCATION QUOTIENT	BASIC ECON ACTIV
1	2.458	5694
2	.57	0
3	1.363	2371
4	.795	0
5	.847	0

```
CONTINUE?


TARGET REGION (REGION 1) SUMMARY:

     TOTAL ECONOMIC ACTIVITY = 36200
     BASIC ECONOMIC ACTIVITY = 8065
     NONBASIC ECON ACTIVITY = 28135
     ECONOMIC BASE MULTIPLIER = 3.48853
     POPULATION = 215000
     POPULATION MULTIPLIER = 5.93923


DO YOU WISH TO MAKE A PROJECTION
(1=YES, 0=NO)? 1

PROJECTED BASIC ECONOMIC ACTIVITY? 150


ECONOMIC BASE PROJECTION:

     BASIC ECONOMIC ACTIVITY = 150
     NONBASIC ECON ACTIVITY = 523
     TOTAL ECONOMIC ACTIVITY = 673
     POPULATION = 3997


DO YOU WISH TO MAKE A PROJECTION
(1=YES, 0=NO)? 0
```

```
ECONOMIC BASE MODEL SAMPLE RUN TWO


ECONOMIC BASE MODEL

OPTIONS FOR BASIC SECTOR ESTIMATION:
    1 - LOCATION QUOTIENT
    2 - MINIMUM REQUIREMENTS

CHOICE OF OPTION? 2

DO YOU WISH TO INCLUDE TARGET REGION
POPULATION (1=YES, 0=NO)? 1

TARGET REGION POPULATION? 215000

NUMBER OF ECON SECTORS (18 MAX)? 5

ENTER TARGET REGION (REGION 1) ECONOMIC
ACTIVITY BY SECTOR
    SECTOR 1 ? 9600
    SECTOR 2 ? 8200
    SECTOR 3 ? 8900
    SECTOR 4 ? 1900
    SECTOR 5 ? 7600

NUMBER OF ADDITIONAL REGIONS? 3

ENTER ECONOMIC ACTIVITY FOR REGION 2
    SECTOR 1 ? 2900
    SECTOR 2 ? 11800
    SECTOR 3 ? 4800
    SECTOR 4 ? 1200
    SECTOR 5 ? 4900

ENTER ECONOMIC ACTIVITY FOR REGION 3
    SECTOR 1 ? 2500
    SECTOR 2 ? 11800
    SECTOR 3 ? 6300
    SECTOR 4 ? 2100
    SECTOR 5 ? 7300

ENTER ECONOMIC ACTIVITY FOR REGION 4
    SECTOR 1 ? 4400
    SECTOR 2 ? 15900
    SECTOR 3 ? 7600
    SECTOR 4 ? 7900
    SECTOR 5 ? 14200
```

```
ECONOMIC ACTIVITY BY REGION AND SECTOR

SECTOR    REGION 1        REGION 2        REGION 3        REGION 4
  1         9600            2900            2500            4400
  2         8200           11800           11800           15900
  3         8900            4800            6300            7600
  4         1900            1200            2100            7900
  5         7600            4900            7300           14200

CONTINUE?


SECTOR        MIN REQ         BASIC
              (PERCENT)       ECON ACTIV
  1            8.33           6583
  2           22.65          0
  3           15.2           3398
  4            4.69           203
  5           19.14           671

CONTINUE?


TARGET REGION (REGION 1) SUMMARY:

     TOTAL ECONOMIC ACTIVITY = 36200
     BASIC ECONOMIC ACTIVITY = 10855
     NONBASIC ECON ACTIVITY = 25345
     ECONOMIC BASE MULTIPLIER = 2.33487
     POPULATION = 215000
     POPULATION MULTIPLIER = 5.93923


DO YOU WISH TO MAKE A PROJECTION
(1=YES, 0=NO)? 1

PROJECTED BASIC ECONOMIC ACTIVITY? 150


ECONOMIC BASE PROJECTION:

     BASIC ECONOMIC ACTIVITY = 150
     NONBASIC ECON ACTIVITY = 350
     TOTAL ECONOMIC ACTIVITY = 500
     POPULATION = 2970


DO YOU WISH TO MAKE A PROJECTION
(1=YES, 0=NO)? 0
```

ECONOMIC BASE MODEL PROGRAM LISTING

```
10 REM ECONOMIC BASE MODEL
20 REM BY JOHN R. OTTENSMANN
30 REM VARIABLES
40 REM      E(I,J) - ECON ACTIVITY, SECTOR I, REGION J
50 REM      L(I) - LOCATION QUOTIENT OR MIN REQUIREMENTS
60 REM      M(I) - BASIC ECONOMIC ACTIVITY
70 REM      B - TOTAL BASIC ECONOMIC ACTIVITY
80 REM      C - CHOICE OF METHOD
90 REM      D - POPULATION INCLUDED? (YES = 1)
100 REM      K - TOTAL NUMBER OF REGIONS
110 REM      N - NUMBER OF SECTORS
120 REM      P - POPULATION
130 REM      Q - POPULATION MULTIPLIER
140 REM      R - ECONOMIC BASE MULTIPLIER
150 REM      S - NONBASIC ECONOMIC ACTIVITY
160 REM      T - TOTAL ECONOMIC ACTIVITY
170 DIM E(19,18), L(18), M(18)
180 REM F SPECIFIES NUMBERS OF COLUMNS IN EXTENDED TABLE
190 REM SEGMENTS
200 REM      F = 5 FOR 80-COLUMN DISPLAY
210 REM      F = 2 FOR 40COLUMN DISPLAY
220 F = 5
230 REM INPUT DATA
240 PRINT
250 PRINT
260 PRINT "ECONOMIC BASE MODEL"
270 PRINT
280 PRINT "OPTIONS FOR BASIC SECTOR ESTIMATION:"
290 PRINT TAB(5); "1 - LOCATION QUOTIENT"
300 PRINT TAB(5); "2 - MINIMUM REQUIREMENTS"
310 PRINT
320 PRINT "CHOICE OF OPTION";
330 INPUT C
340 PRINT
350 PRINT "DO YOU WISH TO INCLUDE TARGET REGION"
360 PRINT "POPULATION (1=YES, 0=NO)";
370 INPUT D
380 GOSUB 4000
390 REM DATA INPUT, COMPUTATIONS, OUTPUT, FOR EACH MODEL
400 IF C <> 1 THEN 470
410 REM LOCATION QUOTIENT MODEL
420 GOSUB 4500
430 GOSUB 1000
440 GOSUB 7000
450 GOTO 510
460 REM MINIMUM REQUIREMENTS MODEL
470 GOSUB 5000
480 GOSUB 1500
490 GOSUB 7500
500 REM BOTH MODELS
```

```
510 GOSUB 8000
520 REM BEGIN PROJECTION PHASE
530 PRINT
540 PRINT
550 PRINT "DO YOU WISH TO MAKE A PROJECTION"
560 PRINT "(1=YES, 0=NO)";
570 INPUT A
580 IF A = 0 THEN 9999
590 PRINT
600 PRINT "PROJECTED BASIC ECONOMIC ACTIVITY";
610 INPUT B
620 GOSUB 8500
630 GOTO 530
980 REM LOCATION QUOTIENT CALCULATION SUBROUTINE ***********
990 REM SUM ECONOMIC ACTIVITY
1000 FOR J = 1 TO 2
1010 E(N+1,J) = 0
1020 FOR I = 1 TO N
1030 E(N+1,J) = E(N+1,J) + E(I,J)
1040 NEXT I
1050 NEXT J
1060 REM COMPUTE LOCATION QUOT AND BASIC ACTIVITY
1070 B = 0
1080 FOR I = 1 TO N
1090 L(I) = (E(I,1)/E(N+1,1)) / (E(I,2)/E(N+1,2))
1100 IF L(I) > 1 THEN 1130
1110 M(I) = 0
1120 GOTO 1150
1130 M(I) = INT(E(I,1) - (E(I,2)/E(N+1,2)) * E(N+1,1) + .5)
1140 B = B + M(I)
1150 L(I) = INT(L(I)*1000 + .5)/1000
1160 NEXT I
1170 T = E(N+1,1)
1180 S = T - B
1190 R = S / B
1200 IF D <> 1 THEN 1220
1210 Q = P / T
1220 RETURN
1480 REM MINIMUM REQUIREMENTS CALCULATION SUBROUTINE *******
1490 REM SUM ECONOMIC ACTIVITY
1500 FOR J = 1 TO K
1510 E(N+1,J) = 0
1520 FOR I = 1 TO N
1530 E(N+1,J) = E(N+1,J) + E(I,J)
1540 NEXT I
1550 NEXT J
1560 REM COMPUTE MINIMUM REQUIREMENTS AND BASIC ACTIVITY
1570 B = 0
1580 FOR I = 1 TO N
1590 L(I) = E(I,1) / E(N+1,1)
1600 FOR J = 2 TO K
1610 IF L(I) <= E(I,J) / E(N+1,J) THEN 1630
1620 L(I) = E(I,J) / E(N+1,J)
```

```
1630 NEXT J
1640 M(I) = INT(E(I,1) - L(I) * E(N+1,1) + .5)
1650 IF M(I) > 0 THEN 1670
1660 M(I) = 0
1670 B = B + M(I)
1680 L(I) = INT(L(I)*10000 + .5)/100
1690 NEXT I
1700 T = E(N+1,1)
1710 S = T - B
1720 R = S / B
1730 IF D <> 1 THEN 1750
1740 Q = P / T
1750 RETURN
3990 REM INITIAL DATA INPUT SUBROUTINE ********************
4000 IF D <> 1 THEN 4040
4010 PRINT
4020 PRINT "TARGET REGION POPULATION";
4030 INPUT P
4040 PRINT
4050 PRINT "NUMBER OF ECON SECTORS (18 MAX)";
4060 INPUT N
4070 PRINT
4080 PRINT "ENTER TARGET REGION (REGION 1) ECONOMIC"
4090 PRINT "ACTIVITY BY SECTOR"
4100 FOR I = 1 TO N
4110 PRINT TAB(5); "SECTOR"; I;
4120 INPUT E(I,1)
4130 NEXT I
4140 RETURN
4490 REM LOCATION QUOTIENT DATA INPUT SUBROUTINE **********
4500 PRINT
4510 PRINT "ENTER NATIONAL ECONOMIC ACTIVITY"
4520 FOR I = 1 TO N
4530 PRINT TAB(5); "SECTOR"; I;
4540 INPUT E(I,2)
4550 NEXT I
4560 RETURN
4990 REM MINIMUM REQUIREMENTS DATA INPUT SUBROUTINE ********
5000 PRINT
5010 PRINT "NUMBER OF ADDITIONAL REGIONS";
5020 INPUT K
5030 K = K + 1
5040 FOR J = 2 TO K
5050 PRINT
5060 PRINT "ENTER ECONOMIC ACTIVITY FOR REGION"; J
5070 FOR I = 1 TO N
5080 PRINT TAB(5); "SECTOR"; I;
5090 INPUT E(I,J)
5100 NEXT I
5110 NEXT J
5120 RETURN
6990 REM LOCATION QUOTIENT OUTPUT SUBROUTINE ***************
7000 PRINT
```

```
7010 PRINT
7020 PRINT "SECTOR"; TAB(13); "TARGET REG";
7030 PRINT TAB(27); "NATIONAL"
7040 PRINT TAB(13); "ECON ACTIV"; TAB(27); "ECON ACTIV"
7050 FOR I = 1 TO N
7060 PRINT I; TAB(13); E(I,1); TAB(27); E(I,2)
7070 NEXT I
7080 GOSUB 9900
7090 PRINT
7100 PRINT
7110 PRINT "SECTOR"; TAB(13); "LOCATION";
7120 PRINT TAB(27); "BASIC"
7130 PRINT TAB(13); "QUOTIENT"; TAB(27); "ECON ACTIV"
7140 FOR I = 1 TO N
7150 PRINT I; TAB(13); L(I); TAB(27); M(I)
7160 NEXT I
7170 GOSUB 9900
7180 RETURN
7490 REM MINIMUM REQUIREMENTS OUTPUT SUBROUTINE ************
7500 F1 = INT (K/F + .99)
7510 PRINT
7520 PRINT
7530 PRINT "ECONOMIC ACTIVITY BY REGION AND SECTOR"
7540 FOR F2 = 1 TO F1
7550 PRINT
7560 PRINT "SECTOR";
7570 F3 = (F2 - 1)*F + 1
7580 F4 = F3 + F - 1
7590 IF F4 <= K THEN 7610
7600 F4 = K
7610 F5 = 9
7620 FOR J = F3 TO F4
7630 PRINT TAB(F5); "REGION"; J;
7640 F5 = F5 + 14
7650 NEXT J
7660 PRINT
7670 FOR I = 1 TO N
7680 F5 = 9
7690 PRINT I;
7700 FOR J = F3 TO F4
7710 PRINT TAB(F5); E(I,J);
7720 F5 = F5 + 14
7730 NEXT J
7740 PRINT
7750 NEXT I
7760 GOSUB 9900
7770 NEXT F2
7780 PRINT
7790 PRINT
7800 PRINT "SECTOR"; TAB(13); "MIN REQ"; TAB(27); "BASIC"
7810 PRINT TAB(13); "(PERCENT)"; TAB(27); "ECON ACTIV"
7820 FOR I = 1 TO N
7830 PRINT I; TAB(13); L(I); TAB(27); M(I)
```

```
7840 NEXT I
7850 GOSUB 9900
7860 RETURN
7990 REM SUMMARY OUTPUT FOR BOTH MODELS SUBROUTINE *********
8000 PRINT
8010 PRINT
8020 PRINT "TARGET REGION (REGION 1) SUMMARY:"
8030 PRINT
8040 PRINT TAB(5); "TOTAL ECONOMIC ACTIVITY ="; T
8050 PRINT TAB(5); "BASIC ECONOMIC ACTIVITY ="; B
8060 PRINT TAB(5); "NONBASIC ECON ACTIVITY ="; S
8070 PRINT TAB(5); "ECONOMIC BASE MULTIPLIER ="; R
8080 IF D <> 1 THEN 8110
8090 PRINT TAB(5); "POPULATION ="; P
8100 PRINT TAB(5); "POPULATION MULTIPLIER =";Q
8110 RETURN
8490 REM PROJECTION OUTPUT SUBROUTINE *********************
8500 PRINT
8510 PRINT
8520 PRINT "ECONOMIC BASE PROJECTION:"
8530 PRINT
8540 PRINT TAB(5); "BASIC ECONOMIC ACTIVITY ="; B
8550 S = INT(B*R + .5)
8560 PRINT TAB(5); "NONBASIC ECON ACTIVITY ="; S
8570 T = B + S
8580 PRINT TAB(5); "TOTAL ECONOMIC ACTIVITY ="; T
8590 IF D <> 1 THEN 8620
8600 P = INT(T*Q + .5)
8610 PRINT TAB(5); "POPULATION ="; P
8620 RETURN
9890 REM PAUSE OUTPUT SUBROUTINE *********************
9900 PRINT
9910 PRINT "CONTINUE";
9920 INPUT A$
9930 RETURN
9999 END
```

Chapter 5

Shift and Share Model

The Model

The shift and share model provides projections of future levels of economic activity in a region using projections of the changes in economic activity by sector at the national level. The simpler approach assumes that regional economic change is a function of the sectoral mix in the regional economy, and that each sector in the regional economy will maintain a constant share of any change in that sector nationally. Alternatively, changes in the regional economy by sector can be compared with changes in the national economy to determine shifts into or out of the region that cause sectors to grow at different rates than in the national economy. By assuming that these shifts remain constant, they can be included in projections of future levels of regional economic activity. In addition to their use in making projections, shift and share models are useful for the analysis of strengths and weaknesses in a regional economy, providing an analytical framework for comparing regional with national economic change.

Projection with a constant share model assumes that each economic sector in the region will change at the same rate as that sector is projected to change nationally. Such change will result in the region maintaining a constant share of the nation's economic activity in each sector. If $R_{i,t}$ is the economic activity in the region in sector i at time t, and g_i is the projected rate of growth in economic activity in sector i from t to $t+1$ in the nation, then the change in economic activity in the region in sector i from t to $t+1$, $\Delta R_{i,t,t+1}$, is as follows:

$$\Delta R_{i,t,t+1} = g_i R_{i,t}$$

Using the constant share model for projection, total economic change in the region will differ from total national economic change due to the economic mix of the region. With a higher proportion of regional economic activity in the more rapidly growing sectors, total regional economic activity will grow more rapidly than in the nation, and vice versa.

The full shift and share model, which provides the basis for the constant shift projection, begins with an analysis of the shifts that have been occurring in the regional economy over a recent period compared with the national economy. The total shift in economic activity in any sector is defined as the difference in the change in the sector and the change that would have occurred if that sector had changed at the same rate as the national economy as a whole. Total shift in the region in sector i is

$$S_i = \Delta R_{i,t-1,t} - \left[\frac{\Delta S_{t-1,t}}{S_{t-1}} \right] R_{i,t-1}$$

where $\Delta R_{i,t-1,t}$ is the change in economic activity in the region in sector i from $t-1$ to t; $\Delta S_{t-1,t}$ is the change in total national economic activity during this period; S_{t-1} is total national economic activity at the start of the period, at $t-1$; and $R_{i,t-1}$ is the economic activity in the region in sector i at the start of the period. The ratio is the rate of growth of the national economy, which when multiplied by economic activity in the region in sector i gives the change that would have been expected had that sector in the region grown at the same rate as the national economy as a whole.

This total shift, or difference between regional performance in sector i and the national economy, can be broken down into two components. If economic activity in the region in sector i changed at the same rate as that sector nationally (the assumption in the constant share model), there would arise a proportional shift reflecting the difference between overall national economic change and national economic change in sector i. This proportional shift is determined by taking the difference in the national rates of change for sector i and for the national economy as a whole and multiplying this by regional activity in sector i at the start of the period. The proportional shift is

$$P_i = \left[\frac{\Delta S_{i,t-1,t}}{S_{i,t-1}} - \frac{\Delta S_{t-1,t}}{S_{t-1}} \right] R_{i,t-1}$$

where $\Delta S_{i,t-1,t}$ is the change in national economic activity in sector i from $t-1$ to t and $S_{i,t-1}$ is the level of national economic activity in sector i at $t-1$. The proportional shift is the change in economic activity in sector i associated with that sector at the national level performing differently from the overall national economy. The sum of the proportional shifts in the region over all sectors provides a measure of the portion of regional change attributable to the economic mix.

The other component of the total shift is a measure of the performance of the regional economy in sector i relative to that same sector nationally. This is called the differential shift. The differences in growth rates in the region in sector i and in the nation in sector i, times initial regional activity, gives this differential shift:

$$D_i = \left[\frac{\Delta R_{i,t-1,t}}{R_{i,t-1}} - \frac{\Delta S_{i,t-1,t}}{S_{i,t-1}} \right] R_{i,t-1}$$

The differential shift is a measure of the gain or loss of economic activity within sector i in the region compared with that sector in the nation as a whole. Thus, the differential shift is an indicator of how the region is performing in competition with other regions. It can be easily shown that the total shift is the sum of the proportional and differential shifts:

$$S_i = P_i + D_i$$

Examination of the proportional and differential shifts for all regions provides an indication of the way in which regional economic performance is influenced by industry mix and by the outcome of competition within sectors with other regions.

Constant shift projections assume that the rate of differential shift observed in the past will remain constant in the future. The projected national growth rates by sector, g_i, incorporate both the projected national economic growth and the proportionality effects—the differences between overall growth and sectoral growth in the nation. In addition, the constant shift model utilizes the differential shift rate by sector:

$$f_i = \left[\frac{\Delta R_{i,t-1,t}}{R_{i,t-1}} - \frac{\Delta S_{i,t-1,t}}{S_{i,t-1}} \right]$$

This is the difference between regional and national rates of change in sector i during the period from $t-1$ to t and represents the shift toward or away from the region in sector i. The differential shift rate is determined using historical data and then is assumed to remain constant. The constant shift projection is then

$$\Delta R_{i,t,t+1} = (f_i + g_i) R_{i,t}$$

The performance of the constant shift method of projection as compared with the constant share method is dependent on the rate of differential shift remaining constant. Empirical studies have raised questions, and a prospective user should examine the issues before choosing a method.

The Program

The Shift and Share Model program allows projections to be made using the constant share method, the constant shift method, or both. Up to 18 economic sectors can be used. The program prompts the user for the necessary data, displays appropriate analyses, and allows repeated projections using different national growth rates.

After the user selects the projection methods to be used, the program prompts for the economic data. When just the constant share projection method has been selected, the only requirement is for data on current levels of economic activity in the region, disaggregated by sector. The constant shift method demands, in addition, comparable data for the nation as a whole and the same information on economic activity in the region and the nation at some earlier point in time. When the constant shift method is used and all of the appropriate data have been entered, the program computes the proportional, differential, and total shifts in economic activity for the region over the time period. This information can be useful in analyzing the strengths and weaknesses in the local economy.

The projection phase begins with a request for the year for which projections are to be made. Any length projection period can be selected; for the constant shift projections, the program automatically adjusts the differential shift rates for the length of the projection period. The user is given two options for the entry of projected national growth rates: Projected annual growth rates—the projected growth by sector per year—may be entered, or projected growth rates for the entire period of the projection—the growth rates over the entire five- or ten-year period (or whatever has been specified) may be used. The appropriate projected national growth rates must be entered for each of the economic sectors. The regional projections are then computed and the projected changes in levels of economic activity and the projected totals are reported for the region by sector using the projection methods selected. The option is provided to repeat the projection phase using different national growth rates.

The structure of the program is very straightforward, with the only complexity arising from the options associated with the choice of the projection method. The main routine, lines 10 to 610, controls the program flow and calls the appropriate subroutines. The menu of projection options comes first, and the choice determines the subroutines to be called. Following this, the subroutine at line 4000 provides for the input of current regional economic activity. If constant shift projections are to be made, the remaining national and regional data required for the current and past periods are input using the subroutine at line 4500. When only the constant share projection has been selected and thus only the data from the subroutine at 4000 entered, the subroutine at 7000 is called to print out the data. Alternatively, with the additional data for a constant shift projection, the subroutine at line 1000 is invoked to compute the shift and share analysis, which is reported by the subroutine at line 7500.

Beginning the projection phase, the subroutine at line 5000 is called to enter projected national growth rates. (This includes the options on entry described above.) These rates are output by the subroutine at line 8000. The actual projections are computed and printed out according to the option originally selected. Subroutines at lines 1500 and 8500 calculate and output the constant share projection, while subroutines at lines 2000 and 9000 do the same for the constant shift projection. The main routine then handles the option of repeating the projection or terminating the program.

Sample Problem

The planner for the same region used in the economic base example wishes to make both constant share and constant shift projections of employment levels for the year 1990. He or she begins with the same data on employment for five sectors in 1980 for the region and the nation:

Sector	Regional Employment	National Employment
1	9,600	6,700,000
2	8,200	24,700,000
3	8,900	11,200,000
4	1,900	4,100,000
5	7,600	15,400,000

Since constant shift projections are to be made, data from an earlier period are required to compute the shifts. Comparable employment data are thus obtained for the year 1970:

Sector	Regional Employment	National Employment
1	8,900	6,000.000
2	7,400	23,700,000
3	7,500	9,900,000
4	1,650	3,500,000
5	6,200	13,100,000

Running the program, projection option 3 is selected to generate projections using both methods. The data on employment are then entered as they are requested. The program prints out the tables of levels of economic activity in 1970 and 1980 and presents the computed shifts over this period. This information is useful in understanding the region's economy. For example, sectors 3 and 5 both had significant positive proportional and differential shifts, meaning that regional employment growth benefited both from above average national growth in these sectors and from shifts in employment from other regions.

Moving on to the making of the projections for the year 1990, the planner has found the following projections of national employment growth by sector for the ten-year period:

Sector	Projected National Growth
1	0.11
2	0.05
3	0.09
4	0.15
5	0.19

Since these rates reflect growth over the entire decade (not annual growth rates), option 2 is selected and the growth rates are entered. The program then reports back these growth rates and prints out the constant share and constant shift projections from 1980 to 1990. Not only do the totals differ (here the constant shift projection is higher), but the distribution of growth by sector varies considerably. This, of course, reflects the rather considerable differential shifts discovered in the previous analysis. The planner now needs to study these patterns and the assumptions of the two projection methods in order to settle on a final projection.

References

Krueckeberg, D. A. and Silvers, A. L., *Urban Planning Analysis: Methods and Models* (New York: John Wiley & Sons, Inc., 1974), Chapter 12, pp. 416–424.

Oppenheim, N., *Applied Models in Urban and Regional Analysis* (Englewood Cliffs, N. J.: Prentice-Hall, Inc., 1980), Chapter 3, pp. 102–107.

```
SHIFT AND SHARE MODEL SAMPLE RUN

SHIFT AND SHARE MODEL

PROJECTION OPTIONS:
      1 - CONSTANT SHARE
      2 - CONSTANT SHIFT
      3 - BOTH METHODS

CHOICE OF OPTION? 3

NUMBER OF SECTORS (MAXIMUM 18)? 5
YEAR FOR CURRENT DATA? 1980

ENTER REGIONAL ECON ACTIVITY FOR 1980
      SECTOR 1 ? 9600
      SECTOR 2 ? 8200
      SECTOR 3 ? 8900
      SECTOR 4 ? 1900
      SECTOR 5 ? 7600

ENTER NATIONAL ECON ACTIVITY FOR 1980
      SECTOR 1 ? 6700000
      SECTOR 2 ? 24700000
      SECTOR 3 ? 11200000
      SECTOR 4 ? 4100000
      SECTOR 5 ? 15400000

YEAR FOR PAST DATA? 1970

ENTER REGIONAL ECON ACTIVITY FOR 1970
      SECTOR 1 ? 8900
      SECTOR 2 ? 7400
      SECTOR 3 ? 7500
      SECTOR 4 ? 1650
      SECTOR 5 ? 6200

ENTER NATIONAL ECON ACTIVITY FOR 1970
      SECTOR 1 ? 6000000
      SECTOR 2 ? 23700000
      SECTOR 3 ? 9900000
      SECTOR 4 ? 3500000
      SECTOR 5 ? 13100000


ECONOMIC ACTIVITY IN 1970
```

SECTOR	REGION	NATION
1	8900	6E+06
2	7400	2.37E+07
3	7500	9.9E+06
4	1650	3.5E+06
5	6200	1.31E+07
TOTAL	31650	5.62E+07

CONTINUE?

ECONOMIC ACTIVITY IN 1980

SECTOR	REGION	NATION
1	9600	6.7E+06
2	8200	2.47E+07
3	8900	1.12E+07
4	1900	4.1E+06
5	7600	1.54E+07
TOTAL	36200	6.21E+07

CONTINUE?

SHIFTS FROM 1970 TO 1980

SECTOR	DIFFERENTIAL	PROPORTIONAL
1	-338	104
2	488	-465
3	415	197
4	-33	110
5	311	438
TOTAL	843	384

CONTINUE?

SECTOR	TOTAL SHIFT
1	-234
2	23
3	612
4	77
5	749
TOTAL	1227

CONTINUE?

PROJECTIONS TO WHAT YEAR? 1990

GROWTH RATE OPTIONS:
    1 - ANNUAL GROWTH RATES
    2 - RATES FOR ENTIRE PERIOD

```
CHOICE OF OPTION? 2

ENTER PROJECTED NATIONAL GROWTH RATES
(IN DECIMAL FORM) FROM 1980 TO 1990
     SECTOR 1 ? .11
     SECTOR 2 ? .05
     SECTOR 3 ? .09
     SECTOR 4 ? .15
     SECTOR 5 ? .19


NATIONAL GROWTH RATES 1980 TO 1990

SECTOR        ENTIRE PERIOD RATE
  1               .11
  2               .05
  3               .09
  4               .15
  5               .19

CONTINUE?

CONSTANT SHARE PROJECTION 1980 TO 1990

SECTOR        CHANGE         ECON ACTIVITY
  1            1056            10656
  2             410             8610
  3             801             9701
  4             285             2185
  5            1444             9044
TOTAL          3996            40196

CONTINUE?


CONSTANT SHIFT PROJECTION 1980 TO 1990

SECTOR        CHANGE         ECON ACTIVITY
  1             691            10291
  2             950             9150
  3            1294            10194
  4             247             2147
  5            1826             9426
TOTAL          5008            41208

CONTINUE?


DO YOU WISH TO REPEAT PROJECTIONS
WITH NEW NATIONAL GROWTH RATES
(1=YES, 0=NO)? 0
```

SHIFT AND SHARE MODEL PROGRAM LISTING


```
10 REM SHIFT AND SHARE MODEL
20 REM BY JOHN R. OTTENSMANN
30 REM VARIABLES
40 REM     C(I) - PROJECTED REGION CHANGE, SECTOR I
50 REM     D(I) - DIFFERENTIAL SHIFT
60 REM     F(I) - DIFFERENTIAL SHIFT RATE
70 REM     G(I) - NATIONAL GROWTH RATES
80 REM     P(I) - PROPORTIONAL SHIFT
90 REM     R(I,J) - REGIONAL ECONOMIC ACTIVITY, TIME J
100 REM     S(I,J) - NATIONAL ECONOMIC ACTIVITY
110 REM     T(I) - TOTAL SHIFT
120 REM     Y(J) - YEARS FOR DATA
130 REM     C - PROJECTION OPTION
140 REM     D - GROWTH RATE OPTION
150 REM     F1 - DIFFERENTIAL SHIFT RATE
160 REM     G1 - GROWTH RATE
170 REM     N - NUMBER OF SECTORS
180 DIM C(19), D(19), F(18), G(18), P(19), R(19,3), S(19,2)
190 DIM T(19), Y(3)
200 REM INPUT DATA
210 PRINT
220 PRINT
230 PRINT "SHIFT AND SHARE MODEL"
240 PRINT
250 PRINT "PROJECTION OPTIONS:"
260 PRINT TAB(5); "1 - CONSTANT SHARE"
270 PRINT TAB(5); "2 - CONSTANT SHIFT"
280 PRINT TAB(5); "3 - BOTH METHODS"
290 PRINT
300 PRINT "CHOICE OF OPTION";
310 INPUT C
320 GOSUB 4000
330 IF C = 1 THEN 360
340 GOSUB 4500
350 REM OUTPUT DATA
360 IF C <> 1 THEN 400
370 GOSUB 7000
380 GOTO 430
390 REM SHIFT-SHARE COMPUTATIONS AND OUTPUT
400 GOSUB 1000
410 GOSUB 7500
420 REM BEGIN PROJECTION - INPUT AND OUTPUT RATES
430 GOSUB 5000
440 GOSUB 8000
450 REM COMPUTE AND OUTPUT PROJECTIONS
460 IF C = 2 THEN 520
470 REM CONSTANT SHARE PROJECTION
480 GOSUB 1500
490 GOSUB 8500
500 IF C = 1 THEN 540
```

```
510 REM CONSTANT SHIFT PROJECTION
520 GOSUB 2000
530 GOSUB 9000
540 PRINT
550 PRINT
560 PRINT "DO YOU WISH TO REPEAT PROJECTIONS"
570 PRINT "WITH NEW NATIONAL GROWTH RATES"
580 PRINT "(1=YES, 0=NO)";
590 INPUT A
600 IF A = 0 THEN 9999
610 GOTO 430
990 REM SHIFT-SHARE COMPUTATION SUBROUTINE *****************
1000 D(N+1) = 0
1010 P(N+1) = 0
1020 T(N+1) = 0
1030 FOR I = 1 TO N
1040 F(I) = (R(I,2)-R(I,1))/R(I,1)-(S(I,2)-S(I,1))/S(I,1)
1050 D(I) = F(I) * R(I,1)
1060 P(I) = (S(I,2)-S(I,1))/S(I,1)
1070 P(I) = (P(I)-(S(N+1,2)-S(N+1,1))/S(N+1,1)) * R(I,1)
1080 D(I) = INT(D(I) + .5)
1090 P(I) = INT(P(I) + .5)
1100 T(I) = D(I) + P(I)
1110 D(N+1) = D(N+1) + D(I)
1120 P(N+1) = P(N+1) + P(I)
1130 T(N+1) = T(N+1) + T(I)
1140 NEXT I
1150 RETURN
1490 REM CONSTANT SHARE PROJECTION SUBROUTINE **************
1500 C(N+1) = 0
1510 R(N+1,3) = 0
1520 FOR I = 1 TO N
1530 G1 = G(I)
1540 IF D <> 1 THEN 1560
1550 G1 = (1 + G1) ^ (Y(3) - Y(2)) - 1
1560 C(I) = R(I,2) * G1
1570 C(I) = INT(C(I) + .5)
1580 R(I,3) = R(I,2) + C(I)
1590 C(N+1) = C(N+1) + C(I)
1600 R(N+1,3) = R(N+1,3) + R(I,3)
1610 NEXT I
1620 RETURN
1990 REM CONSTANT SHIFT PROJECTION SUBROUTINE **************
2000 C(N+1) = 0
2010 R(N+1,3) = 0
2020 FOR I = 1 TO N
2030 F1 = (1 + F(I)) ^ ((Y(3)-Y(2))/(Y(2)-Y(1))) - 1
2040 G1 = G(I)
2050 IF D <> 1 THEN 2070
2060 G1 = (1 + G1) ^ (Y(3) - Y(2)) - 1
2070 C(I) = (F1 + G1) * R(I,2)
2080 C(I) = INT(C(I) + .5)
2090 R(I,3) = R(I,2) + C(I)
```

```
2100 C(N+1) = C(N+1) + C(I)
2110 R(N+1,3) = R(N+1,3) + R(I,3)
2120 NEXT I
2130 RETURN
3990 REM INITIAL DATA INPUT SUBROUTINE **********************
4000 PRINT
4010 PRINT "NUMBER OF SECTORS (MAXIMUM 18)";
4020 INPUT N
4030 PRINT "YEAR FOR CURRENT DATA";
4040 INPUT Y(2)
4050 PRINT
4060 PRINT "ENTER REGIONAL ECON ACTIVITY FOR"; Y(2)
4070 R(N+1,2) = 0
4080 FOR I = 1 TO N
4090 PRINT TAB(5); "SECTOR"; I;
4100 INPUT R(I,2)
4110 R(N+1,2) = R(N+1,2) + R(I,2)
4120 NEXT I
4130 RETURN
4490 REM CONSTANT SHIFT DATA INPUT SUBROUTINE **************
4500 PRINT
4510 PRINT "ENTER NATIONAL ECON ACTIVITY FOR"; Y(2)
4520 S(N+1,2) = 0
4530 FOR I = 1 TO N
4540 PRINT TAB(5); "SECTOR"; I;
4550 INPUT S(I,2)
4560 S(N+1,2) = S(N+1,2) + S(I,2)
4570 NEXT I
4580 PRINT
4590 PRINT "YEAR FOR PAST DATA";
4600 INPUT Y(1)
4610 PRINT
4620 PRINT "ENTER REGIONAL ECON ACTIVITY FOR"; Y(1)
4630 R(N+1,1) = 0
4640 FOR I = 1 TO N
4650 PRINT TAB(5); "SECTOR"; I;
4660 INPUT R(I,1)
4670 R(N+1,1) = R(N+1,1) + R(I,1)
4680 NEXT I
4690 PRINT
4700 PRINT "ENTER NATIONAL ECON ACTIVITY FOR"; Y(1)
4710 S(N+1,1) = 0
4720 FOR I = 1 TO N
4730 PRINT TAB(5); "SECTOR"; I;
4740 INPUT S(I,1)
4750 S(N+1,1) = S(N+1,1) + S(I,1)
4760 NEXT I
4770 RETURN
4990 REM PROJECTED NATIONAL GROWTH INPUT SUBROUTINE ********
5000 PRINT
5010 PRINT
5020 PRINT "PROJECTIONS TO WHAT YEAR";
5030 INPUT Y(3)
```

```
5040 PRINT
5050 PRINT "GROWTH RATE OPTIONS:"
5060 PRINT TAB(5); "1 - ANNUAL GROWTH RATES"
5070 PRINT TAB(5); "2 - RATES FOR ENTIRE PERIOD"
5080 PRINT
5090 PRINT "CHOICE OF OPTION";
5100 INPUT D
5110 PRINT
5120 PRINT "ENTER PROJECTED NATIONAL GROWTH RATES"
5130 PRINT "(IN DECIMAL FORM) FROM"; Y(2); "TO"; Y(3)
5140 FOR I = 1 TO N
5150 PRINT TAB(5); "SECTOR"; I;
5160 INPUT G(I)
5170 NEXT I
5180 RETURN
6990 REM OPTION 1 DATA OUTPUT SUBROUTINE *******************
7000 PRINT
7010 PRINT
7020 PRINT "ECONOMIC ACTIVITY IN"; Y(2)
7030 PRINT
7040 PRINT "SECTOR"; TAB(13); "REGION"
7050 FOR I = 1 TO N
7060 PRINT I; TAB(13); R(I,2)
7070 NEXT I
7080 PRINT "TOTAL"; TAB(13); R(N+1,2)
7090 GOSUB 9900
7100 RETURN
7490 REM SHIFT-SHARE OUTPUT SUBROUTINE ********************
7500 FOR J = 1 TO 2
7510 PRINT
7520 PRINT
7530 PRINT "ECONOMIC ACTIVITY IN"; Y(J)
7540 PRINT
7550 PRINT "SECTOR"; TAB(13); "REGION"; TAB(27); "NATION"
7560 FOR I = 1 TO N
7570 PRINT I; TAB(13); R(I,J); TAB(27); S(I,J)
7580 NEXT I
7590 PRINT "TOTAL"; TAB(13); R(N+1,J); TAB(27); S(N+1,J)
7600 GOSUB 9900
7610 NEXT J
7620 PRINT
7630 PRINT
7640 PRINT "SHIFTS FROM "; Y(1); "TO"; Y(2)
7650 PRINT
7660 PRINT "SECTOR"; TAB(13); "DIFFERENTIAL";
7670 PRINT TAB(27); "PROPORTIONAL"
7680 FOR I = 1 TO N
7690 PRINT I; TAB(13); D(I); TAB(27); P(I)
7700 NEXT I
7710 PRINT "TOTAL"; TAB(13); D(N+1); TAB(27); P(N+1)
7720 GOSUB 9900
7730 PRINT
7740 PRINT "SECTOR"; TAB(13); "TOTAL SHIFT"
```

```
7750 FOR I = 1 TO N
7760 PRINT I; TAB(13); T(I)
7770 NEXT I
7780 PRINT "TOTAL"; TAB(13); T(N+1)
7790 GOSUB 9900
7800 RETURN
7990 REM NATIONAL GROWTH RATE OUTPUT SUBROUTINE ************
8000 PRINT
8010 PRINT
8020 PRINT
8030 PRINT "NATIONAL GROWTH RATES"; Y(2); "TO"; Y(3)
8040 PRINT
8050 PRINT "SECTOR"; TAB(13);
8060 IF D<> 1 THEN 8090
8070 PRINT "ANNUAL RATE"
8080 GOTO 8100
8090 PRINT "ENTIRE PERIOD RATE"
8100 FOR I = 1 TO N
8110 PRINT I; TAB(13); G(I)
8120 NEXT I
8130 GOSUB 9900
8140 RETURN
8490 REM CONSTANT SHARE PROJECTION OUTPUT SUBROUTINE *******
8500 PRINT
8510 PRINT "CONSTANT SHARE PROJECTION"; Y(2); "TO"; Y(3)
8520 GOSUB 9500
8530 RETURN
8990 REM CONSTANT SHIFT PROJECTION OUTPUT SUBROUTINE *******
9000 PRINT
9010 PRINT
9020 PRINT "CONSTANT SHIFT PROJECTION"; Y(2); "TO"; Y(3)
9030 GOSUB 9500
9040 RETURN
9490 REM PROJECTION OUTPUT SUBROUTINE *********************
9500 PRINT
9510 PRINT "SECTOR"; TAB(13); "CHANGE";
9520 PRINT TAB(27); "ECON ACTIVITY"
9530 FOR I = 1 TO N
9540 PRINT I; TAB(13); C(I); TAB(27); R(I,3)
9550 NEXT I
9560 PRINT "TOTAL"; TAB(13); C(N+1); TAB(27); R(N+1,3)
9570 GOSUB 9900
9580 RETURN
9890 REM PAUSE OUTPUT SUBROUTINE ***********************
9900 PRINT
9910 PRINT "CONTINUE";
9920 INPUT A$
9930 RETURN
9999 END
```

Chapter 6

Input–Output Model

The Model

The input–output model provides one of the more comprehensive frameworks for analyzing and projecting regional economic activity. The local economy is broken down into industry sectors, and an input–output table describes the flows of goods and services from one sector to another, as well as the inputs from external sectors and the outputs to the final demand sectors. Thus, interrelationships among industries within the region can be taken into account in the analysis and projection. The levels of regional economic activity are assumed to be dependent on the final demand for goods and services, and the input–output model can be used to determine the total output required by each industry to produce a specified level of final demand.

The point of departure for analysis is the input–output table showing the dollar value of goods and services flowing from each industry sector to each other industry sector. An illustration of an input–output table with two industry sectors is shown in Table 6.1. The entries down the left-hand side of the table show the sources of these flows, while entries across the top show the destinations. First, consider the outputs across the rows. Industry 1, for example, produces q_{11} worth of output which is sold to and purchased by other firms in the same industry. Industry 1 also produces q_{12} of output which is sold to and used as an input by industry 2. An additional x_1 of the output of industry 1 goes to the final demand sector. Adding these three values, across the row, gives the total output y_1 for industry 1:

$$q_{11} + q_{12} + x_1 = y_1$$

Alternatively, consider the inputs by looking down the columns. Industry 1 purchases q_{11} of its inputs from industry 1, q_{21} of its inputs from industry

2, and s_1 of its inputs from the external input sector, for a total of y_1 of inputs. Note that total inputs must equal total outputs in an input–output table.

Table 6.1 Input–Output Table with Two Industry Sectors

From Industry	To Industry 1	To Industry 2	Final Demand	Total Output
1	q_{11}	q_{12}	x_1	y_1
2	q_{21}	q_{22}	x_2	y_2
External Supply	s_1	s_2		
Total Input	y_1	y_2		$y_1 + y_2$

The final demand sector bears some relationship to the basic sector in the economic base model. Final demand includes the export or sale of goods and services outside of the region. Likewise, the external input sector includes the import or purchase of goods and services from outside of the region. Depending on how the input–output table is constructed, however, final demand can also include the sale of goods and services to households within the region for consumption. In this case, the external input sector would include the purchase of labor and the payment of wages to those households. Alternatively, households may be included as a sector within the interindustry portion of the table, in which case input of labor and output to local consumption would appear there. Additional final demand sectors, such as government, may also be specified. The issues involved in setting up an input–output table are too complex to be treated in this brief introduction.

Dividing the interindustry flows q_{ij} by the total inputs y_j for each industry gives the dollar value of inputs required to produce one dollar of output. These interindustry production coefficients or technical coefficients are denoted a_{ij} and are defined as

$$a_{ij} = \frac{q_{ij}}{y_j}$$

For example, a_{12} is the dollar value of inputs from industry 1 (less than one dollar) required to produce one dollar's worth of output from industry 2. The relationship among these technical coefficients, final demand, and total output for industry 1 is then

$$a_{11}y_1 + a_{12}y_2 + x_1 = y_1$$

Likewise, external input coefficients can be computed in the same manner as measures of the dollar value of inputs from this sector required to produce one dollar's worth of output in any given industry sector. These coefficients will be denoted b_j and will be defined as

$$b_j = \frac{s_j}{y_j}$$

The relationship among the interindustry coefficients, final demand, and total output can be expressed more compactly using the notation of linear (matrix) algebra, which is important for presenting further developments.[1] Let $\mathbf{A}$ be the square matrix of the interindustry coefficients a_{ij}:

$$\mathbf{A} = \begin{bmatrix} a_{11} & a_{12} \\ a_{21} & a_{22} \end{bmatrix}$$

$\mathbf{X}$ and $\mathbf{Y}$ are vectors of the final demand values, x_i, and the total output, y_i:

$$\mathbf{X} = \begin{bmatrix} x_1 \\ x_2 \end{bmatrix}, \qquad \mathbf{Y} = \begin{bmatrix} y_1 \\ y_2 \end{bmatrix}$$

The relationship for an input–output model with any number of sectors is then simply

$$\mathbf{A}\mathbf{Y} + \mathbf{X} = \mathbf{Y}$$

Determining the total output $\mathbf{Y}$ that would result from meeting any given final demand $\mathbf{X}$ involves solving this equation for $\mathbf{Y}$. The process is equivalent to solving a system of simultaneous linear equations, but can be expressed more directly using linear algebra:

$$\mathbf{Y} = (\mathbf{I} - \mathbf{A})^{-1}\mathbf{X}$$

The matrix $\mathbf{I}$ is the identity matrix, with ones on the diagonal and zeroes elsewhere. The matrix $(\mathbf{I} - \mathbf{A})^{-1}$ is called the Leontief inverse and is central to the input–output model. Computation requires the determination of the inverse of the matrix $(\mathbf{I} - \mathbf{A})$. Given a projection of final demand by industry, the vector $\mathbf{X}$, this can be multiplied by the matrix $(\mathbf{I} - \mathbf{A})^{-1}$ to obtain the projected vector $\mathbf{Y}$ of total output for each industry. To obtain the entire matrix of interindustry flows, the total input to each industry (the same as the output) needs only to be multiplied by the interindustry coefficient:

$$q_{ij} = a_{ij}y_j$$

The quantity of external inputs needed by each sector to produce that total output is computed in a similar fashion using the external supply coefficient:

$$s_j = b_j y_j$$

Application of the input—output model begins with the table of current interindustry flows, the q_{ij}'s, and the final demand, the x_i's. This information is used to compute the interindustry coefficients, the a_{ij}, and the external supply coefficients, the b_j. The matrix **A** of the interindustry coefficients is used to compute the Leontief inverse, $(\mathbf{I} - \mathbf{A})^{-1}$. Then, given a projection of the new final demand, **X**, the inverse matrix is multiplied by that vector to calculate the quantities of total outputs, **Y**, required for the production of this final demand. Finally, the technical coefficients and the external input coefficients are multiplied by the projected total output to complete the projected input—output table.

The Program

The Input—Output Model program provides for the entry of an initial table of current flows, computes and presents the elements of the input—output model, and allows the making of projections using these values. In making a projection, the user enters the projected final demand for each industry. The program computes and displays the complete input—output table for this final demand.

The Input—Output Model program can handle up to 16 industry sectors, but is limited to one final demand sector and one external supply sector. The treatment of households is left to the user of the program. Outputs to consumption can be included in the final demand totals by industry or households can be included in the interindustry portion of the model by specifying an additional industry sector. In the latter case, outputs to households in the form of consumption and inputs from households in the form of labor must be entered for each industry for the industry sector designated for households. Input and output values are rounded to the nearest integer within the program, and coefficients are presented to four decimal places (though greater accuracy is retained internally).

Operation of the program is straightforward. After specifying the number of sectors, the user is prompted to enter the interindustry flows and the final demand for the current input—output table. The remainder of the table is computed and the entire table is displayed. Interindustry production coefficients, external input coefficients, and the $(\mathbf{I} - \mathbf{A})^{-1}$ matrix are then calculated and presented. To make a projection, the user must enter the projected final demand by industry. The entire projected input—output table is then computed and displayed. An option is provided for making multiple projections.

To increase the legibility of the output, the program is designed to display as many columns across the screen as can be accommodated on the video display. Systems with 80-column displays can handle five columns, while 40-column displays are limited to two columns. The number of columns can be set by assigning the appropriate value to F in line 130. Whatever number of columns is specified, the program automatically takes care of dividing larger tables into parts, displaying them appropriately.

Despite the relative complexity of some routines, the program is quite straightforward. Understanding the data structure is the key to following the program. The entire input–output table is stored in a single array X. The interindustry portion is in the first N rows and columns, external inputs and final demand are in the $N + 1$ row and column, respectively, and total inputs and outputs are in the $N + 2$ row and column. Likewise, the interindustry coefficients are stored in the first N rows and columns of Y, with external supply coefficients in the $N + 1$ row. The $(I - A)^{-1}$ matrix is stored in Z. All output, however, is through the matrix X, using a call to a matrix output routine specifying the number of rows and columns to be printed. Values from Y and Z are placed in X for output.

The main routine in lines 10 through 400 calls all of the necessary subroutines. First, the subroutine at line 4000 handles the input of initial interindustry flows and final demand. The subroutine at line 1000 calculates the remaining values in the input–output table, which is then printed by the subroutine at line 7000. This subroutine, like all of the output subroutines, makes a further call to the general matrix output subroutine at line 9000, which handles the actual printing of the values placed in the array X. Next, interindustry and external input coefficients are computed by the subroutine at 1500 and are output by the subroutine at 7500. Computation of the inverse matrix is handled by the subroutine at line 2000, which employs a standard Gaussian elimination algorithm. The results are output by the subroutine at 8000. For the projection phase, projected final demand is entered through the subroutine at 4500. The new input–output table is computed by the subroutine at 2500 and is output by the subroutine at 8500.

Sample Problem

A four-industry input–output table is available for a regional economy and is to be used in making projections. The interindustry flows are as follows:

From Industry	To Industry			
	1	2	3	4
1	900	1200	850	30
2	780	2900	1840	680
3	410	750	1490	570
4	330	1190	920	1670

In addition, data are needed on the final demand for each industry:

Industry	Final Demand
1	1120
2	3600
3	3380
4	1590

Running the Input–Output Model program, the user enters this information for the input–output table. The program then computes and presents the following information: (1) the completed input–output table; (2) the interindustry production coefficients and the external input coefficients; and (3) the $(I - A)^{-1}$ Leontief inverse matrix.

At this point, the user is given the option of making a projection. For the example region, projected final demand for some future year is

Industry	Final Demand
1	1230
2	3800
3	3890
4	1720

When this information has been entered, the complete input–output table is projected and displayed, including total outputs, interindustry flows, and external inputs.

References

Isard, W., *Methods of Regional Analysis: An Introduction to Regional Science* (Cambridge, Mass.: M.I.T. Press, 1960), Chapter 8, pp. 309–374.

Krueckeberg, D. A. and Silvers, A. L., *Urban Planning Analysis: Methods and Models* (New York: John Wiley & Sons, Inc., 1974), Chapter 12, pp. 406–416.

Masser, I., *Analytical Models for Urban and Regional Planning* (Newton Abbot: David & Charles, 1972), Chapter 3, pp. 69–79.

Oppenheim, N., *Applied Models in Urban and Regional Analysis* (Englewood Cliffs, N. J.: Prentice-Hall, Inc., 1980), Chapter 3, pp. 77–87.

Wilson, A. G., *Urban and Regional Models in Geography and Planning* (London: John Wiley & Sons, 1974), Chapter 8, pp. 112–116.

Note

[1] Brief introductions to matrix algebra are presented in most of the texts introducing input–output analysis that are listed in the References above.

```
INPUT-OUTPUT MODEL SAMPLE RUN

INPUT-OUTPUT MODEL

NUMBER OF INDUSTRY SECTORS (MAX 16)? 4

ENTER INTER-INDUSTRY FLOWS BY ROW

     FROM IND 1 TO IND 1 ? 900
     FROM IND 1 TO IND 2 ? 1200
     FROM IND 1 TO IND 3 ? 850
     FROM IND 1 TO IND 4 ? 30

     FROM IND 2 TO IND 1 ? 780
     FROM IND 2 TO IND 2 ? 2900
     FROM IND 2 TO IND 3 ? 1840
     FROM IND 2 TO IND 4 ? 680

     FROM IND 3 TO IND 1 ? 410
     FROM IND 3 TO IND 2 ? 750
     FROM IND 3 TO IND 3 ? 1490
     FROM IND 3 TO IND 4 ? 570

     FROM IND 4 TO IND 1 ? 330
     FROM IND 4 TO IND 2 ? 1190
     FROM IND 4 TO IND 3 ? 920
     FROM IND 4 TO IND 4 ? 1670

ENTER FINAL DEMAND

     INDUSTRY 1 ? 1120
     INDUSTRY 2 ? 3600
     INDUSTRY 3 ? 3380
     INDUSTRY 4 ? 1590


INPUT-OUTPUT TABLE
```

FR IND	TO IND 1	TO IND 2	TO IND 3	TO IND 4
1	900	1200	850	30
2	780	2900	1840	680
3	410	750	1490	570
4	330	1190	920	1670
EXT INP	1680	3760	1500	2750
TOT INP	4100	9800	6600	5700

```
CONTINUE?
```

```
FR IND     FINAL DEM     TOTAL OUT

1          1120          4100
2          3600          9800
3          3380          6600
4          1590          5700
EXT INP
TOT INP                  26200

CONTINUE?
```

INTER-INDUSTRY PRODUCTION COEFFICIENTS

```
FR IND     TO IND 1      TO IND 2      TO IND 3      TO IND 4
1          .2195         .1224         .1288         .0053
2          .1902         .2959         .2788         .1193
3          .1           .0765         .2258         .1
4          .0805         .1214         .1394         .293

CONTINUE?
```

EXTERNAL INPUT COEFFICIENTS

```
INDUSTRY   COEFFICIENT
1          .4098
2          .3837
3          .2273
4          .4825

CONTINUE?
```

(I - A) INVERSE MATRIX

```
FR IND     TO IND 1      TO IND 2      TO IND 3      TO IND 4
1          1.4142        .3052         .3657         .1138
2          .5438         1.6651        .7608         .3927
3          .2763         .2518         1.4739        .253
4          .3089         .3703         .4629         1.5447

CONTINUE?


DO YOU WISH TO MAKE A PROJECTION WITH
NEW FINAL DEMAND (1=YES, 0=NO)? 1
```

```
ENTER PROJECTED FINAL DEMAND

    INDUSTRY 1 ? 1230
    INDUSTRY 2 ? 3800
    INDUSTRY 3 ? 3890
    INDUSTRY 4 ? 1720


PROJECTED INPUT-OUTPUT TABLE
```

FR IND	TO IND 1	TO IND 2	TO IND 3	TO IND 4
1	992	1302	961	33
2	859	3146	2081	745
3	452	814	1685	625
4	364	1291	1041	1830
EXT INP	1851	4079	1697	3013
TOT INP	4517	10631	7465	6245

```
CONTINUE?
```

FR IND	FINAL DEM	TOTAL OUT
1	1230	4517
2	3800	10631
3	3890	7465
4	1720	6245
EXT INP		
TOT INP		28858

```
CONTINUE?


DO YOU WISH TO MAKE A PROJECTION WITH
NEW FINAL DEMAND (1=YES, 0=NO)? 0
```

INPUT-OUTPUT MODEL PROGRAM LISTING

```
10 REM INPUT-OUTPUT MODEL
20 REM BY JOHN R. OTTENSMANN
30 REM VARIABLES
40 REM     X(I,J) - WORKING AND OUTPUT MATRIX
50 REM     Y(I,J) - PRODUCTION COEFFICIENTS
60 REM     Z(I,J) - INVERSE MATRIX
70 REM     K - SIZE OF MATRIX TO BE OUTPUT
80 REM     N - NUMBER OF INDUSTRY SECTORS
90 DIM X(18,18), Y(17,16), Z(16,16)
100 REM F SPECIFIES NUMBER OF FIELDS IN TABLE SEGMENTS
110 REM     F=5 FOR 80-COLUMN DISPLAY
120 REM     F=2 FOR 40-COLUMN DISPLAY
130 F = 5
140 REM INPUT I/O TABLE
150 PRINT
160 PRINT
170 PRINT "INPUT-OUTPUT MODEL"
180 GOSUB 4000
190 REM COMPLETE AND OUTPUT TABLE
200 GOSUB 1000
210 GOSUB 7000
220 REM COMPUTE AND OUTPUT COEFFICIENTS
230 GOSUB 1500
240 GOSUB 7500
250 REM INVERT AND OUTPUT MATRIX
260 GOSUB 2000
270 GOSUB 8000
280 REM PROJECTION PHASE
290 PRINT
300 PRINT
310 PRINT "DO YOU WISH TO MAKE A PROJECTION WITH"
320 PRINT "NEW FINAL DEMAND (1=YES, 0=NO)";
330 INPUT A
340 IF A = 0 THEN 9999
350 REM INPUT NEW FINAL DEMAND
360 GOSUB 4500
370 REM PROJECT NEW I/O TABLE AND OUTPUT
380 GOSUB 2500
390 GOSUB 8500
400 GOTO 290
980 REM COMPLETE I/O TABLE SUBROUTINE *********************
990 REM SUM OUTPUTS
1000 X(N+2,N+2) = 0
1010 FOR I = 1 TO N
1020 X(I,N+2) = 0
1030 FOR J = 1 TO N + 1
1040 X(I,N+2) = X(I,N+2) + X(I,J)
1050 NEXT J
1060 X(N+2,N+2) = X(N+2,N+2) + X(I,N+2)
1070 X(N+2,I) = X(I,N+2)
```

```
1080 NEXT I
1090 REM CALCULATE EXTERNAL INPUTS
1100 FOR J = 1 TO N
1110 X(N+1,J) = X(N+2,J)
1120 FOR I = 1 TO N
1130 X(N+1,J) = X(N+1,J) - X(I,J)
1140 NEXT I
1150 NEXT J
1160 RETURN
1490 REM COMPUTE COEFFICIENTS SUBROUTINE *******************
1500 FOR J = 1 TO N
1510 FOR I = 1 TO N + 1
1520 Y(I,J) = X(I,J) / X(N+2,J)
1530 X(I,J) = INT(Y(I,J) * 10000 + .5) / 10000
1540 NEXT I
1550 NEXT J
1560 RETURN
1980 REM MATRIX INVERSION SUBROUTINE ***********************
1990 REM CREATE (I - A) MATRIX
2000 FOR I = 1 TO N
2010 FOR J = 1 TO N
2020 X(I,J) = -X(I,J)
2030 Z(I,J) = 0
2040 NEXT J
2050 X(I,I) = 1 + X(I,I)
2060 Z(I,I) = 1
2070 NEXT I
2080 REM INVERT MATRIX
2090 FOR I = 1 TO N
2100 W = X(I,I)
2110 FOR J = 1 TO N
2120 X(I,J) = X(I,J) / W
2130 Z(I,J) = Z(I,J) / W
2140 NEXT J
2150 FOR J = 1 TO N
2160 IF J = I THEN 2220
2170 W = X(J,I)
2180 FOR K = 1 TO N
2190 X(J,K) = X(J,K) - X(I,K) * W
2200 Z(J,K) = Z(J,K) - Z(I,K) * W
2210 NEXT K
2220 NEXT J
2230 NEXT I
2240 REM PUT INVERTED MATRIX INTO X
2250 FOR I = 1 TO N
2260 FOR J = 1 TO N
2270 X(I,J) = INT(Z(I,J) * 10000 + .5) / 10000
2280 NEXT J
2290 NEXT I
2300 RETURN
2480 REM CALCULATE PROJECTED I/O TABLE SUBROUTINE **********
2490 REM COMPUTE TOTAL OUTPUT
2500 X(N+2,N+2) = 0
```

```
2510 FOR I = 1 TO N
2520 X(I,N+2) = 0
2530 FOR J = 1 TO N
2540 X(I,N+2) = X(I,N+2) + Z(I,J) * X(J,N+1)
2550 NEXT J
2560 X(I,N+2) = INT(X(I,N+2) + .5)
2570 X(N+2,N+2) = X(N+2,N+2) + X(I,N+2)
2580 X(N+2,I) = X(I,N+2)
2590 NEXT I
2600 REM COMPUTE INTER-IND AND EXT INPUT VALUES
2610 FOR J = 1 TO N
2620 FOR I = 1 TO N + 1
2630 X(I,J) = Y(I,J) * X(N+2,J)
2640 X(I,J) = INT(X(I,J) + .5)
2650 NEXT I
2660 NEXT J
2670 RETURN
3990 REM SUBROUTINE TO INPUT BASIC TABLE ********************
4000 PRINT
4010 PRINT "NUMBER OF INDUSTRY SECTORS (MAX 16)";
4020 INPUT N
4030 PRINT
4040 PRINT "ENTER INTER-INDUSTRY FLOWS BY ROW"
4050 FOR I = 1 TO N
4060 PRINT
4070 FOR J = 1 TO N
4080 PRINT TAB(5); "FROM IND"; I; "TO IND"; J;
4090 INPUT X(I,J)
4100 NEXT J
4110 NEXT I
4120 PRINT
4130 PRINT "ENTER FINAL DEMAND"
4140 PRINT
4150 FOR I = 1 TO N
4160 PRINT TAB(5); "INDUSTRY"; I;
4170 INPUT X(I,N+1)
4180 NEXT I
4190 RETURN
4490 REM INPUT PROJECTED FINAL DEMAND SUBROUTINE ***********
4500 PRINT
4510 PRINT
4520 PRINT "ENTER PROJECTED FINAL DEMAND"
4530 PRINT
4540 FOR I = 1 TO N
4550 PRINT TAB(5); "INDUSTRY"; I;
4560 INPUT X(I,N+1)
4570 NEXT I
4580 RETURN
6990 REM INITIAL I/O TABLE OUTPUT SUBROUTINE ***************
7000 PRINT
7010 PRINT
7020 PRINT "INPUT-OUTPUT TABLE"
7030 K = N + 2
```

```
·7040 GOSUB 9000
 7050 RETURN
 7490 REM PRODUCTION COEFFICIENTS OUTPUT SUBROUTINE *********
 7500 PRINT
 7510 PRINT
 7520 PRINT "INTER-INDUSTRY PRODUCTION COEFFICIENTS"
 7530 K = N
 7540 GOSUB 9000
 7550 PRINT
 7560 PRINT "EXTERNAL INPUT COEFFICIENTS"
 7570 PRINT
 7580 PRINT "INDUSTRY"; TAB(11); "COEFFICIENT"
 7590 FOR J = 1 TO N
 7600 PRINT J; TAB(11); X(N+1,J)
 7610 NEXT J
 7620 GOSUB 9900
 7630 RETURN
 7990 REM INVERSE OUTPUT SUBROUTINE ************************
 8000 PRINT
 8010 PRINT
 8020 PRINT "(I - A) INVERSE MATRIX"
 8030 K = N
 8040 GOSUB 9000
 8050 RETURN
 8490 REM PROJECTED I/O TABLE OUTPUT SUBROUTINE *************
 8500 PRINT
 8510 PRINT
 8520 PRINT "PROJECTED INPUT-OUTPUT TABLE"
 8530 K = N + 2
 8540 GOSUB 9000
 8550 RETURN
 8990 REM GENERAL MATRIX OUTPUT SUBROUTINE ******************
 9000 F1 = INT (K/F + .99)
 9010 FOR F2 = 1 TO F1
 9020 F3 = (F2 - 1) * F + 1
 9030 F4 = F3 + F - 1
 9040 IF F4 <= K THEN 9060
 9050 F4 = K
 9060 F5 = 11
 9070 REM PRINT HEADING
 9080 PRINT
 9090 PRINT "FR IND";
 9100 FOR J = F3 TO F4
 9110 IF J > N THEN 9140
 9120 PRINT TAB(F5); "TO IND"; J;
 9130 GOTO 9180
 9140 IF J > N + 1 THEN 9170
 9150 PRINT TAB(F5); "FINAL DEM";
 9160 GOTO 9180
 9170 PRINT TAB(F5); "TOTAL OUT"
 9180 F5 = F5 + 14
 9190 NEXT J
 9200 PRINT
```

```
9210 REM PRINT BODY OF TABLE
9220 FOR I = 1 TO N
9230 PRINT I;
9240 F5 = 11
9250 FOR J = F3 TO F4
9260 PRINT TAB(F5); X(I,J);
9270 F5 = F5 + 14
9280 NEXT J
9290 PRINT
9300 NEXT I
9310 REM PRINT BOTTOM ROWS IF NEEDED
9320 IF K = N THEN 9490
9330 PRINT "EXT INP";
9340 F5 = 11
9350 FOR J = F3 TO F4
9360 IF J > N THEN 9390
9370 PRINT TAB(F5); X(N+1,J);
9380 F5 = F5 + 14
9390 NEXT J
9400 PRINT
9410 PRINT "TOT INP";
9420 F5 = 11
9430 FOR J = F3 TO F4
9440 IF J = N + 1 THEN 9460
9450 PRINT TAB(F5); X(N+2,J);
9460 F5 = F5 + 14
9470 NEXT J
9480 PRINT
9490 GOSUB 9900
9500 NEXT F2
9510 RETURN
9890 REM PAUSE OUTPUT SUBROUTINE **************************
9900 PRINT
9910 PRINT "CONTINUE";
9920 INPUT A$
9930 RETURN
9999 END
```

Chapter 7

Single-Constrained Gravity Model

The Model

Spatial interaction models are used to predict the flows between locations in space. The gravity model is the most commonly used form of spatial interaction model. Gravity models can be applied to a variety of problems ranging from the determination of travel patterns to the prediction of locations of activities. The Single-Constrained Gravity Model program, presented in this chapter, can be used for predicting the locations of residential activities in an urban area, retail trade volumes, recreational facility utilization, and a variety of other locational patterns where those locations are dependent on interactions with other locations. Chapter 8 presents the Double-Constrained Gravity Model program for predicting the patterns of travel between origins and destinations.

The basic, general form of the gravity model assumes that the volume of trips from an origin to a destination is proportional to the total numbers of origins and destinations and to some inverse function of distance or some other measure of separation such as time or cost of travel. The model can be expressed as follows:

$$T_{ij} = k_i l_j O_i D_j f(d_{ij})$$

where T_{ij} is the number of trips from origin i to destination j; O_i is the number of trips beginning at origin i; D_j is the number of trips ending at destination j; d_{ij} is the distance from origin i to destination j; $f(d_{ij})$ is some inverse function of distance; and k_i and l_j are empirically determined parameters associated with the origins and destinations. While a variety of functions might be employed for $f(d_{ij})$, two are used most often. The original formulation of the gravity model used an inverse power function, where

$$f(d_{ij}) = d_{ij}^{-a} = 1/d_{ij}^a$$

Also frequently used is the negative exponential function,

$$f(d_{ij}) = e^{-ad_{ij}}$$

where $e = 2.71828\ldots$ is the base of the natural logarithms. Of course, travel time or cost between origins and destinations can be substituted for distance.

Use of the gravity model frequently requires the addition of constraints on the model. For example, if shoppers travel from their residences to retail establishments to shop, the total volume of shopping is constrained by the number of residents or by some measure of their purchasing power. The gravity model serves to allocate this total from all origins to the various possible retailing destinations based on their locations and their attractiveness to shoppers, perhaps the number of square feet of retail space at each destination. The gravity model would be used primarily to predict the volume of shopping—the total number of destinations—at each location.

Because the number of origins is fixed while the number of destinations can vary and is to be predicted, this application requires an origin-constrained gravity model. Applying such a constraint to the basic model gives this formula predicting trips from origin i to destination j:

$$T_{ij} = KO_i \frac{A_j f(d_{ij})}{\sum\limits_{j=1}^{n} A_j f(d_{ij})}$$

The notation follows that used before, except that A_j is a measure of the attractiveness of destination j; n is the number of destinations; and K is a single constant of proportionality. The origin- and destination-specific k_i and l_j parameters drop out in the single-constrained form. In this formulation, the trips from any origin i are allocated to the various destinations j in proportion to each destination's combination of attractiveness and accessibility, $A_j f(d_{ij})$. Summing the trips to destination j over all origins gives the final form for the single-constrained gravity model used here:

$$D_j = \sum_{i=1}^{m} T_{ij} = K \sum_{i=1}^{m} \frac{O_i A_j f(d_{ij})}{\sum\limits_{j=1}^{n} A_j f(d_{ij})}$$

where m is the number of origin locations.

The need for the constant of proportionality in the single-constrained gravity model arises from the fact that origins and destinations may be expressed in dissimilar units. In the shopping example, numbers of residents or total income might be used as the measure of origins, while numbers of shoppers or dollar volume of sales might be used as the measure of destinations. In such cases, the total number of origins to be allocated will not equal the total number of destinations, so the constant of proportionality is needed. This can be defined simply as follows:

$$K = \sum_{j=1}^{n} D_j \Big/ \sum_{i=1}^{m} O_i .$$

Then the total number of destinations will equal the constant of proportionality times the total number of origins.

Use of the origin-constrained gravity model requires the fitting of the model to available data, including the actual measures of destinations. Different values for the parameter in the distance function may be tried, and perhaps different forms for the function as well. The goal is to arrive at the model that best predicts the known pattern of destinations and to determine whether the fit of the model—the closeness of the predictions—warrants the use of the model for projecting future values. This requires a measure of the goodness-of-fit of the model. The mean squared error (MSE) in predicting numbers of destinations is one reasonable measure of goodness-of-fit:

$$MSE = \sum_{j=1}^{n} (D_j - \hat{D}_j)^2$$

where D_j is the actual number of destinations at j and $\hat{D}_j$ is the number predicted by the model.

The origin-constrained gravity model can be applied to a variety of planning problems in addition to the projection of retail activity. One of the most important is the projection of residential population distributions, with the locations of residences being seen as linked to places of employment by the home–work trip. If employment locations are taken as the origins (which are fixed), employees can be allocated to various residential locations (destinations) using an origin-constrained gravity model. The urban area is divided into a series of zones, and the quantity of land available for residential development can be used as a measure of attractiveness to residences. (More complex attractiveness measures may also be used.)

Instead of the number of origins being constrained, certain problems involve a constraint on the numbers of destinations, which must then be allocated among the various origins. The gravity model for the destination-constrained problem has exactly the same form as that for the origin-constrained model, except that origins and destinations are interchanged.

The Program

The Single-Constrained Gravity Model program and its companion in Chapter 8, the Double-Constrained Gravity Model program, are the longest programs in this book. The length arises both from the complexity of the procedures and from the variety of options provided to allow these programs to be used for a range of problems. Both programs allow information on the separations of origins and destinations to be entered in a variety of ways. The programs may be used to fit the models to known data and to predict future values. The user may select either an inverse power function or a negative exponential function of distance. Options for repetition allow parameter and function changes when fitting a model, a shift from model fitting to projection, and the changing of the basic problem.

The distances (or other measures of separation such as time or cost) between origins and destinations are required by all gravity models. Different planning problems pose very different situations. Origins or destinations may be discrete locations, such as shopping centers, or an area may be divided into zones, with the numbers of origins or destinations reported for each zone. The latter method would generally be employed for residential population, for example. With a system of zones, the zone centroid (usually estimated) is taken as the location of all origins or destinations in a zone. Origins and destinations may be at the same locations (as when the same system of zones is used for both), or they may be at different locations. Actual distances between origins and destinations (or other measures of separation) may be available, or the coordinates of the origins and destinations may be used to compute the direct (airline) distances between them.

The distance input routines in the Single-Constrained Gravity Model program and the Double-Constrained Gravity Model program are identical and include provisions for handling all of these alternatives in a convenient and efficient manner. The user is first asked for the number of origins and the number of destinations (with a maximum of 18 for each). If these values are equal, the program then asks if origins and destinations are at the same locations. (When numbers of origins and destinations are not equal, they cannot all be at the same locations.) The purpose of this query is to ease data entry by eliminating the entering of redundant information. Two options are then offered for data entry, the input of coordinates (for distance calculation by the program) or the input of actual distances.

The programs then begin prompting the user for the appropriate information. With the coordinate option, x- and y- coordinates are requested for each origin and destination. However, if origins and destinations are at the same locations, coordinates are required only for the origins. With the distance option, the user is asked the distance from each origin to each destination. Again, if origins and destinations are the same, redundant information is not requested. Once the distance from origin 1 to destination 2 has been entered, the program does not ask for the distance from origin 2 to destination 1.

When origins and destinations coincide, a problem arises in determining the distance from an origin to the same destination, for example, from origin 1 to destination 1. A value of zero is seldom appropriate. Assuming the origins and destinations represent zone centroids, the average distance between actual origins and destinations, scattered within the zone, is certainly greater than zero. Terminal times or other fixed costs are associated with any trip or interaction, no matter how small the distance. A technical problem arises as well if the inverse power function is to be used, for a zero distance leads to an attempted division by zero. When the user enters the distances, he or she must be certain that all distances are greater than zero. When coordinate entry is used for origins and destinations at the same locations, however, such zero distances would automatically be computed for the distance from each origin to the destination at the same point. One commonly used procedure to deal with this problem is to set these intrazonal distances to one-half the distances to the next-nearest zones. Using coordinate entry, the programs automatically follow this procedure. Whenever the distance from an origin to a destination is zero (meaning their coordinates are the same), the distance from that origin to the destination is assigned the value of one-half the distance from that origin to the next-nearest destination.

After the distance information has been entered, both programs report the coordinates of the origins and destinations, if entered, and the distances from each origin to each destination, either as entered or as computed from the coordinates.

The Single-Constrained Gravity Model program is set up to handle an origin-constrained model. Users needing a destination-constrained model need only enter destinations in place of origins and vice versa. After the distance information entry, the user is given the choice of either fitting the model to existing data or making predictions of destinations. Fitting requires, of course, the known destinations, while prediction requires the appropriate parameters, including the constant of proportionality. The user must then enter the information to set up the problem: the numbers of origins, attractiveness of destinations, and numbers of destinations (if fitting the model). A selection must be made of either the inverse power function or the negative exponential function and the parameter must be entered. For the inverse power function, values in the range of one to three will be most common. The negative exponential function will generally require values much less than one, though the magnitude will depend on the distance measures and the scale of the problem. When the prediction option has been selected, the constant of proportionality is requested at this point.

The program then goes through the actual computations and displays the information entered on origins, attractiveness, and destinations, and the predicted numbers of destinations. The parameters of the model are reported, along with the mean squared error if the model is being fitted to a set of known destinations.

This concludes the computation and presentation of the results for the single-constrained gravity model, and the program now provides various options for their repetition. The first choice is to repeat the same problem with a different distance function. The numbers of origins, attractiveness, and destinations are not changed. The user is asked to select the distance function and enter the parameter, and a new set of predictions is made. The procedure will be most useful in fitting the model, where the parameter (and even the functional form) can be changed to assess the impact on the prediction of the destinations. In many instances, the user will proceed through multiple repetitions in an attempt to minimize the mean squared error.

The second option is intended for making predictions of destinations after the model has successfully been fit to existing data. The model specification—the form of the distance function, distance parameter, and constant of proportionality— are retained from the last run through the model. The user is asked for the numbers of origins and the attractiveness of the destinations associated with the prediction. The results, including the predicted numbers of destinations, are reported. A third option allows entry of an entirely new problem, essentially starting from scratch while preserving the information on distances between origins and destinations.

The main routine of the program, from lines 10 through 790, controls the flow of the program, calls the subroutines, and presents several of the major options. The subroutine at 4000 acquires the basic data for establishing the format of the distance input. If input of coordinates is selected, the subroutine at 4500 provides for entry, distances are computed by the subroutine at 1000, coordinates are printed back by the subroutine at 7000, and the distances are printed out by the subroutine at 7500. With distance input, the distances are entered through the subroutine at 5000 and output by the subroutine at 7500.

The projection phase begins by determining whether fitting or prediction is to be done. In either instance, the subroutine at 5500 provides for the input of origins and attractiveness. If fitting, the subroutine at 6000 is called for the entry of destinations. The distance function is specified by the user through the subroutine at 6000, and then the subroutine at 1500 computes the values of the distance function and stores these in the array F. Finally, the gravity model computations are carried out by the subroutine at line 2000, and the results are displayed by the subroutine at 8000.

On repetition, option 1 transfers control back to the point of distance function definition, and option 3 goes back to the start of the projection phase. For option 2, prediction after fitting, a call is made to the subroutine at 5500 for the entry of the data for the prediction, and control is then transferred directly to the point for model computation and output.

The program provides for the distance matrix to be output using as many columns as can fit on the video display. Following the standard procedures, the variable F must be assigned the number of fields to be displayed, such as $F = 5$ for an 80-column display. This is accomplished in line 220.

Sample Problem

An imaginary state has most of its population concentrated into five urban centers, and the recreational needs of this population are served by three state parks, as shown in Figure 7.1. The distances from the cities to the parks is shown in the following table:

City	Park A	Park B	Park C
1	35	108	138
2	119	38	155
3	104	161	60
4	130	154	36
5	163	107	91

Current average daily attendance at the three parks is

Park	Attendance
A	450
B	390
C	770

The state is contemplating the expansion of park A, near its largest population center, and wishes to ascertain the impact on attendance at the three parks.

An origin-constrained gravity model with trips having their origins at the urban centers and destinations at the parks will be used for this analysis. The populations in the cities will be used as the measures of the numbers of origins and are as follows:

City	Population
1	610,000
2	54,000
3	81,000
4	98,000
5	170,000

The size of each park in acres will be employed as the measure of attractiveness:

Park	Acres
A	340
B	980
C	1920

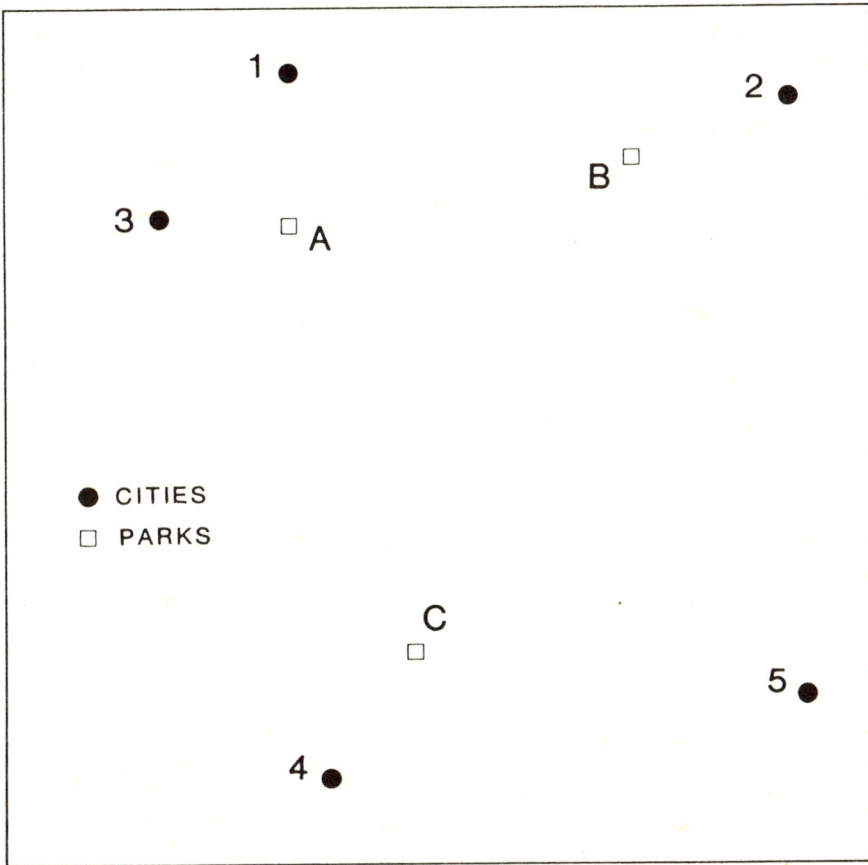

Figure 7.1   Locations of cities and parks for the Single-Constrained Gravity Model example.

The proposal is to expand park *A* from 340 to 1270 acres through acquisition of adjacent land. The current attendance figures are, of course, the measures of destinations.

The Single-Constrained Gravity Model program first asks for the number of origins and destinations. The user then selects the distance input option and enters the 15 distances from cities to parks as they are requested.

Next comes the fitting of the model to the current data. For numbers of origins, city populations are entered. The initial park sizes are provided in response to the destination attractiveness request, and attendance figures provide the destinations. The negative exponential function of distance is chosen, using a parameter value of 0.02. This completes data entry, and the

the program displays the data, the predicted destinations, and the mean squared error.

In this example, the predicted values are quite close to the actual values, and the mean squared error of 614 is quite low. In general, multiple attempts with different parameter values will be required to obtain the best results. For this sample problem, this trial-and-error process was completed prior to the run of the model that is presented.

Since the fit of the model to the data is quite good, the option of making a prediction using the parameter values is selected. No significant population changes are expected, so the same values are entered for the origins. (This is not, in general, required by the model.) For attractiveness, the increased size of park A is entered along with the unchanged values for the remaining parks. The prediction of destinations shows a great increase in the attendance at park A, as would be expected. Park B shows the greatest proportional drop in attendance, possibly raising questions about the utilization of this facility. Of course, the additional park capacity might attract greater overall attendance, which is to say that origins are not completely constrained.

References

Krueckeberg, D. A. and Silvers, A. L., *Urban Planning Analysis: Methods and Models* (New York: John Wiley & Sons, Inc., 1974), Chapter 9, pp. 288–314.

Masser, I., *Analytical Models for Urban and Regional Planning* (Newton Abbot: David & Charles, 1972), Chapter 4, pp. 84–109.

Oppenheim, N., *Applied Models in Urban and Regional Analysis* (Englewood Cliffs, N. J.: Prentice-Hall, Inc., 1980), Chapter 4, pp. 111–123.

Reif, B., *Models in Urban and Regional Planning* (New York: Intertext Educational Publishers, 1973), Chapter 6, pp. 94–102.

Thomas, R. W. and Huggett, R. J., *Modelling in Geography: A Mathematical Approach* (Totowa, N. J.: Barnes & Noble Books, 1980), Chapter 5, pp. 132–148.

Wilson, A. G., *Urban and Regional Models in Geography and Planning* (London: John Wiley & Sons, 1974), Chapter 6, pp. 63–75.

```
SINGLE-CONSTRAINED GRAVITY MODEL SAMPLE RUN


SINGLE-CONSTRAINED GRAVITY MODEL

NUMBER OF ORIGINS (MAXIMUM 18)? 5
NUMBER OF DESTINATIONS (MAXIMUM 18)? 3

OPTIONS FOR DISTANCE DATA ENTRY:
    1 - COORDINATES OF ORIGINS, DESTS
    2 - DISTANCES FROM ORIGINS TO DESTS

CHOICE OF OPTION? 2

ENTER DISTANCES BETWEEN ORIGINS AND
DESTINATIONS

FROM ORIGIN 1 TO DESTINATION 1 ? 35
FROM ORIGIN 1 TO DESTINATION 2 ? 108
FROM ORIGIN 1 TO DESTINATION 3 ? 138

FROM ORIGIN 2 TO DESTINATION 1 ? 119
FROM ORIGIN 2 TO DESTINATION 2 ? 38
FROM ORIGIN 2 TO DESTINATION 3 ? 155

FROM ORIGIN 3 TO DESTINATION 1 ? 104
FROM ORIGIN 3 TO DESTINATION 2 ? 161
FROM ORIGIN 3 TO DESTINATION 3 ? 60

FROM ORIGIN 4 TO DESTINATION 1 ? 130
FROM ORIGIN 4 TO DESTINATION 2 ? 154
FROM ORIGIN 4 TO DESTINATION 3 ? 36

FROM ORIGIN 5 TO DESTINATION 1 ? 163
FROM ORIGIN 5 TO DESTINATION 2 ? 107
FROM ORIGIN 5 TO DESTINATION 3 ? 91


DISTANCES FROM ORIGINS TO DESTINATIONS

ORIGIN     DEST 1        DEST 2        DEST 3
  1          35           108           138
  2         119            38           155
  3         104           161            60
  4         130           154            36
  5         163           107            91

CONTINUE?
```

```
DO YOU WISH TO--
    1 - FIT MODEL TO DATA
          (DESTINATIONS NEEDED)
    2 - PREDICT DESTINATIONS
          (MODEL PARAMETERS NEEDED)

CHOICE OF OPTION? 1


ENTER NUMBERS OF ORIGINS
     ORIGIN 1 ? 610000
     ORIGIN 2 ? 54000
     ORIGIN 3 ? 81000
     ORIGIN 4 ? 98000
     ORIGIN 5 ? 170000

ENTER ATTRACTIVENESS OF DESTINATIONS
     DESTINATION 1 ? 340
     DESTINATION 2 ? 980
     DESTINATION 3 ? 1920

ENTER NUMBERS OF DESTINATIONS
     DESTINATION 1 ? 450
     DESTINATION 2 ? 390
     DESTINATION 3 ? 770


OPTIONS FOR DISTANCE FUNCTION:
    1 - INVERSE POWER FUNCTION
    2 - NEGATIVE EXPONENTIAL FUNCTION

CHOICE OF OPTION? 2

DISTANCE FUNCTION PARAMETER
(POSITIVE NUMBER)? .02


ORIGIN        NO. OF ORIGINS
  1              610000
  2              54000
  3              81000
  4              98000
  5              170000

CONTINUE?

DEST          ATTRACTION
  1              340
  2              980
  3              1920

CONTINUE?
```

```
DEST         NO. OF DESTS   PRED DESTS
  1            450            431
  2            390            425
  3            770            754

CONTINUE?


MEAN SQUARED ERROR = 614

NEGATIVE EXPONENTIAL FUNCTION OF DISTANCE
PARAMETER = .02

CONSTANT OF PROPORTIONALITY = 1.58934E-03

CONTINUE?


OPTIONS FOR REPEATING:
    1 - SAME PROB, CHANGE DIST FUNCTION
    2 - MAKE PREDICTIONS USING SAME
             PARAMETERS
    3 - NEW PROBLEM, SAME DISTANCES
    4 - STOP

CHOICE OF OPTION? 2


ENTER NUMBERS OF ORIGINS
    ORIGIN 1 ? 610000
    ORIGIN 2 ? 54000
    ORIGIN 3 ? 81000
    ORIGIN 4 ? 98000
    ORIGIN 5 ? 170000

ENTER ATTRACTIVENESS OF DESTINATIONS
    DESTINATION 1 ? 1270
    DESTINATION 2 ? 980
    DESTINATION 3 ? 1920


ORIGIN      NO. OF ORIGINS
  1            610000
  2            54000
  3            81000
  4            98000
  5            170000

CONTINUE?
```

```
DEST          ATTRACTION    PRED DESTS
  1             1270          790
  2              980          265
  3             1920          556
```

CONTINUE?

NEGATIVE EXPONENTIAL FUNCTION OF DISTANCE
PARAMETER = .02

CONSTANT OF PROPORTIONALITY = 1.58934E-03

CONTINUE?

OPTIONS FOR REPEATING:
    1 - SAME PROB, CHANGE DIST FUNCTION
    2 - MAKE PREDICTIONS USING SAME
            PARAMETERS
    3 - NEW PROBLEM, SAME DISTANCES
    4 - STOP

CHOICE OF OPTION? 4

SINGLE-CONSTRAINED GRAVITY MODEL PROGRAM LISTING

```
10 REM SINGLE-CONSTRAINED GRAVITY MODEL
20 REM BY JOHN R. OTTENSMANN
30 REM VARIABLES
40 REM     A(J) - ATTRACTIVENESS OF DESTINATION J
50 REM     D(J) - DESTINATIONS (ACTUAL) AT J
60 REM     E(J) - PREDICTED DESTINATIONS AT J
70 REM     F(I,J) - FUNCTION OF DISTANCE FROM I TO J
80 REM     R(I) - ORIGINS AT I
90 REM     X(I,J) - COORDINATES OF ORIGINS AND DESTINATIONS
100 REM    Z(I,J) - DISTANCE FROM I TO J
110 REM    B - FUNCTIION PARAMETER
120 REM    C1, C2, ... - CHOICE VARIABLES
130 REM    K - CONSTANT OF PROPORTIONALITY
140 REM    N1 - NUMBER OF ORIGINS
150 REM    N2 - NUMBER OF DESTINATIONS
160 REM    P - ERROR IN PREDICTION
170 DIM A(18), D(19), E(19), F(18,18), R(19), X(18,4)
180 DIM Z(18,18)
190 REM F SPECIFIES NUMBER OF FIELDS IN TABLE SEGMENTS
200 REM    F=5 FOR 80-COLUMN DISPLAYS
210 REM    F=2 FOR 40-COLUMN DISPLAYS
220 F = 5
230 REM DISTANCE DATA INPUT AND OUTPUT
240 PRINT
250 PRINT
260 PRINT "SINGLE-CONSTRAINED GRAVITY MODEL"
270 GOSUB 4000
280 IF C2 = 2 THEN 350
290 REM COORDINATE INPUT
300 GOSUB 4500
310 GOSUB 1000
320 GOSUB 7000
330 GOTO 370
340 REM DISTANCE INPUT
350 GOSUB 5000
360 REM DISTANCE OUTPUT
370 GOSUB 7500
380 REM BEGIN PROJECTION PHASE
390 PRINT
400 PRINT
410 PRINT "DO YOU WISH TO--"
420 PRINT TAB(5); "1 - FIT MODEL TO DATA"
430 PRINT TAB(12); "(DESTINATIONS NEEDED)"
440 PRINT TAB(5); "2 - PREDICT DESTINATIONS"
450 PRINT TAB(12); "(MODEL PARAMETERS NEEDED)"
460 PRINT
470 PRINT "CHOICE OF OPTION";
480 INPUT C3
490 REM ENTER DATA FOR MODEL
500 GOSUB 5500
```

```
510 IF C3 <> 1 THEN 540
520 GOSUB 6000
530 REM ESTABLISH DISTANCE FUNCTION
540 GOSUB 6500
550 GOSUB 1500
560 REM COMPUTE AND OUTPUT RESULTS
570 GOSUB 2000
580 GOSUB 8000
590 PRINT
600 PRINT
610 PRINT "OPTIONS FOR REPEATING:"
620 PRINT TAB(5); "1 - SAME PROB, CHANGE DIST FUNCTION"
630 PRINT TAB(5); "2 - MAKE PREDICTIONS USING SAME"
640 PRINT TAB(12); "PARAMETERS"
650 PRINT TAB(5); "3 - NEW PROBLEM, SAME DISTANCES"
660 PRINT TAB(5); "4 - STOP"
670 PRINT
680 PRINT "CHOICE OF OPTION";
690 INPUT C5
700 IF C5 <> 1 THEN 720
710 GOTO 540
720 IF C5 <> 2 THEN 760
730 C3 = 2
740 GOSUB 5500
750 GOTO 570
760 IF C5 <> 3 THEN 780
770 GOTO 390
780 IF C5 <> 4 THEN 590
790 GOTO 9999
990 REM DISTANCE COMPUTATION SUBROUTINE ********************
1000 FOR I = 1 TO N1
1010 FOR J = 1 TO N2
1020 Z(I,J) = SQR((X(I,1)-X(J,3))^2+(X(I,2)-X(J,4))^2)
1030 NEXT J
1040 NEXT I
1050 REM SET ZEROS TO 1/2 DISTANCE TO NEAREST DEST
1060 FOR I = 1 TO N1
1070 FOR J = 1 TO N2
1080 IF Z(I,J) > 0 THEN 1150
1090 Z(I,J) = 1E+20
1100 FOR J2 = 1 TO N2
1110 IF Z(I,J2) >= Z(I,J) THEN 1130
1120 Z(I,J) = Z(I,J2)
1130 NEXT J2
1140 Z(I,J) = Z(I,J) / 2
1150 NEXT J
1160 NEXT I
1170 RETURN
1490 REM DISTANCE FUNCTION COMPUTATION SUBROUTINE **********
1500 FOR I = 1 TO N1
1510 FOR J = 1 TO N2
1520 IF C4 <> 1 THEN 1550
1530 F(I,J) = 1 / Z(I,J) ^ B
```

```
1540 GOTO 1560
1550 F(I,J) = EXP(-B * Z(I,J))
1560 NEXT J
1570 NEXT I
1580 RETURN
1990 REM MODEL COMPUTATION SUBROUTINE **********************
2000 IF C3 <> 1 THEN 2110
2010 R(N1+1) = 0
2020 FOR I = 1 TO N1
2030 R(N1+1) = R(N1+1) + R(I)
2040 NEXT I
2050 D(N2+1) = 0
2060 FOR J = 1 TO N2
2070 D(N2+1) = D(N2+1) + D(J)
2080 NEXT J
2090 K = D(N2+1) / R(N1+1)
2100 REM CALCULATE SUM OVER J OF A(J) * F(I,J)
2110 FOR I = 1 TO N1
2120 X(I,1) = 0
2130 FOR J = 1 TO N2
2140 X(I,1) = X(I,1) + A(J) * F(I,J)
2150 NEXT J
2160 NEXT I
2170 REM MAKE PREDICTIONS OF DESTINATIONS
2180 FOR J = 1 TO N2
2190 E(J) = 0
2200 FOR I = 1 TO N1
2210 E(J) = E(J) + R(I) * F(I,J) / X(I,1)
2220 NEXT I
2230 E(J) = INT(K * A(J) * E(J) + .5)
2240 NEXT J
2250 REM CALCULATE ERROR
2260 IF C3 <> 1 THEN 2320
2270 P = 0
2280 FOR J = 1 TO N2
2290 P = P + (D(J) - E(J)) ^ 2
2300 NEXT J
2310 P = P / N2
2320 RETURN
3990 REM INITIAL DISTANCE INPUT ROUTINE ********************
4000 PRINT
4010 PRINT "NUMBER OF ORIGINS (MAXIMUM 18)";
4020 INPUT N1
4030 C1 = 0
4040 PRINT "NUMBER OF DESTINATIONS (MAXIMUM 18)";
4050 INPUT N2
4060 IF N1 <> N2 THEN 4110
4070 PRINT
4080 PRINT "ARE ORIGINS AND DESTINATIONS AT SAME"
4090 PRINT "LOCATIONS (1=YES, 0=NO)";
4100 INPUT C1
4110 PRINT
4120 PRINT "OPTIONS FOR DISTANCE DATA ENTRY:"
```

```
4130 PRINT TAB(5); "1 - COORDINATES OF ORIGINS, DESTS"
4140 PRINT TAB(5); "2 - DISTANCES FROM ORIGINS TO DESTS"
4150 PRINT
4160 PRINT "CHOICE OF OPTION";
4170 INPUT C2
4180 RETURN
4490 REM COORDINATE INPUT SUBROUTINE ***********************
4500 PRINT
4510 PRINT "ENTER COORDINATES OF ORIGINS AND"
4520 PRINT "DESTINATIONS"
4530 FOR I = 1 TO N1
4540 PRINT
4550 PRINT "ORIGIN"; I
4560 PRINT TAB(5); "X COORDINATE";
4570 INPUT X(I,1)
4580 PRINT TAB(5); "Y COORDINATE";
4590 INPUT X(I,2)
4600 NEXT I
4610 IF C1 = 1 THEN 4710
4620 FOR J = 1 TO N2
4630 PRINT
4640 PRINT "DESTINATION"; J
4650 PRINT TAB(5); "X COORDINATE";
4660 INPUT X(J,3)
4670 PRINT TAB(5); "Y COORDINATE";
4680 INPUT X(J,4)
4690 NEXT J
4700 GOTO 4750
4710 FOR I = 1 TO N1
4720 X(I,3) = X(I,1)
4730 X(I,4) = X(I,2)
4740 NEXT I
4750 RETURN
4990 REM DISTANCE INPUT SUBROUTINE *************************
5000 PRINT
5010 PRINT "ENTER DISTANCES BETWEEN ORIGINS AND"
5020 PRINT "DESTINATIONS"
5030 FOR I = 1 TO N1
5040 PRINT
5050 J2 = 1
5060 IF C1 <> 1 THEN 5080
5070 J2 = I
5080 FOR J = J2 TO N2
5090 PRINT "FROM ORIGIN"; I; "TO DESTINATION"; J;
5100 INPUT Z(I,J)
5110 IF C1 <> 1 THEN 5130
5120 Z(J,I) = Z(I,J)
5130 NEXT J
5140 NEXT I
5150 RETURN
5490 REM ORIGINS AND ATTRACTIVENESS INPUT SUBROUTINE *******
5500 PRINT
5510 PRINT
```

```
5520 PRINT "ENTER NUMBERS OF ORIGINS"
5530 FOR I = 1 TO N1
5540 PRINT TAB(5); "ORIGIN"; I;
5550 INPUT R(I)
5560 NEXT I
5570 PRINT
5580 PRINT "ENTER ATTRACTIVENESS OF DESTINATIONS"
5590 FOR J = 1 TO N2
5600 PRINT TAB(5); "DESTINATION"; J;
5610 INPUT A(J)
5620 NEXT J
5630 RETURN
5990 REM DESTINATION INPUT SUBROUTINE *********************
6000 PRINT
6010 PRINT "ENTER NUMBERS OF DESTINATIONS"
6020 FOR J = 1 TO N2
6030 PRINT TAB(5); "DESTINATION"; J;
6040 INPUT D(J)
6050 NEXT J
6060 RETURN
6490 REM OPTIONS FOR DISTANCE FUNCTION SUBROUTINE **********
6500 PRINT
6510 PRINT
6520 PRINT "OPTIONS FOR DISTANCE FUNCTION:"
6530 PRINT TAB(5); "1 - INVERSE POWER FUNCTION"
6540 PRINT TAB(5); "2 - NEGATIVE EXPONENTIAL FUNCTION"
6550 PRINT
6560 PRINT "CHOICE OF OPTION";
6570 INPUT C4
6580 PRINT
6590 PRINT "DISTANCE FUNCTION PARAMETER"
6600 PRINT "(POSITIVE NUMBER)";
6610 INPUT B
6620 IF C3 = 1 THEN 6670
6630 PRINT
6640 PRINT "CONSTANT OF PROPORTIONALITY BETWEEN"
6650 PRINT "ORIGINS AND DESTINATIONS";
6660 INPUT K
6670 RETURN
6990 REM COORDINATE OUTPUT SUBROUTINE *********************
7000 PRINT
7010 PRINT
7020 PRINT "COORDINATES OF ORIGINS AND DESTINATIONS"
7030 PRINT
7040 PRINT "ORIGIN"; TAB(13); "X COORDINATE";
7050 PRINT TAB(27); "Y COORDINATE"
7060 FOR I = 1 TO N1
7070 PRINT I; TAB(13); X(I,1); TAB(27); X(I,2)
7080 NEXT I
7090 GOSUB 9900
7100 IF C1 = 1 THEN 7180
7110 PRINT
7120 PRINT "DEST"; TAB(13); "X COORDINATE";
```

```
7130 PRINT TAB(27); "Y COORDINATE"
7140 FOR J = 1 TO N2
7150 PRINT J; TAB(13); X(J,3); TAB(27); X(J,4)
7160 NEXT J
7170 GOSUB 9900
7180 RETURN
7490 REM DISTANCE MATRIX OUTPUT SUBROUTINE ******************
7500 PRINT
7510 PRINT
7520 PRINT "DISTANCES FROM ORIGINS TO DESTINATIONS"
7530 F1 = INT(N2/F + .99)
7540 FOR F2 = 1 TO F1
7550 PRINT
7560 PRINT "ORIGIN";
7570 F3 = (F2 - 1) * F + 1
7580 F4 = F3 + F - 1
7590 IF F4 <= N2 THEN 7610
7600 F4 = N2
7610 F5 = 11
7620 FOR J = F3 TO F4
7630 PRINT TAB(F5); "DEST"; J;
7640 F5 = F5 + 14
7650 NEXT J
7660 PRINT
7670 FOR I = 1 TO N1
7680 PRINT I;
7690 F5 = 11
7700 FOR J = F3 TO F4
7710 PRINT TAB(F5); Z(I,J);
7720 F5 = F5 + 14
7730 NEXT J
7740 PRINT
7750 NEXT I
7760 GOSUB 9900
7770 NEXT F2
7780 RETURN
7990 REM MODEL RESULTS OUTPUT SUBROUTINE ******************
8000 PRINT
8010 PRINT
8020 PRINT "ORIGIN"; TAB(13); "NO. OF ORIGINS"
8030 FOR I = 1 TO N1
8040 PRINT I; TAB(13); R(I)
8050 NEXT I
8060 GOSUB 9900
8070 PRINT
8080 IF C3 <> 1 THEN 8250
8090 PRINT "DEST"; TAB(13); "ATTRACTION"
8100 FOR J = 1 TO N2
8110 PRINT J; TAB(13); A(J)
8120 NEXT J
8130 GOSUB 9900
8140 PRINT
8150 PRINT "DEST"; TAB(13); "NO. OF DESTS";
```

```
8160 PRINT TAB(27); "PRED DESTS"
8170 FOR J = 1 TO N2
8180 PRINT J; TAB(13); D(J); TAB(27); E(J)
8190 NEXT J
8200 GOSUB 9900
8210 PRINT
8220 PRINT
8230 PRINT "MEAN SQUARED ERROR ="; P
8240 GOTO 8320
8250 PRINT "DEST"; TAB(13); "ATTRACTION";
8260 PRINT TAB(27); "PRED DESTS"
8270 FOR J = 1 TO N2
8280 PRINT J; TAB(13); A(J); TAB(27); E(J)
8290 NEXT J
8300 GOSUB 9900
8310 PRINT
8320 PRINT
8330 IF C4 <> 1 THEN 8360
8340 PRINT "INVERSE POWER FUNCTION OF DISTANCE"
8350 GOTO 8370
8360 PRINT "NEGATIVE EXPONENTIAL FUNCTION OF DISTANCE"
8370 PRINT "PARAMETER ="; B
8380 PRINT
8390 PRINT "CONSTANT OF PROPORTIONALITY ="; K
8400 GOSUB 9900
8410 RETURN
9890 REM PAUSE OUTPUT SUBROUTINE ***************************
9900 PRINT
9910 PRINT "CONTINUE";
9920 INPUT A$
9930 RETURN
9999 END
```

Chapter 8

Double-Constrained Gravity Model

The Model

In making predictions of travel patterns, the number of origins and destinations are assumed to be given, and the gravity model is used to predict the number of trips from each origin to each destination. This is the trip distribution phase of the standard transportation planning process. It follows trip generation, which makes the prediction of the numbers of origins and destinations in each zone.

The general form of the gravity model to be used is the same as in the previous chapter:

$$T_{ij} = k_i l_j O_i D_j f(d_{ij})$$

where T_{ij} is the number of trips from origin i to destination j; O_i is the number of trips with origins at i; D_j is the number of trips with destinations at j; d_{ij} is the distance from i to j; $f(d_{ij})$ is some inverse function of distance; and k_i and l_j are empirically determined parameters associated with the origins and destinations. As before, $f(d_{ij})$ can be an inverse power function or a negative exponential function of distance.

In using the gravity model for trip distribution, both numbers of origins and numbers of destinations are known. Trip distribution thus calls for a double-constrained gravity model, with constraints on both the origins and destinations. This requires establishing values for the parameters k_i and l_j so that the sum of all trips predicted as having origins at i equals the actual origins at i:

$$\sum_{j=1}^{n} T_{ij} = O_i$$

and so that the sum of all trips predicted as having destinations at j equals the actual destinations at j:

$$\sum_{i=1}^{m} T_{ij} = D_j$$

Satisfying these constrains requires that the k_i and l_j have the following values:

$$k_i = \frac{1}{\sum_{j=1}^{n} l_j D_j f(d_{ij})}$$

$$l_j = \frac{1}{\sum_{i=1}^{m} k_i O_i f(d_{ij})}$$

These k_i and l_j parameters are used to adjust or balance the projected trips to match the trip totals and are thus sometimes referred to as balancing factors. Since the k_i values depend on the l_j values and vice versa, these parameters cannot be computed directly. Instead, an iterative procedure is followed. Arbitrary values (in the program, all ones) are assigned to the k_i parameters. These are used to compute the values for the l_j parameters. These l_j values are used in turn to compute new values for the k_i parameters. As the process is repeated, the values of the parameters converge upon stable values that satisfy the original origin and destination constraints. Iteration is continued until the change in the parameters from one round to the next is less than some arbitrarily small value.

The double-constrained gravity model is used to predict the matrix of trips from all origins to all destinations. Error in prediction—the fit of the model—is determined by comparing the predicted trip matrix to the similar matrix of actual trips. While a variety of measures may be used for this purpose, for consistency the mean squared error (MSE) is again used as the goodness-of-fit measure:

$$MSE = \sum_{i=1}^{m} \sum_{j=1}^{n} (T_{ij} - \hat{T}_{ij})^2$$

where T_{ij} is the actual number of trips from i to j and $\hat{T}_{ij}$ is the number predicted by the model.

As with the single-constrained gravity model, the model would first be fit using a known trip distribution. Then, after the functional form and the distance parameter have been established and it has been determined that the model fits the data sufficiently well, the model can be used for predicting trip distributions from given patterns of origins and destinations.

The Program

The Double-Constrained Gravity Model program provides for the fitting of the model and the prediction of trips for up to 18 origins and destinations. The full range of options for distance input provided in the Single-Constrained Gravity Model program are provided in this program as well. Likewise, either the inverse power function or the negative exponential function may be chosen. Repetition can be for the same problem changing only the distance function, for prediction using parameters from fitting the model, or for brand new problems, preserving the distance matrix.

The initial stages of the program involve entering the information on distances from origins to destinations. This functions exactly like the Single-Constrained Gravity Model, so the procedure is not repeated here. Readers are referred to Chapter 7 for an explanation.

Entering the projection phase presents the user with the option of either fitting the model to data or predicting trips. The former requires the information on actual trips from each origin to each destination, and the user would be prompted to enter these, one at a time. Prediction requires only the total trips ending at each origin and each destination, along with the appropriate distance function. The program asks the user for the total numbers of origins or destinations at each location. Note that if the overall total of origins does not equal the overall total of destinations, the program will detect the error and ask that all information be reentered. With either fitting or projection, prompting for the form of the distance function and the parameter follows, as in the Single-Constrained Gravity Model program.

The program then computes the k_i and l_j parameters (the balancing factors). For larger models with more origins and destinations, this computation can take a significant amount of time. The user is so warned by the program. For example, a problem with 15 origins and destinations required up to two and one-half minutes for these computations using Microsoft BASIC-80 under CP/M with a Z-80 running at four megahertz.

The output includes the matrix of actual trips (if fitting) and the predicted trip matrix. These predicted trips are rounded to the nearest whole number. The total numbers of origins and destinations in the predicted trip matrix may not exactly match the actual values because of numerical and rounding errors. Next are reported the mean squared error (if fitting), the form of the distance function and the parameters, and the calculated values for the balancing factors.

The options for repetition work in the same manner for the Single-Constrained Gravity Model and the Double-Constrained Gravity Model programs. The first option repeats the current problem while allowing changes to be made to the distance function. This will most often be used in finding the best fit of the model to the data on actual trips. Option 2 allows a prediction to be made with new origins and destinations while retaining the distance function from the last run (presumably a successful fitting). The third option allows for a restart of the projection phase with a new problem while retaining the distance information.

The main routine, lines 10 to 850, controls program flow and calls the subroutines. The distance input section of the program, lines 250 to 380, functions exactly like the Single-Constrained Gravity Model program. Indeed, the associated subroutines with entry points at lines 1000, 4000, 4500, 5000, 7000, and 7500 are identical for the two programs and may be copied to avoid retyping. (The subroutine at line 1500, used for the distance function computation, is also the same in both programs.)

After distance input, the program enters the projection phase, determining whether fitting or prediction is to be undertaken. Fitting requires the entry of the entire trip matrix, handled by the subroutine at 5500, while prediction needs only origins and destinations, entered through the subroutine at 6000. The distance function is then chosen and the parameter entered in response to the subroutine at 6500, and the subroutine at 1500 computes the distance function matrix. The main routine displays the message requesting patience and then goes to the subroutine at 2000 for the iterative computation of the balancing factors and the prediction of the trips. Results are displayed by the subroutine at 8000. Processing of the repetition options is very similar to that for the Single-Constrained Gravity Model program in the preceding chapter.

Both the distance matrix and all trip matrices are displayed in a horizontally extended format using as many columns as will fit on the screen. The number of fields to be printed (five for an 80-column display) is specified by assigning the value to F in line 210.

The iterative refinement of the k_i and l_j balancing factors is continued until all differences from one round to the next are less than the maximum convergence error, E. The value of E is defined as $E = .0001$ in line 230. This should be appropriate for most applications. E could, however, be changed by the user to obtain more or less accurate convergence.

Sample Problem

A fairly standard trip distribution problem is posed for a hypothetical small city subdivided into four zones, as shown in Figure 8.1. The coordinates of these zones are as follows:

Zone	X-Coordinate	Y-Coordinate
1	8	13
2	25	16
3	19	9
4	22	4

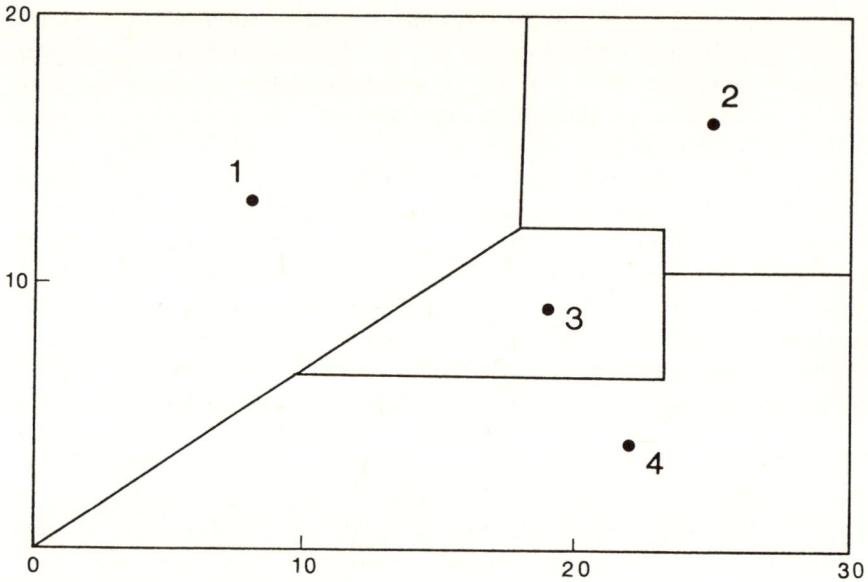

Figure 8.1   System of zones with centroids for the Double-Constrained Gravity Model example.

The distribution of current travel among the four zones, obtained from a recent survey, is

Origin Zone	Destination Zone			
	1	2	3	4
1	2470	390	560	240
2	320	3280	740	310
3	490	1010	4230	790
4	110	190	680	960

The planners wish to fit a double-constrained gravity model to these data and then predict the pattern of travel for the year 1995. Their trip generation model has already produced this projection of 1995 origins and destinations by zone:

Zone	Origins	Destinations
1	4010	4060
2	3940	4110
3	7830	7730
4	3370	3250

Running the Double-Constrained Gravity Model program first requires the entry of the distance information. The user indicates that there are four origins and destinations that are the same. The program then requests the four coordinate pairs and prints out the coordinates and the distances that have been computed. Note that the intrazonal distances (such as that from origin 1 to destination 1) are not zero but one-half the distance to the next-closest destination.

Operation continues with the user selecting option 1 to fit the model and then entering all of the values from the actual trip matrix. For the distance function, the inverse power function is selected and a parameter of 1.6 is used. (Actually, multiple trials were made using different parameter values in developing the example and only the best is shown.) The program prints out the actual and the predicted trips, and the prediction is quite reasonable. The mean squared error of 3762 is much better than for the other parameters tried earlier. Given the reasonable fit of the model to the actual data, option 2 is then selected to make a prediction. The total numbers of origins and destinations for 1995 are entered and the predicted trips for that year are computed and displayed.

References

Foot, D., *Operational Urban Models: An Introduction* (London: Methuen, 1981), Chapter 4, pp. 87–99.

Masser, I., *Analytical Models for Urban and Regional Planning* (Newton Abbot: David & Charles, 1972), Chapter 4, pp. 84–109.

Oppenheim, N., *Applied Models in Urban and Regional Analysis* (Englewood Cliffs, N. J.: Prentice-Hall, Inc., 1980), Chapter 4, pp. 123–134.

Reif, B., *Models in Urban and Regional Planning* (New York: Intertext Educational Publishers, 1973), Chapter 6, pp. 94–102.

Thomas, R. W. and Huggett, R. J., *Modelling in Geography: A Mathematical Approach* (Totowa, N. J.: Barnes & Noble Books, 1980), Chapter 5, pp. 148–153.

Wilson, A. G., *Urban and Regional Models in Geography and Planning* (London: John Wiley & Sons, 1974), Chapter 6, pp. 63–75.

```
DOUBLE-CONSTRAINED GRAVITY MODEL SAMPLE RUN


DOUBLE-CONSTRAINED GRAVITY MODEL

NUMBER OF ORIGINS (MAXIMUM 18)? 4
NUMBER OF DESTINATIONS (MAXIMUM 18)? 4

ARE ORIGINS AND DESTINATIONS AT SAME
LOCATIONS (1=YES, 0=NO)? 1

OPTIONS FOR DISTANCE DATA ENTRY:
    1 - COORDINATES OF ORIGINS, DESTS
    2 - DISTANCES FROM ORIGINS TO DESTS

CHOICE OF OPTION? 1

ENTER COORDINATES OF ORIGINS AND
DESTINATIONS

ORIGIN 1
    X COORDINATE? 8
    Y COORDINATE? 13

ORIGIN 2
    X COORDINATE? 25
    Y COORDINATE? 16

ORIGIN 3
    X COORDINATE? 19
    Y COORDINATE? 9

ORIGIN 4
    X COORDINATE? 22
    Y COORDINATE? 4


COORDINATES OF ORIGINS AND DESTINATIONS

ORIGIN      X COORDINATE  Y COORDINATE
  1           8             13
  2           25            16
  3           19            9
  4           22            4

CONTINUE?
```

```
DISTANCES FROM ORIGINS TO DESTINATIONS

ORIGIN     DEST 1            DEST 2            DEST 3            DEST 4
1          5.85235           17.2627           11.7047           16.6433
2          17.2627           4.60977           9.21954           12.3693
3          11.7047           9.21954           2.91548           5.83095
4          16.6433           12.3693           5.83095           2.91548

CONTINUE?


DO YOU WISH TO--
    1 - FIT MODEL TO DATA
          (FULL TRIP MATRIX NEEDED)
    2 - PREDICT TRIPS
          (MODEL PARAMETERS NEEDED)

CHOICE OF OPTION? 1


ENTER TRIPS FROM ORIGINS TO
DESTINATIONS

    FROM ORIGIN 1 TO DEST 1 ? 2470
    FROM ORIGIN 1 TO DEST 2 ? 390
    FROM ORIGIN 1 TO DEST 3 ? 560
    FROM ORIGIN 1 TO DEST 4 ? 240

    FROM ORIGIN 2 TO DEST 1 ? 320
    FROM ORIGIN 2 TO DEST 2 ? 3280
    FROM ORIGIN 2 TO DEST 3 ? 740
    FROM ORIGIN 2 TO DEST 4 ? 310

    FROM ORIGIN 3 TO DEST 1 ? 490
    FROM ORIGIN 3 TO DEST 2 ? 1010
    FROM ORIGIN 3 TO DEST 3 ? 4230
    FROM ORIGIN 3 TO DEST 4 ? 790

    FROM ORIGIN 4 TO DEST 1 ? 110
    FROM ORIGIN 4 TO DEST 2 ? 190
    FROM ORIGIN 4 TO DEST 3 ? 680
    FROM ORIGIN 4 TO DEST 4 ? 960


OPTIONS FOR DISTANCE FUNCTION:
    1 - INVERSE POWER FUNCTION
    2 - NEGATIVE EXPONENTIAL FUNCTION

CHOICE OF OPTION? 1

DISTANCE FUNCTION PARAMETER
(POSITIVE NUMBER)? 1.6
```

```
COMPUTING BALANCING FACTORS
THIS MAY TAKE A WHILE


ACTUAL TRIPS FROM ORIGINS TO DESTS
```

ORIGIN	DEST 1	DEST 2	DEST 3	DEST 4
1	2470	390	560	240
2	320	3280	740	310
3	490	1010	4230	790
4	110	190	680	960
TOTAL	3390	4870	6210	2300

```
CONTINUE?
```

ORIGIN	TOTAL
1	3660
2	4650
3	6520
4	1940
TOTAL	16770

```
CONTINUE?


PREDICTED TRIPS FROM ORIGINS TO DESTS
```

ORIGIN	DEST 1	DEST 2	DEST 3	DEST 4
1	2350	468	633	209
2	349	3243	777	281
3	560	923	4229	808
4	131	236	571	1002
TOTAL	3390	4870	6210	2300

```
CONTINUE?
```

ORIGIN	TOTAL
1	3660
2	4650
3	6520
4	1940
TOTAL	16770

```
CONTINUE?


MEAN SQUARED ERROR = 3761.87

INVERSE POWER FUNCTION OF DISTANCE
PARAMETER = 1.6

CONTINUE?
```

```
BALANCING (K AND L) FACTORS

ORIGIN       K FACTOR
  1          1.7613
  2          1.16154
  3          .714613
  4          .983062

CONTINUE?

DEST         L FACTOR
  1          1.81691E-03
  2          1.42175E-03
  3          8.09766E-04
  4          1.26603E-03

CONTINUE?


OPTIONS FOR REPEATING:
    1 - SAME PROB, CHANGE DIST FUNCTION
    2 - MAKE PREDICTIONS USING SAME
            PARAMETERS
    3 - NEW PROBLEM, SAME DISTANCES
    4 - STOP

CHOICE OF OPTION? 2


ENTER TOTAL NUMBERS OF ORIGINS
      ORIGIN 1 ? 4010
      ORIGIN 2 ? 3940
      ORIGIN 3 ? 7830
      ORIGIN 4 ? 3370

ENTER TOTAL NUMBERS OF DESTINATIONS
      DESTINATION 1 ? 4060
      DESTINATION 2 ? 4110
      DESTINATION 3 ? 7730
      DESTINATION 4 ? 3250


COMPUTING BALANCING FACTORS
THIS MAY TAKE A WHILE


PREDICTED TRIPS FROM ORIGINS TO DESTS
```

ORIGIN	DEST 1	DEST 2	DEST 3	DEST 4
1	2706	392	689	223
2	371	2511	781	277
3	734	880	5234	981
4	248	327	1026	1768
TOTAL	4059	4110	7730	3249

CONTINUE?

ORIGIN	TOTAL
1	4010
2	3940
3	7829
4	3369
TOTAL	19148

CONTINUE?

INVERSE POWER FUNCTION OF DISTANCE
PARAMETER = 1.6

CONTINUE?

BALANCING (K AND L) FACTORS

ORIGIN	K FACTOR
1	1.70241
2	1.34107
3	.717002
4	.990181

CONTINUE?

DEST	L FACTOR
1	1.64958E-03
2	1.33326E-03
3	6.68243E-04
4	9.0341E-04

CONTINUE?

OPTIONS FOR REPEATING:
    1 - SAME PROB, CHANGE DIST FUNCTION
    2 - MAKE PREDICTIONS USING SAME
            PARAMETERS
    3 - NEW PROBLEM, SAME DISTANCES
    4   STOP

CHOICE OF OPTION? 4

DOUBLE-CONSTRAINED GRAVITY MODEL PROGRAM LISTING

```
10 REM DOUBLE-CONSTRAINED GRAVITY MODEL
20 REM BY JOHN R. OTTENSMANN
30 REM VARIABLES
40 REM     F(I,J) - FUNCTION OF DISTANCE, I TO J
50 REM     K(I) - BALANCING FACTORS, ORIGIN I
60 REM     L(J) - BALANCING FACTORS, DESTINATION J
70 REM     T(I,J) - ACTUAL TRIPS FROM I TO J
80 REM     U(I,J) - PREDICTED TRIPS FROM I TO J
90 REM     X(I,J) - COORDINATES OF ORIGINS AND DESTINATIONS
100 REM     Z(I,J) - DISTANCE FROM I TO J
110 REM     B - FUNCTION PARAMETER
120 REM     C1, C2, ... - CHOICE VARIABLES
130 REM     N1 - NUMBER OF ORIGINS
140 REM     N2 - NUMBER OF DESTINATIONS
150 REM     P - ERROR IN PREDICTION
160 DIM F(18,18), K(18), L(18), T(19,19), U(19,19)
170 DIM X(18,4), Z(18,18)
180 REM F SPECIFIES NUMBER OF FIELDS IN TABLE SEGMENTS
190 REM     F=5 FOR 80-COLUMN DISPLAYS
200 REM     F=2 FOR 40-COLUMN DISPLAYS
210 F = 5
220 REM E IS CONVERGENCE ERROR IN SOLUTION
230 E = .0001
240 REM DISTANCE DATA INPUT AND OUTPUT
250 PRINT
260 PRINT
270 PRINT "DOUBLE-CONSTRAINED GRAVITY MODEL"
280 GOSUB 4000
290 IF C2 = 2 THEN 360
300 REM COORDINATE INPUT
310 GOSUB 4500
320 GOSUB 1000
330 GOSUB 7000
340 GOTO 380
350 REM DISTANCE INPUT
360 GOSUB 5000
370 REM DISTANCE OUTPUT
380 GOSUB 7500
390 REM BEGIN PROJECTION PHASE
400 PRINT
410 PRINT
420 PRINT "DO YOU WISH TO--"
430 PRINT TAB(5); "1 - FIT MODEL TO DATA"
440 PRINT TAB(12); "(FULL TRIP MATRIX NEEDED)"
450 PRINT TAB(5); "2 - PREDICT TRIPS"
460 PRINT TAB(12); "(MODEL PARAMETERS NEEDED)"
470 PRINT
480 PRINT "CHOICE OF OPTION";
490 INPUT C3
500 REM ENTER DATA FOR MODEL
```

```
510 IF C3 <> 1 THEN 540
520 GOSUB 5500
530 GOTO 560
540 GOSUB 6000
550 REM ESTABLISH DISTANCE FUNCTION
560 GOSUB 6500
570 GOSUB 1500
580 REM COMPUTE AND OUTPUT RESULTS
590 PRINT
600 PRINT
610 PRINT "COMPUTING BALANCING FACTORS"
620 PRINT "THIS MAY TAKE A WHILE"
630 GOSUB 2000
640 GOSUB 8000
650 PRINT
660 PRINT
670 PRINT "OPTIONS FOR REPEATING:"
680 PRINT TAB(5); "1 - SAME PROB, CHANGE DIST FUNCTION"
690 PRINT TAB(5); "2 - MAKE PREDICTIONS USING SAME"
700 PRINT TAB(12); "PARAMETERS"
710 PRINT TAB(5); "3 - NEW PROBLEM, SAME DISTANCES"
720 PRINT TAB(5); "4 - STOP"
730 PRINT
740 PRINT "CHOICE OF OPTION";
750 INPUT C5
760 IF C5 <> 1 THEN 780
770 GOTO 560
780 IF C5 <> 2 THEN 820
790 C3 = 2
800 GOSUB 6000
810 GOTO 590
820 IF C5 <> 3 THEN 840
830 GOTO 400
840 IF C5 <> 4 THEN 650
850 GOTO 9999
990 REM DISTANCE COMPUTATION SUBROUTINE *********************
1000 FOR I = 1 TO N1
1010 FOR J = 1 TO N2
1020 Z(I,J) = SQR((X(I,1)-X(J,3))^2+(X(I,2)-X(J,4))^2)
1030 NEXT J
1040 NEXT I
1050 REM SET ZEROS TO 1/2 DISTANCE TO NEAREST DEST
1060 FOR I = 1 TO N1
1070 FOR J = 1 TO N2
1080 IF Z(I,J) > 0 THEN 1150
1090 Z(I,J) = 1E+20
1100 FOR J2 = 1 TO N2
1110 IF Z(I,J2) >= Z(I,J) THEN 1130
1120 Z(I,J) = Z(I,J2)
1130 NEXT J2
1140 Z(I,J) = Z(I,J) / 2
1150 NEXT J
1160 NEXT I
```

```
1170 RETURN
1490 REM DISTANCE FUNCTION COMPUTATION SUBROUTINE **********
1500 FOR I = 1 TO N1
1510 FOR J = 1 TO N2
1520 IF C4 <> 1 THEN 1550
1530 F(I,J) = 1 / Z(I,J) ^ B
1540 GOTO 1560
1550 F(I,J) = EXP(-B * Z(I,J))
1560 NEXT J
1570 NEXT I
1580 RETURN
1980 REM MODEL CALCULATION SUBROUTINE *********************
1990 REM SUM ORIGINS AND DESTINATIONS IF FITTING
2000 IF C3 <> 1 THEN 2140
2010 FOR I = 1 TO N1
2020 T(I,N2+1) = 0
2030 FOR J = 1 TO N2
2040 T(I,N2+1) = T(I,N2+1) + T(I,J)
2050 NEXT J
2060 NEXT I
2070 FOR J = 1 TO N2
2080 T(N1+1,J) = 0
2090 FOR I = 1 TO N1
2100 T(N1+1,J) = T(N1+1,J) + T(I,J)
2110 NEXT I
2120 NEXT J
2130 REM SUM TOTAL TRIPS AND SET K = 1
2140 T(N1+1,N2+1) = 0
2150 FOR I = 1 TO N1
2160 K(I) = 1
2170 T(N1+1,N2+1) = T(N1+1,N2+1) + T(I,N2+1)
2180 NEXT I
2190 REM DETERMINE K AND L FACTORS--BEGIN LOOP
2200 E1 = 0
2210 REM COMPUTE L FROM K
2220 FOR J = 1 TO N2
2230 L1 = 0
2240 FOR I = 1 TO N1
2250 L1 = L1 + K(I) * T(I,N2+1) * F(I,J)
2260 NEXT I
2270 L1 = 1 / L1
2280 IF ABS(L(J) - L1) < E THEN 2300
2290 E1 = 1
2300 L(J) = L1
2310 NEXT J
2320 REM COMPUTE K FROM L
2330 FOR I = 1 TO N1
2340 K1 = 0
2350 FOR J = 1 TO N2
2360 K1 = K1 + L(J) * T(N1+1,J) * F(I,J)
2370 NEXT J
2380 K1 = 1 / K1
2390 IF ABS(K(I) - K1) < E THEN 2410
```

```
2400 E1 = 1
2410 K(I) = K1
2420 NEXT I
2430 IF E1 = 1 THEN 2200
2440 REM COMPUTE PREDICTED TRIPS
2450 FOR I = 1 TO N1 + 1
2460 U(I,N2+1) = 0
2470 NEXT I
2480 FOR J = 1 TO N2 + 1
2490 U(N1+1,J) = 0
2500 NEXT J
2510 FOR I = 1 TO N1
2520 FOR J = 1 TO N2
2530 U1 = K(I) * L(J) * T(I,N2+1) * T(N1+1,J) * F(I,J)
2540 U1 = INT(U1 + .5)
2550 U(I,J) = U1
2560 U(I,N2+1) = U(I,N2+1) + U1
2570 U(N1+1,J) = U(N1+1,J) + U1
2580 U(N1+1,N2+1) = U(N1+1,N2+1) + U1
2590 NEXT J
2600 NEXT I
2610 REM IF FITTING, COMPUTE ERROR
2620 IF C3 <> 1 THEN 2700
2630 P = 0
2640 FOR I = 1 TO N1
2650 FOR J = 1 TO N2
2660 P = P + (T(I,J) - U(I,J)) ^ 2
2670 NEXT J
2680 NEXT I
2690 P = P / (N1 * N2)
2700 RETURN
3990 REM INITIAL DISTANCE INPUT ROUTINE ********************
4000 PRINT
4010 PRINT "NUMBER OF ORIGINS (MAXIMUM 18)";
4020 INPUT N1
4030 C1 = 0
4040 PRINT "NUMBER OF DESTINATIONS (MAXIMUM 18)";
4050 INPUT N2
4060 IF N1 <> N2 THEN 4110
4070 PRINT
4080 PRINT "ARE ORIGINS AND DESTINATIONS AT SAME"
4090 PRINT "LOCATIONS (1=YES, 0=NO)";
4100 INPUT C1
4110 PRINT
4120 PRINT "OPTIONS FOR DISTANCE DATA ENTRY:"
4130 PRINT TAB(5); "1 - COORDINATES OF ORIGINS, DESTS"
4140 PRINT TAB(5); "2 - DISTANCES FROM ORIGINS TO DESTS"
4150 PRINT
4160 PRINT "CHOICE OF OPTION";
4170 INPUT C2
4180 RETURN
4490 REM COORDINATE INPUT SUBROUTINE ***********************
4500 PRINT
```

```
4510 PRINT "ENTER COORDINATES OF ORIGINS AND"
4520 PRINT "DESTINATIONS"
4530 FOR I = 1 TO N1
4540 PRINT
4550 PRINT "ORIGIN"; I
4560 PRINT TAB(5); "X COORDINATE";
4570 INPUT X(I,1)
4580 PRINT TAB(5); "Y COORDINATE";
4590 INPUT X(I,2)
4600 NEXT I
4610 IF C1 = 1 THEN 4710
4620 FOR J = 1 TO N2
4630 PRINT
4640 PRINT "DESTINATION"; J
4650 PRINT TAB(5); "X COORDINATE";
4660 INPUT X(J,3)
4670 PRINT TAB(5); "Y COORDINATE";
4680 INPUT X(J,4)
4690 NEXT J
4700 GOTO 4750
4710 FOR I = 1 TO N1
4720 X(I,3) = X(I,1)
4730 X(I,4) = X(I,2)
4740 NEXT I
4750 RETURN
4990 REM DISTANCE INPUT SUBROUTINE ************************
5000 PRINT
5010 PRINT "ENTER DISTANCES BETWEEN ORIGINS AND"
5020 PRINT "DESTINATIONS"
5030 FOR I = 1 TO N1
5040 PRINT
5050 J2 = 1
5060 IF C1 <> 1 THEN 5080
5070 J2 = I
5080 FOR J = J2 TO N2
5090 PRINT "FROM ORIGIN"; I; "TO DESTINATION"; J;
5100 INPUT Z(I,J)
5110 IF C1 <> 1 THEN 5130
5120 Z(J,I) = Z(I,J)
5130 NEXT J
5140 NEXT I
5150 RETURN
5490 REM TRIP MATRIX INPUT SUBROUTINE *********************
5500 PRINT
5510 PRINT
5520 PRINT "ENTER TRIPS FROM ORIGINS TO"
5530 PRINT "DESTINATIONS"
5540 FOR I = 1 TO N1
5550 PRINT
5560 FOR J = 1 TO N2
5570 PRINT TAB(5); "FROM ORIGIN"; I; "TO DEST"; J;
5580 INPUT T(I,J)
5590 NEXT J
```

```
5600 NEXT I
5610 RETURN
5990 REM ORIGINS AND DESTINATIONS INPUT SUBROUTINE ********;
6000 PRINT
6010 PRINT
6020 PRINT "ENTER TOTAL NUMBERS OF ORIGINS"
6030 T(N1+1,N2+1) = 0
6040 FOR I = 1 TO N1
6050 PRINT TAB(5); "ORIGIN"; I;
6060 INPUT T(I,N2+1)
6070 T(N1+1,N2+1) = T(N1+1,N2+1) + T(I,N2+1)
6080 NEXT I
6090 PRINT
6100 PRINT "ENTER TOTAL NUMBERS OF DESTINATIONS"
6110 T1 = 0
6120 FOR J = 1 TO N2
6130 PRINT TAB(5); "DESTINATION"; J;
6140 INPUT T(N1+1,J)
6150 T1 = T1 + T(N1+1,J)
6160 NEXT J
6170 IF T1 = T(N1+1,N2+1) THEN 6250
6180 PRINT
6190 PRINT "TOTAL NUMBER OF ORIGINS DOES NOT"
6200 PRINT "EQUAL TOTAL NUMBER OF DESTINATIONS"
6210 PRINT
6220 PRINT "REPEAT ENTRY WITH TOTAL ORIGINS"
6230 PRINT "EQUAL TO TOTAL DESTINATIONS"
6240 GOTO 6000
6250 RETURN
6490 REM OPTIONS FOR DISTANCE FUNCTION SUBROUTINE **********
6500 PRINT
6510 PRINT
6520 PRINT "OPTIONS FOR DISTANCE FUNCTION:"
6530 PRINT TAB(5); "1 - INVERSE POWER FUNCTION"
6540 PRINT TAB(5); "2 - NEGATIVE EXPONENTIAL FUNCTION"
6550 PRINT
6560 PRINT "CHOICE OF OPTION";
6570 INPUT C4
6580 PRINT
6590 PRINT "DISTANCE FUNCTION PARAMETER"
6600 PRINT "(POSITIVE NUMBER)";
6610 INPUT B
6620 RETURN
6990 REM COORDINATE OUTPUT SUBROUTINE *********************
7000 PRINT
7010 PRINT
7020 PRINT "COORDINATES OF ORIGINS AND DESTINATIONS"
7030 PRINT
7040 PRINT "ORIGIN"; TAB(13); "X COORDINATE";
7050 PRINT TAB(27); "Y COORDINATE"
7060 FOR I = 1 TO N1
7070 PRINT I; TAB(13); X(I,1); TAB(27); X(I,2)
7080 NEXT I
```

```
7090 GOSUB 9900
7100 IF C1 = 1 THEN 7180
7110 PRINT
7120 PRINT "DEST"; TAB(13); "X COORDINATE";
7130 PRINT TAB(27); "Y COORDINATE"
7140 FOR J = 1 TO N2
7150 PRINT J; TAB(13); X(J,3); TAB(27); X(J,4)
7160 NEXT J
7170 GOSUB 9900
7180 RETURN
7490 REM DISTANCE MATRIX OUTPUT SUBROUTINE *****************
7500 PRINT
7510 PRINT
7520 PRINT "DISTANCES FROM ORIGINS TO DESTINATIONS"
7530 F1 = INT(N2/F + .99)
7540 FOR F2 = 1 TO F1
7550 PRINT
7560 PRINT "ORIGIN";
7570 F3 = (F2 - 1) * F + 1
7580 F4 = F3 + F - 1
7590 IF F4 <= N2 THEN 7610
7600 F4 = N2
7610 F5 = 11
7620 FOR J = F3 TO F4
7630 PRINT TAB(F5); "DEST"; J;
7640 F5 = F5 + 14
7650 NEXT J
7660 PRINT
7670 FOR I = 1 TO N1
7680 PRINT I;
7690 F5 = 11
7700 FOR J = F3 TO F4
7710 PRINT TAB(F5); Z(I,J);
7720 F5 = F5 + 14
7730 NEXT J
7740 PRINT
7750 NEXT I
7760 GOSUB 9900
7770 NEXT F2
7780 RETURN
7990 REM MODEL OUTPUT SUBROUTINE **************************
8000 F1 = INT((N2 + 1)/F + .99)
8010 FOR I1 = 1 TO 2
8020 IF C3 = 1 THEN 8040
8030 IF I1 = 1 THEN 8440
8040 PRINT
8050 PRINT
8060 IF I1 <> 1 THEN 8090
8070 PRINT "ACTUAL";
8080 GOTO 8100
8090 PRINT "PREDICTED";
8100 PRINT " TRIPS FROM ORIGINS TO DESTS"
8110 FOR F2 = 1 TO F1
```

```
8120 PRINT
8130 PRINT "ORIGIN";
8140 F3 = (F2 - 1) * F + 1
8150 F4 = F3 + F - 1
8160 IF F4 <= N2 + 1 THEN 8180
8170 F4 = N2 + 1
8180 F5 = 11
8190 FOR J = F3 TO F4
8200 IF J = N2 + 1 THEN 8230
8210 PRINT TAB(F5); "DEST"; J;
8220 GOTO 8240
8230 PRINT TAB(F5); "TOTAL";
8240 F5 = F5 + 14
8250 NEXT J
8260 PRINT
8270 FOR I = 1 TO N1 + 1
8280 F5 = 11
8290 IF I = N1 + 1 THEN 8320
8300 PRINT I;
8310 GOTO 8330
8320 PRINT "TOTAL";
8330 FOR J = F3 TO F4
8340 IF I1 <> 1 THEN 8370
8350 PRINT TAB(F5); T(I,J);
8360 GOTO 8380
8370 PRINT TAB(F5); U(I,J);
8380 F5 = F5 + 14
8390 NEXT J
8400 PRINT
8410 NEXT I
8420 GOSUB 9900
8430 NEXT F2
8440 NEXT I1
8450 REM MATERIAL FOLLOWING BIG TABLES
8460 PRINT
8470 PRINT
8480 IF C3 <> 1 THEN 8510
8490 PRINT "MEAN SQUARED ERROR ="; P
8500 PRINT
8510 IF C4 <> 1 THEN 8540
8520 PRINT "INVERSE POWER FUNCTION OF DISTANCE"
8530 GOTO 8550
8540 PRINT "NEGATIVE EXPONENTIAL FUNCTION OF DISTANCE"
8550 PRINT "PARAMETER ="; B
8560 GOSUB 9900
8570 PRINT
8580 PRINT
8590 PRINT "BALANCING (K AND L) FACTORS"
8600 PRINT
8610 PRINT "ORIGIN"; TAB(13); "K FACTOR"
8620 FOR I = 1 TO N1
8630 PRINT I; TAB(13); K(I)
8640 NEXT I
```

```
8650 GOSUB 9900
8660 PRINT
8670 PRINT "DEST"; TAB(13); "L FACTOR"
8680 FOR J = 1 TO N2
8690 PRINT J; TAB(13); L(J)
8700 NEXT J
8710 GOSUB 9900
8720 RETURN
9890 REM PAUSE OUTPUT SUBROUTINE **************************
9900 PRINT
9910 PRINT "CONTINUE";
9920 INPUT A$
9930 RETURN
9999 END
```

Chapter 9

Facility Location on a Plane Model

The Model

A common planning problem involves the determination of appropriate sites for public facilities that provide a service to a variety of locations in space. The service might be provided by travel from the facilities to those locations where the service is needed, as occurs when fire trucks or ambulances respond to emergencies. Alternatively, users of the service may be the ones who do the traveling, to the facility, as is the case with parks or social service centers. Facility location concerns are not limited to activities providing services directly to the public. For example, a parks department might also be concerned with finding the best sites for centralized maintenance facilities from which employees will be dispatched to care for larger numbers of parks.

In all such cases, the desire is to locate one or more facilities so as to in some way minimize the travel required. A variety of criteria may be applied to these problems. In emergency response situations, for example, planners often seek locations that will minimize the maximum response distance or time (the minimax criterion) or that will ensure that all potential emergencies can be reached in less than some predetermined maximum time. Perhaps the most frequently employed criterion, however, is the minimization of total (or average) distance or time. Facility locations are sought that minimize the total amount of travel either by the producers or by the consumers of the service.

Facility location problems can be posed either on a plane in continuous space or on a network of links interconnecting the locations of the recipients of the service and possible locations for facilities. In facility location on a plane, the facilities may be located at any points on the continuous surface. The performance of any facility location is dependent on the distances in space to those locations being served. Facility location on a network may be more realistic by acknowledging the necessity of traveling over a system of roads between the facilities and those served. Furthermore, travel times along the network can be employed just as easily as physical distances; the problem on the continuous plane is necessarily limited to physical distance. Thus, addressing facility location problems on a network would appear to be superior. However, such problems can be extremely demanding in terms of the data required to specify the network. Locations on a plane, on the other hand, are easily specified by pairs of coordinates. For many problems, the simpler approach of addressing facility location on a plane may be entirely satisfactory. The programs presented in this chapter and the next are used to determine locations for one or more public facilities that will minimize the total travel between these facilities and the locations of the recipients of the services. The Facility Location on a Plane Model program presented in this chapter provides for location in continuous space and thus will usually need less data. Chapter 10 presents the Facility Location on a Network Model program, which allows the realism and flexibility of the network formulation, but requires the data for the complete specification of the network.

The problem of locating facilities on a plane begins with the specification of the locations of those to be served by the facilities. Assume that those to be served are at n locations, which will be termed demand points. The location of demand point i in space is given by the coordinates x_i and y_i, for $i = 1, \ldots, n$. In addition, each of these points can have a different demand associated with it, reflecting the numbers of service recipients or the rate of utilization of the service. This demand or weight of the demand point, w_i, is a measure of the number of trips required from the demand point to the facility (or vice versa) in any given period of time.

For problems in which very large numbers of actual individual demanders are spread widely across the entire plane, a system of zones might be employed. All of the demanders in a zone could be assumed to be located at the zone centroid, which is taken as a demand point. The weight of that demand point would then be the number of trips required by the demanders located within the zone.

For the general problem, m facilities are to be located to serve these n demand points. The coordinates of these facilities will be p_j and q_j $(j = 1, \ldots, m)$ for the x- and y-axes, respectively. The direct or airline distance is used as the measure of travel between a demand point and a facility. This is determined using the Pythagorean theorem, so that the distance d_{ij} from demand point i to facility j is

$$d_{ij} = \sqrt{(x_i - p_j)^2 + (y_i - q_j)^2}$$

If total travel is to be minimized, each demand point must be served by the nearest facility. To indicate this allocation of demand points to facilities, let the variable $a_{ij} = 1$ when facility j is the closest facility to demand point i, and let $a_{ij} = 0$ otherwise. Then d_{ij} is the distance from i to j; $w_i d_{ij}$ is the travel that would be required if i were served by j; and $a_{ij} w_i d_{ij}$ is that travel if j is the closest facility to i, and zero otherwise. The goal is to minimize the total distance traveled,

$$\text{Minimize} \sum_{i=1}^{n} \sum_{j=1}^{m} a_{ij} w_i d_{ij}$$

Minimizing the total travel requires finding locations p_j and q_j for the facilities that satisfy this criterion.

No direct solution exists for determining the facility locations p_j and q_j. For the location of a single facility, the coordinates p_1 and q_1 can be determined using an iterative procedure. This single-facility location problem is sometimes called the Weber problem after the industrial location problem first described by Alfred Weber. Begin with any starting locations p_1 and q_1 for the facility. Compute the distances d_{i1} to the demand points. Then the following equations are used to compute new estimates p_1^* and q_1^* for the facility coordinates:

$$p_1^* = \sum_{i=1}^{n} \frac{w_i x_i}{d_{i1}} \bigg/ \sum_{i=1}^{n} \frac{w_i}{d_{i1}}$$

$$q_1^* = \sum_{i=1}^{n} \frac{w_i y_i}{d_{i1}} \bigg/ \sum_{i=1}^{n} \frac{w_i}{d_{i1}}$$

The process is repeated using these new estimates, and the values converge on the values of p_1 and q_1 that minimize the total distance. The iterative procedure would be repeated until the change in coordinate locations or total distance from one step to the next is less than some arbitrarily small value. This iterative process has been proven to always converge on the optimal distance-minimizing facility location.

No such guaranteed procedure is available for the location of multiple facilities. Instead, heuristic algorithms must be employed that *may* lead to the best solution. The program makes use of a procedure called the alternating algorithm. Once again, arbitrary starting locations are assumed for each of the m facilities to be located, with the coordinates p_j and q_j. The distance from each facility to each demand point is computed to determine the values of the d_{ij}. Each of the demand points is assigned to the nearest facility, producing the allocation specified in a_{ij}. Then, using the set of demand points assigned to each facility, that facility location is adjusted to minimize the total distance of that facility to those demand points. This adjustment employs the iterative procedure used in the single-facility case. The generalized equations for this procedure are

$$p_j^* = \sum_{i=1}^{n} \frac{a_{ij} w_i x_i}{d_{ij}} \bigg/ \sum_{i=1}^{n} \frac{a_{ij} w_i}{d_{ij}}$$

$$q_j^* = \sum_{i=1}^{n} \frac{a_{ij} w_i y_i}{d_{ij}} \bigg/ \sum_{i=1}^{n} \frac{a_{ij} w_i}{d_{ij}}$$

The iterative process is repeated for each facility and its assigned demand points until the convergence criterion has been met for each set. Then the entire process is repeated. The distances from the demand points to the new facility locations are computed, and demand points are reassigned to the nearest facilities, which may have changed. Each facility location is once again adjusted to minimize the total distance to its assigned demand points. This process continues, alternating between the demand point reassignment and the facility relocation (hence the name of the algorithm), until no further changes in the assignment of demand points to facilities are made.

The final solution produced by the alternating algorithm may or may not be the optimal set of locations that minimizes total distance. The final solution will be better than the starting solution, and the total distance required will often be, if not the minimum, at least not too much greater than the minimum. However, facilities may be located very differently than in the optimal solution. Since the final solution is dependent on the starting facility locations, one should do multiple runs with the starting points located in different patterns to increase the chances of reaching the optimal solution. There is no guarantee, however, and one has no way of knowing whether the best solution obtained is actually the optimum.

The Program

The Facility Location on a Plane Model program uses the alternating algorithm to attempt to determine locations for multiple facilities that will minimize total travel to a set of weighted demand points. To provide the capacity to handle realistic problems, the program can handle up to 50 demand points and can locate up to 10 facilities. Provisions for repetition allow alternative sets of starting locations to be readily employed, making it easy to search for the optimal solution.

Operation of the program is very simple and straightforward. The program begins by asking for the number of demand points and then requests the x- and y-coordinates and weights of those demand points. These are displayed in a table.

Conducting a facility location requires entry of the number of facilities to be located and the coordinates of the starting locations of those facilities. In addition, the program requires specification of a convergence limit for the single-facility iterative location algorithm. (More on this below.)

After computation has been completed, the program reports the facility locations that have been determined. The total travel distance and the average distance for the required trips are also reported, along with the assignment of the facilities to the demand points and the distances from the demand points to their nearest facilities. If desired, the problem can be repeated using the same demand points but specifying a different number of facilities or different starting locations.

The single-center location process—the adjustment of the facility location to minimize total distance to its assigned demand points—converges iteratively. The procedure must be repeated until any changes are sufficiently small. The program uses the total distances before and after each step and continues until the proportional reduction in distance is less than some convergence limit E. If D is the total distance at the beginning of an iteration and D^* is the distance at the end, the convergence criterion is

$$\frac{D - D^*}{D} < E$$

The use of proportional reduction of distance makes the criterion independent of the magnitude of the distances.

The time required for the computations in the model—which can be substantial—is highly dependent on the convergence error selected. A smaller limit requires more rounds of computation and more time in producing a more accurate result. Larger convergence limits are less accurate but faster. The convergence limit of 0.0001 is suggested to the user by the program. This cuts off the iterative process when distances decline by less than one- hundredth of one percent and gives quite accurate results with reasonable computation time. Users trying many sets of starting locations might wish to speed up the process by choosing a larger value for the convergence limit, while those seeking highly accurate results might select a smaller value.

Because of the large numbers of iterations required, computation time may be considerable on a microcomputer. The program warns of the possible delay. For example, a problem with 15 demand points involving the location of three or four facilities required nearly a minute and a half for the computation of some of the solutions. This came running the program using Microsoft BASIC-80 under CP/M with a four megahertz Z-80. The convergence error was set to the usual value of 0.0001. Larger problems would require even more time. Users should be patient. Most microcomputers can compute along on a problem for many minutes with complete reliability.

The printing of the results is dependent on the screen size. With a 40-column display and the number of fields specified as $F = 2$ in line 240, the table of demand points must be broken into two parts. For any greater value of F, all information on coordinates and weights are reported more conveniently in a single table. With up to 50 demand points allowed, tabular information on demand points must be broken into segments vertically to avoid information scrolling off the top of the screen. The program automatically handles this. The number of lines that can be displayed on the scrollable portion of the screen, generally 24, must be specified in line 260, for example with $L = 24$.

The overall structure of the program is simpler than many of the others, with fewer subroutines. The main routine, lines 10 to 470, calls the subroutines and handles repetition. The subroutine at line 4000 handles the entry of the demand points, with the subroutine at 7000 printing out the information. The facility location problem is specified through the subroutine at 4500, calculation of the facility locations is carried out by the subroutine at 1000, and results are printed out by the subroutine at 7500.

The model computation subroutine at 1000 is fairly lengthy. The major loop for the repetition of the alternating algorithm extends from lines 1070 to 1550. The first section computes distances from demand points to facilities and allocates the demand points to the nearest facility. A check is made as to whether any changes in allocation have been made since the last round; if there are none, the process has been completed and the program exits this major loop. Next comes the iterative single- facility location procedure for the Weber problem. This is carried out for all facilities by the loop from 1290 to 1540. For each facility, the location is readjusted until the change in total distance meets the convergence criterion in line 1510, so yet another loop handles this iterative process in lines 1300 to 1530.

All of the earlier programs were limited in the sizes of the problems that could be handled by the number of display lines on the screen, and array dimensions were set accordingly. This program includes the logic required to break long tables into multiple parts. The limit of 50 demand points and the dimensioning of the arrays accordingly is arbitrary. The arrays could be set for problems as large as desired, as long as they fit into available memory. The program should still work fine, though output would be lengthy and the process of input would become extremely tedious. The program structure and data structures are sufficiently simple that alternatives that perhaps read demand points from a disk file could be easily implemented.

Sample Problem

A state has seven state parks, located as shown in Figure 9.1. The coordinates of these parks are as follows:

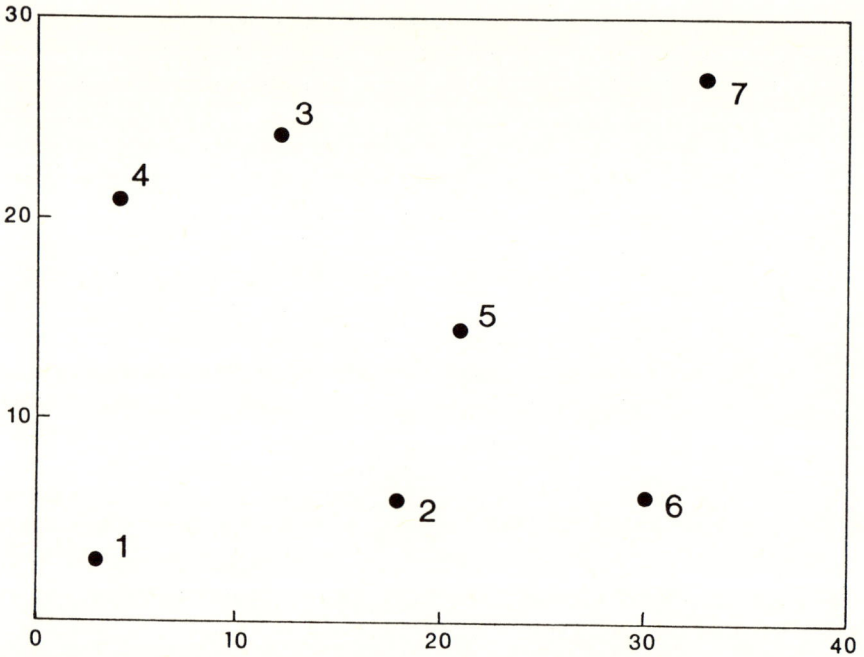

Figure 9.1   Locations of state parks for the Facility Location on a Plane example.

Park	X-Coordinate	Y-Coordinate
1	3	3
2	18	6
3	12	24
4	6	21
5	21	15
6	30	6
7	33	27

Two central maintenance facilities are to be established, with crews traveling from the facilities to the parks to perform regular maintenance. The average number of maintenance trips required by each park in a week are

Park	Maintenance Trips
1	15
2	25
3	20
4	20
5	15
6	25
7	25

Locations are sought for the two facilities that will minimize the total travel required.

Running the Facility Location on a Plane Model program first requires the information that there are seven demand points and then the coordinates and maintenance trips (demand weights) for each park. Two facilities are to be located, and starting coordinates of (12, 12) and (27, 15) are entered. The normal convergence limit of 0.0001 is used.

The results place facility 1 at coordinates of about (6, 21), that is, at park 4. This facility would also serve parks 1 and 3. The remaining parks would be served by a facility at (24.6, 11.3), in the middle between parks 2, 5, and 6, with park 7 requiring a longer trip.

A single repetition cannot provide any indication as to how good this solution might be. However, several additional repetitions using different starting points produced either the same solution or different facility locations with greater total and average distances. For any multiple facility location problem, such experimentation should be undertaken.

References

Rushton, G., *Optimal Location of Facilities* (Wentworth, N. H.: COMPress, Inc., 1979), Chapter 2, pp. 41–63, and Chapter 3, pp. 79–107.

Rushton, G., Goodchild, M. F., and Ostresh, Jr., L. M., *Computer Programs for Loacation-Allocation Problems*, Monograph Number 6 (Iowa City: Department of Geography, University of Iowa, 1973), Chapter 1, pp. 1–9, and Chapter 4, pp. 55–61.

FACILITY LOCATION ON A PLANE MODEL SAMPLE RUN

FACILITY LOCATION ON A PLANE

NUMBER OF DEMAND POINTS (MAX 50)? 7

ENTER DATA FOR DEMAND POINTS

DEMAND POINT 1
     X COORDINATE? 3
     Y COORDINATE? 3
     WEIGHT? 15

DEMAND POINT 2
     X COORDINATE? 18
     Y COORDINATE? 6
     WEIGHT? 25

DEMAND POINT 3
     X COORDINATE? 12
     Y COORDINATE? 24
     WEIGHT? 20

DEMAND POINT 4
     X COORDINATE? 6
     Y COORDINATE? 21
     WEIGHT? 20

DEMAND POINT 5
     X COORDINATE? 21
     Y COORDINATE? 15
     WEIGHT? 15

DEMAND POINT 6
     X COORDINATE? 30
     Y COORDINATE? 6
     WEIGHT? 25

DEMAND POINT 7
     X COORDINATE? 33
     Y COORDINATE? 27
     WEIGHT? 25

DEMAND POINTS

POINT	X COORD	Y COORD	WEIGHT
1	3	3	15
2	18	6	25
3	12	24	20
4	6	21	20
5	21	15	15
6	30	6	25
7	33	27	25

CONTINUE?

NUMBER OF FACILITIES TO BE LOCATED
(MAXIMUM 10)? 2

STARTING LOCATION OF FACILITY 1
     X COORDINATE? 12
     Y COORDINATE? 12

STARTING LOCATION OF FACILITY 2
     X COORDINATE? 27
     Y COORDINATE? 15

CONVERGENCE LIMIT--
     MINIMUM PROPORTIONAL
     REDUCTION OF DISTANCE
     (FOR EXAMPLE, .0001)? .0001

DETERMINING BEST FACILITY LOCATIONS
THIS MAY TAKE A WHILE

FACILITY LOCATIONS

FACILITY	X COORD	Y COORD
1	6.04176	20.9844
2	24.5697	11.2865

TOTAL DISTANCE = 1331.39
AVERAGE DISTANCE = 9.18203

CONTINUE?

```
ASSIGNMENT OF DEMAND POINTS
TO NEAREST FACILITIES

DEMAND          NEAREST         DISTANCE
POINT           FACILITY
  1                1            18.2398
  2                2            8.43256
  3                1            6.67792
  4                1            .0445925
  5                2            5.15097
  6                2            7.57864
  7                2            17.8321

CONTINUE?


DO YOU WISH TO REPEAT USING SAME
DEMAND POINTS (1=YES, 0=NO)? 0
```

FACILITY LOCATION ON A PLANE MODEL PROGRAM LISTING

```
10 REM FACILITY LOCATION ON A PLANE
20 REM BY JOHN R. OTTENSMANN
30 REM VARIABLES
40 REM     A(I) - NEAREST FACILITY TO DEMAND POINT I
50 REM     C(J) - TOTAL TRAVEL TO FACILITY J
60 REM     D(I) - DISTANCE FACILITY TO I
70 REM     P(J) - X COORDINATE FACILITY J
80 REM     Q(J) - Y COORDINATE FACILITY J
90 REM     W(I) - WEIGHT FOR DEMAND POINT I
100 REM     X(I) - X COORDINATE FOR DEMAND POINT I
110 REM     Y(I) - Y COORDINATE FOR DEMAND POINT I
120 REM     D1 - TOTAL TRAVEL
130 REM     D2 - AVERAGE DISTANCE
140 REM     E - CONVERGENCE ERROR
150 REM     M - NUMBER OF FACILITIES
160 REM     N - NUMBER OF DEMAND POINTS
170 REM     W1 - TOTAL WEIGHTS
180 DIM A(50), C(10), D(50), P(10), Q(10), W(50), X(50)
190 DIM Y(50)
200 REM F SPECIFIES MAXIMUM NUMBER OF FIELDS IN TABLE
210 REM SEGMENTS
220 REM     F=5 FOR 80-COLUMN DISPLAY
230 REM     F=2 FOR 40-COLUMN DISPLAY
240 F = 5
250 REM L SPECIFIES NUMBER OF LINES ON SCREEN
260 L = 24
270 REM INPUT DEMAND POINTS AND OUTPUT
280 PRINT
290 PRINT
300 PRINT "FACILITY LOCATION ON A PLANE"
310 GOSUB 4000
320 GOSUB 7000
330 REM SPECIFY PROBLEM, COMPUTE, AND OUTPUT
340 GOSUB 4500
350 PRINT
360 PRINT
370 PRINT "DETERMINING BEST FACILITY LOCATIONS"
380 PRINT "THIS MAY TAKE A WHILE"
390 GOSUB 1000
400 GOSUB 7500
410 PRINT
420 PRINT
430 PRINT "DO YOU WISH TO REPEAT USING SAME"
440 PRINT "DEMAND POINTS (1=YES, 0=NO)";
450 INPUT B
460 IF B = 0 THEN 9999
470 GOTO 340
980 REM MODEL COMPUTATION SUBROUTINE **********************
990 REM SUM WEIGHT, INITIALIZE A(I)
1000 W1 = 0
```

```
1010 FOR I = 1 TO N
1020 W1 = W1 + W(I)
1030 A(I) = 0
1040 NEXT I
1050 REM BEGIN MAJOR ITERATIVE LOOP
1060 REM COMPUTE DISTANCES AND MAKE ASSIGNMENTS
1070 G = 0
1080 FOR J = 1 TO M
1090 C(J) = 0
1100 NEXT J
1110 FOR I = 1 TO N
1120 J1 = 0
1130 D3 = 1E+10
1140 FOR J = 1 TO M
1150 D4 = SQR((X(I)-P(J))^2 + (Y(I)-Q(J))^2)
1160 IF D4 > D3 THEN 1190
1170 D3 = D4
1180 J1 = J
1190 NEXT J
1200 D(I) = D3
1210 C(J1) = C(J1) + D3 * W(I)
1220 IF A(I) = J1 THEN 1250
1230 G = 1
1240 A(I) = J1
1250 NEXT I
1260 REM IF ASSIGNMENTS UNCHANGED, EXIT
1270 IF G = 0 THEN 1570
1280 REM WEBER PROBLEM - OPTIMIZE FACILITIES
1290 FOR J = 1 TO M
1300 S1 = 0
1310 S2 = 0
1320 S3 = 0
1330 FOR I = 1 TO N
1340 IF A(I) <> J THEN 1390
1350 IF D(I) = 0 THEN 1390
1360 S1 = S1 + W(I) * X(I) / D(I)
1370 S2 = S2 + W(I) * Y(I) / D(I)
1380 S3 = S3 + W(I) / D(I)
1390 NEXT I
1400 IF S3 = 0 THEN 1540
1410 P(J) = S1 / S3
1420 Q(J) = S2 / S3
1430 REM COMPUTE NEW DISTANCES
1440 C1 = 0
1450 FOR I = 1 TO N
1460 IF A(I) <> J THEN 1490
1470 D(I) = SQR((X(I) - P(J))^2 + (Y(I) - Q(J))^2)
1480 C1 = C1 + D(I) * W(I)
1490 NEXT I
1500 REM TEST TO REPEAT
1510 IF (C(J) - C1) / C(J) < E THEN 1540
1520 C(J) = C1
1530 GOTO 1300
```

```
1540 NEXT J
1550 GOTO 1070
1560 REM FINAL ADDING UP OF DISTANCES
1570 D1 = 0
1580 FOR I = 1 TO N
1590 D1 = D1 + W(I) * D(I)
1600 NEXT I
1610 D2 = D1 / W1
1620 RETURN
3990 REM DEMAND POINT INPUT SUBROUTINE ********************
4000 PRINT
4010 PRINT "NUMBER OF DEMAND POINTS (MAX 50)";
4020 INPUT N
4030 PRINT
4040 PRINT "ENTER DATA FOR DEMAND POINTS"
4050 FOR I = 1 TO N
4060 PRINT
4070 PRINT "DEMAND POINT"; I
4080 PRINT TAB(5); "X COORDINATE";
4090 INPUT X(I)
4100 PRINT TAB(5); "Y COORDINATE";
4110 INPUT Y(I)
4120 PRINT TAB(5); "WEIGHT";
4130 INPUT W(I)
4140 NEXT I
4150 RETURN
4490 REM FACILITY PROBLEM SPECIFICATION SUBROUTINE *********
4500 PRINT
4510 PRINT
4520 PRINT "NUMBER OF FACILITIES TO BE LOCATED"
4530 PRINT "(MAXIMUM 10)";
4540 INPUT M
4550 FOR J = 1 TO M
4560 PRINT
4570 PRINT "STARTING LOCATION OF FACILITY"; J
4580 PRINT TAB(5); "X COORDINATE";
4590 INPUT P(J)
4600 PRINT TAB(5); "Y COORDINATE";
4610 INPUT Q(J)
4620 NEXT J
4630 PRINT
4640 PRINT "CONVERGENCE LIMIT--"
4650 PRINT TAB(5); "MINIMUM PROPORTIONAL"
4660 PRINT TAB(5); "REDUCTION OF DISTANCE"
4670 PRINT TAB(5); "(FOR EXAMPLE, .0001)";
4680 INPUT E
4690 RETURN
6990 REM DEMAND POINT OUTPUT SUBROUTINE ********************
7000 PRINT
7010 PRINT
7020 PRINT "DEMAND POINTS"
7030 F0 = L - 5
7040 F1 = INT(N/F0 + .99)
```

```
7050 FOR F2 = 1 TO F1
7060 PRINT
7070 PRINT "POINT"; TAB(13); "X COORD"; TAB(27); "Y COORD";
7080 IF F = 2 THEN 7100
7090 PRINT TAB(41); "WEIGHT";
7100 PRINT
7110 F3 = (F2 - 1) * F0 + 1
7120 F4 = F3 + F0 - 1
7130 IF F4 <= N THEN 7150
7140 F4 = N
7150 FOR I = F3 TO F4
7160 PRINT I; TAB(13); X(I); TAB(27); Y(I);
7170 IF F = 2 THEN 7190
7180 PRINT TAB(41); W(I);
7190 PRINT
7200 NEXT I
7210 GOSUB 9900
7220 NEXT F2
7230 IF F <> 2 THEN 7360
7240 FOR F2 = 1 TO F1
7250 PRINT
7260 PRINT "POINT"; TAB(13); "WEIGHT"
7270 F3 = (F2 - 1) * F0 + 1
7280 F4 = F3 + F0 - 1
7290 IF F4 <= N THEN 7310
7300 F4 = N
7310 FOR I = F3 TO F4
7320 PRINT I; TAB(13); W(I)
7330 NEXT I
7340 GOSUB 9900
7350 NEXT F2
7360 RETURN
7490 REM RESULTS OUTPUT SUBROUTINE *************************
7500 PRINT
7510 PRINT
7520 PRINT "FACILITY LOCATIONS"
7530 PRINT
7540 PRINT "FACILITY"; TAB(13); "X COORD"; TAB(27);
7550 PRINT "Y COORD"
7560 FOR J = 1 TO M
7570 PRINT J; TAB(13); P(J); TAB(27); Q(J)
7580 NEXT J
7590 PRINT
7600 PRINT "TOTAL DISTANCE ="; D1
7610 PRINT "AVERAGE DISTANCE ="; D2
7620 GOSUB 9900
7630 PRINT
7640 PRINT
7650 PRINT "ASSIGNMENT OF DEMAND POINTS"
7660 PRINT "TO NEAREST FACILITIES"
7670 F0 = L - 7
7680 F1 = INT(N/F0 + .99)
7690 FOR F2 = 1 TO F1
```

```
7700 PRINT
7710 PRINT "DEMAND"; TAB(13); "NEAREST"; TAB(27); "DISTANCE"
7720 PRINT "POINT"; TAB(13); "FACILITY"
7730 F3 = (F2 - 1) * F0 + 1
7740 F4 = F3 + F0 - 1
7750 IF F4 <= N THEN 7770
7760 F4 = N
7770 FOR I = F3 TO F4
7780 PRINT I; TAB(13); A(I); TAB(27); D(I)
7790 NEXT I
7800 GOSUB 9900
7810 NEXT F2
7820 RETURN
9890 REM PAUSE OUTPUT SUBROUTINE ***************************
9900 PRINT
9910 PRINT "CONTINUE";
9920 INPUT A$
9930 RETURN
9999 END
```

Chapter 10

Facility Location on a Network Model

The Model

The optimal locations of public facilities to service demand at numbers of locations can be determining by considering travel distances, times, or costs over a network on which demand points and facilities are located and over which travel must take place. Applying the same criterion used for the Facility Location on a Plane Model in the preceding chapter, facility locations can be selected that will minimize the total travel between the facilities and the demand points. This is the objective of the Facility Location on a Network Model program presented in this chapter.

Specification of a problem begins with a network of paths along which travel can take place, interconnecting the various demand points. An example of such a network is shown later in this chapter in Figure 10.1, which illustrates the network for the sample problem. The network will most often be the set of road segments providing automobile transportation. Public transit or other networks may also be used when appropriate.

A network is described in terms of nodes, links, and the lengths of those links. Each link connects two nodes. Nodes are the points at the intersections of two or more links or points at the ends of links. All demand points are located at nodes on the network. The weight w_i represents the weight of the demand point at node i, the number of trips to or from the facility that are required by i. Not all nodes in a network need be demand points. Some nodes may just be the intersections of several links. In such cases, the nodes would have demand weights of zero.

Each of the links in the network connects exactly two nodes. A link can be identified by specifying the two nodes connected. Every link has a length, which is the distance (or time or cost) of traveling from one node to the other using this link. (It is being assumed here that travel distance or time—the length of the link—is the same for travel in both directions.)

This specifies the problem. Demand points are located at some or all of the nodes on the network. Locations are to be found for facilities on that network that will minimize the total travel over the network between those facilities and the demand points. Fortunately, it has been proven that such distance-minimizing locations must be located at nodes on the network. The problem then becomes the identification of those nodes at which the facilities must be located to minimize total travel.

Given the network of nodes, links, and the lengths of those links, it is necessary to determine first the shortest paths from every node in the network to every other node and to determine the distances associated with those minimum paths. A reasonably efficient search algorithm exists for such minimum-path problems and can be employed to find the shortest path from any given node to all of the other nodes in a network. The algorithm is a combination of a labeling and search technique and proceeds as follows:

1. The starting node is labeled as "reached" and is given a distance from the starting node (from itself) of zero.
2. All of the nodes in the network are examined to see if they can be reached from an already "reached" node by traveling over a single link. If so, the distance from the starting node is determined by adding the length of that connecting link to the distance of the already "reached" node from the starting node.
3. After all nodes have been so examined, the distances of all the newly reached nodes are compared. The node with the shortest distance to the starting node is labeled as "reached" and the distance to the starting node is saved. (This is the distance of the minimum path.)
4. The procedure is repeated, returning to step 2, until all of the nodes have been labeled as "reached."

The distances associated with each of the nodes at the conclusion of this procedure are the minimum distances to the starting node. The algorithm can be repeated using each of the other nodes as a starting node. The result is the matrix of the minimum distances from each node to every other node over the network.

Given these minimum distances, the location of a single facility to minimize total travel to the demand points is accomplished by examining each node in turn. The distances from any node to each of the demand point nodes is multiplied by the weights of the demand points, and these values are summed. This gives the travel that would be associated with a facility serving the demand points from that node. This distance computation is carried out for each of the nodes. The node with the lowest total weighted distance to the demand points is then the optimal location for the single facility, minimizing travel to the demand points.

The location of multiple facilities poses greater problems. A set of nodes must be found for the facility locations. Travel will be between each demand point and the closest facility node. Evaluation of all possible combinations of facility nodes will be impractical for reasonable-sized problems, since the number of possible combinations and the volume of the computations required would tax even very large computers. Instead, a heuristic algorithm designed to search out the best solution must be employed, but there can be no guarantee that the solution will be optimal, with the minimum travel between the demand points and the nearest facilities.

The Facility Location on a Network Model employs the Teitz and Bart vertex substitution or nodal interchange algorithm to seek the set of facility nodes producing minimum travel. The algorithm involves the swapping of nodes not currently in the facility location set with the facility locations, keeping those swaps that produce the greatest reduction in travel in serving the demand points. The algorithm works as follows:

1. An arbitrary set of starting nodes is chosen as the initial set of locations for the facilities.
2. The total travel from the demand points to the nearest facilities in this initial facility set is computed.
3. The next node not currently in the set of facility locations (beginning with the first node) is temporarily swapped with each of the nodes in the facility location set. The total distances from the demand points to the nearest facility nodes are then computed for the facility sets resulting from each of these swaps. If any of the swaps results in a lower total amount of travel, that combination with the lowest value is chosen and that swap is made permanent, giving an altered set of facility nodes.
4. The procedure in step 3 is repeated for each node not currently in the set of facility nodes.
5. The entire procedure in steps 3 and 4 is repeated until one complete examination of all nodes not currently in the facility set produces no reductions in total travel and no swaps are made permanent.

Thus, the final solution is one in which no single facility can be moved to another location and result in a lowering of the total travel required to service the demand points. This is not necessarily the optimal, minimum travel solution, for it may be possible that moving two or more facilities simultaneously could result in an improvement. Nevertheless, this algorithm generally yields facility locations that are either optimal or have total travel not far from the minimum value.

The Program

The Facility Location on a Network Model program is used to find the locations for public facilities that will minimize the total travel required in serving demand locations on a network. The program allows problems with moderately sized networks with up to 50 nodes and 150 links. Locations for up to 10 facilities can be determined.

Operation of the program is very direct and simple. However, the user will benefit from having the information on the network assembled in an organized fashion so that nodes or links are not inadvertently missed, duplicated, or otherwise incorrectly entered. The program refers to the nodes and links by number, so the user should begin by numbering each of the nodes and links. Numbering can be arbitrary, in any order. The program does not require that nodes or links be entered in any special order.

At the start, the program begins by requesting the number of nodes in the network and then prompts the user to enter the demand weights for each node. If a demand point is not located at any given node, the demand is zero and that weight should be entered. Next, the program asks for the number of links in the network. Then, for each link, the program requests the nodes which that link connects and the length of that link. The nodes are referred to as the origin and destination nodes, but the designation is arbitrary. Either of the end nodes of a link can be entered first. Data on the nodes and links are reported in tables.

This completes the entry of the data on the demand and the network. The program then proceeds to compute the minimum paths through the network from each node to every other node. For larger networks, this can take a considerable amount of time. The user is cautioned to be patient.

Next comes the specification of the facility location problem. This requires entry of the number of facilities to be located and the starting nodes at which the facilities are to be placed. The program then proceeds to determine the best locations for these facilities using the Teitz and Bart vertex substitution algorithm. Once again, the process may take a while and a message cautions the user to that effect.

When the computation has been completed, the program prints out the nodes at which the facilities have been located and the total and average distances associated with this solution. Another table lists, for each node in the network, the facility node that is closest (and hence would serve any demand at that node), along with the distance from each node to that closest facility node. The process can be repeated, allowing the specification of different numbers of facilities or different starting points for a problem on the original network.

Tables listing nodes and links will be automatically divided into multiple segments if they are too long to fit on the screen. This keeps information from scrolling off the top of the screen. For this purpose, the number of lines on the screen must be specified. This will most often be 24 lines, in which case line 190 would be $L1 = 24$.

As already mentioned, both the minimum path computation and the vertex substitution algorithm can require considerable amounts of time when the program is executed on a microcomputer. To check this, a sample problem was entered with 15 nodes and 20 links. The program was run using Microsoft BASIC-80 under CP/M on a four megahertz Z-80 system. The computation of the minimum paths required 58 seconds. The time required to locate facilities varied with the number of facilities to be located and the choice of the starting points. For the location of two facilities, computation time varied from 45 seconds to about one minute. Five facilities, however, required from three and one-half to nearly five minutes for a solution. For larger problems, one would probably need to enter the problem and then take a break, allowing the computer to work away for an extended period of time.

The overall structure of the program is quite simple. The main routine, lines 10 to 480, calls the subroutines and provides for the repetition. First, the subroutines at lines 4000 and 7000 provide for the entry of the data on nodes and links and display the information that has been entered. The minimum paths through the network are determined by the subroutine at 1000. Next, the subroutine at 4500 is called for entry of the number of facilities to be located and the starting nodes. The solution is produced by the subroutine at 1500, which in turn uses a small subroutine at 2000. Display of the final results is handled by the subroutine at 7500.

The minimum path subroutine produces a matrix D of distances between nodes. The minimum paths are determined row by row, with minimum distances from the node designated by the row determined to all of the nodes designated by columns. However, since the minimum path from node 1 to 2, for example, is also the minimum from 2 to 1, the columns are also filled in. Thus, the procedure need only determine minimum distances from the starting or row node in each row to the higher-numbered nodes, saving considerable time. The major loop beginning at line 1000 goes through all rows except the last, using these as starting nodes. The problem is then set up, with the starting node labeled reached (with a one in U) and given a distance of zero, with all other nodes labeled unreached (zeroes in U) and given distances of "infinity" ($M9$). Then $N - I$ distances must be determined to the nodes numbered higher than I; this loop begins at 1100. For determining each distance, it is necessary to examine all of the links, using the loop from 1140 to 1320. Each link is examined to determine if it serves as a link from a reached node to an unreached node. If so, the distance to the starting node is determined and kept for that node if less than an earlier value. The node is retained as a possible reached node if the distance is less than the current minimum distance for the round. After all links have been examined, that node with the lowest distance is marked as reached and the search repeats for the next minimum path. A check is made during this process: If the minimum path has the value of "infinity," not all of the nodes are interconnected. The program reports the problem and stops. After all minimum distances have been generated in D, they are multiplied by the weights of the row nodes, as these products are required by the vertex substitution routine.

The starting nodes are provided to the vertex substitution routine in a short array A containing the facility node numbers. An additional array U of all nodes is created with the value one for facility nodes and zero if the node is not currently the location of a facility. The subroutine at 2000 is called to compute the total distance associated with the starting facility location. The major loop from 1590 to 1840 processes the main iterations and repeats until a round has been completed in which no swaps have been made. Within this, the loop from 1610 to 1820 goes through all of the nodes (but skips those currently in the facility set) to determine whether the solution might be improved by swapping with a current facility node. Then the loop from 1660 to 1750 swaps the candidate node with each of the facility nodes, gets the distance from the subroutine at 2000, and determines which swap yields the minimum distance. Finally, this distance is compared with the total distance for the current facility set. If the new distance is lower, the new node is permanently substituted for the appropriate node in the facility set, and a flag, $S1$, is set to indicate that a swap has been made on this round. Finally, the subroutine concludes after a round has been completed without any swaps and determines which facility node is closest to each node; this information is stored in C.

The output routines automatically segment the printing of node and link tables so that information will not scroll off the screen. Thus, the only limit on the number of nodes and links is the dimensioning of the arrays to 50 for arrays holding node data and 150 for the link arrays. The capacity of the program can thus be increased simply by changing the DIMension statement and increasing these values. The only limit is the available memory for array storage.

Sample Problem

Two social service outreach centers, each to be open one day a week, are to be located in a rural county so as to minimize travel by clients utilizing the

facilities. The population of the county resides in seven villages, interconnected by roads as shown in Figure 10.1. The numbers of clients of the
social service agency in the villages are as follows:

Village	Clients
1	12
2	14
3	10
4	8
5	20
6	7
7	16

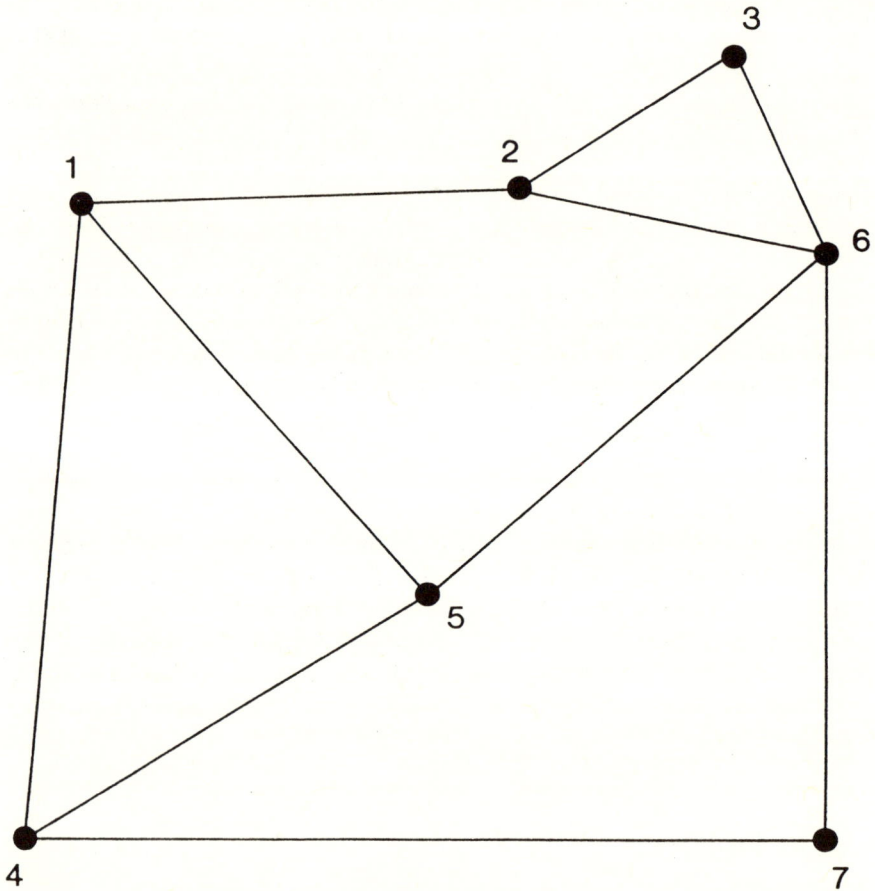

Figure 10.1   Network of villages and interconnecting roads for the
Facility Location on a Network example.

The mileages for the road segments are as follows:

Road Segment	Villages Connected	Mileage
1	1, 2	8
2	1, 4	12
3	1, 5	10
4	2, 3	5
5	2, 5	8
6	2, 6	6
7	3, 6	4
8	4, 5	9
9	4, 7	15
10	5, 6	10
11	6, 7	11

Using the Facility Location on a Network program requires the entry of this information. There are seven nodes, with the number of clients being the demand at each node. For each of the 11 links in the network, the nodes or villages that the road segment connects must be entered, along with the length or mileage. Two facilities are to be located, with the starting points arbitrarily specified as nodes 2 and 4.

The solution places the outreach centers in villages 5 and 6, with the center in 5 serving the clients in villages 1, 4, and 5, and the center in 6 serving the others. The average distance to be traveled by clients to reach the nearest center will be approximately 5.7 miles.

References

Goodchild, M. F. and Noronha, V. T., *Location-Allocation for Small Computers*, Monograph Number 8 (Iowa City: Department of Geography, University of Iowa, 1983).

Oppenheim, N., *Applied Models in Urban and Regional Analysis* (Englewood Cliffs, N. J.: Prentice-Hall, Inc., 1980), Chapter 4, pp. 157–163 (shortest path algorithm only).

Rushton, G., *Optimal Location of Facilities* (Wentworth, N. H.: COMPress, Inc., 1979), Chapter 2, pp. 64–78; Chapter 4, pp. 109–154; and Chapter 5, pp. 155–163.

Rushton, G., Goodchild, M. F., and Ostresh, Jr., L. M., *Computer Programs for Location-Allocation Problems*, Monograph Number 6 (Iowa City: Department of Geography, University of Iowa, 1973), Chapter 8, pp. 141–150, and Chapter 9, pp. 163–179.

FACILITY LOCATION ON A NETWORK MODEL SAMPLE RUN

FACILITY LOCATION ON A NETWORK

NUMBER OF NODES IN NETWORK
(MAXIMUM 50)? 7

ENTER DEMAND WEIGHTS FOR EACH NODE
(ZERO IF NO DEMAND)
     NODE 1 ? 12
     NODE 2 ? 14
     NODE 3 ? 10
     NODE 4 ? 8
     NODE 5 ? 20
     NODE 6 ? 7
     NODE 7 ? 16

NUMBER OF LINKS IN NETWORK
(MAXIMUM 150)? 11

ENTER DATA FOR LINK 1
     ORIGIN NODE? 1
     DESTINATION NODE? 2
     LENGTH OF LINK? 8

ENTER DATA FOR LINK 2
     ORIGIN NODE? 1
     DESTINATION NODE? 4
     LENGTH OF LINK? 12

ENTER DATA FOR LINK 3
     ORIGIN NODE? 1
     DESTINATION NODE? 5
     LENGTH OF LINK? 10

ENTER DATA FOR LINK 4
     ORIGIN NODE? 2
     DESTINATION NODE? 3
     LENGTH OF LINK? 5

ENTER DATA FOR LINK 5
     ORIGIN NODE? 2
     DESTINATION NODE? 5
     LENGTH OF LINK? 8

ENTER DATA FOR LINK 6
     ORIGIN NODE? 2
     DESTINATION NODE? 6
     LENGTH OF LINK? 6

```
ENTER DATA FOR LINK 7
    ORIGIN NODE? 3
    DESTINATION NODE? 6
    LENGTH OF LINK? 4

ENTER DATA FOR LINK 8
    ORIGIN NODE? 4
    DESTINATION NODE? 5
    LENGTH OF LINK? 9

ENTER DATA FOR LINK 9
    ORIGIN NODE? 4
    DESTINATION NODE? 7
    LENGTH OF LINK? 15

ENTER DATA FOR LINK 10
    ORIGIN NODE? 5
    DESTINATION NODE? 6
    LENGTH OF LINK? 10

ENTER DATA FOR LINK 11
    ORIGIN NODE? 6
    DESTINATION NODE? 7
    LENGTH OF LINK? 11


NODES IN NETWORK

NODE NO.   DEMAND
   1          12
   2          14
   3          10
   4          8
   5          20
   6          7
   7          16

CONTINUE?
```

```
LINKS IN NETWORK

LINK        ORIGIN      DEST        LENGTH
NUMBER      NODE        NODE
1           1           2           8
2           1           4           12
3           1           5           10
4           2           3           5
5           2           5           8
6           2           6           6
7           3           6           4
8           4           5           9
9           4           7           15
10          5           6           10
11          6           7           11

CONTINUE?


COMPUTING MINIMUM PATHS IN NETWORK
THIS MAY TAKE A WHILE


NUMBER OF FACILITIES TO BE LOCATED
(MAXIMUM 10)? 2

STARTING LOCATIONS OF FACILITIES
(ENTER NODE NUMBERS)
     FACILITY 1 ? 2
     FACILITY 2 ? 4


DETERMINING BEST FACILITY LOCATIONS
THIS MAY TAKE A WHILE


FACILITY LOCATIONS

FACILITY     NODE
 1            6
 2            5

TOTAL DISTANCE = 492
AVERAGE DISTANCE = 5.65517

CONTINUE?
```

```
ASSIGNMENT OF DEMAND POINTS
TO NEAREST FACILITIES
```

DEMAND NODE	FACILITY NODE	DISTANCE
1	5	10
2	6	6
3	6	4
4	5	9
5	5	0
6	6	0
7	6	11

```
CONTINUE?


DO YOU WISH TO REPEAT USING SAME
NETWORK (1=YES, 0=NO)? 0
```

FACILITY LOCATION ON A NETWORK MODEL
PROGRAM LISTING

```
10 REM FACILITY LOCATION ON A NETWORK
20 REM BY JOHN R. OTTENSMANN
30 REM VARIABLES
40 REM    A(J) - NODE OF FACILITY J
50 REM    C(I) - NODE OF CLOSEST FACILITY TO I
60 REM    D(I,J) - WEIGHTED DISTANCE NODE I TO J
70 REM    Q(K) - ORIGIN NODE OF LINK K
80 REM    R(K) - DESTINATION NODE OF LINK K
90 REM    S(K) - LENGTH OF LINK K
100 REM   U(I) - WORK VECTOR
110 REM   W(I) - WEIGHT OF NODE I
120 REM   D1, D2 - DISTANCE VARIABLES
130 REM   L - NUMBER OF LINKS
140 REM   M - NUMBER OF FACILITIES
150 REM   N - NUMBER OF NODES
160 DIM A(10), C(50), D(50,50), Q(150), R(150), S(150)
170 DIM U(50), W(50)
180 REM L1 SPECIFIES NUMBER OF LINES ON SCREEN
190 L1 = 24
200 REM M9 SPECIFIES VERY LARGE VALUE FOR INFINITY
210 M9 = 1E+20
220 REM INPUT NETWORK AND OUTPUT
230 PRINT
240 PRINT
250 PRINT "FACILITY LOCATION ON A NETWORK"
260 GOSUB 4000
270 GOSUB 7000
280 REM FIND MINIMUM PATHS
290 PRINT
300 PRINT
310 PRINT "COMPUTING MINIMUM PATHS IN NETWORK"
320 PRINT "THIS MAY TAKE A WHILE"
330 GOSUB 1000
340 REM SPECIFY PROBLEM, COMPUTE, AND OUTPUT
350 GOSUB 4500
360 PRINT
370 PRINT
380 PRINT "DETERMINING BEST FACILITY LOCATIONS"
390 PRINT "THIS MAY TAKE A WHILE"
400 GOSUB 1500
410 GOSUB 7500
420 PRINT
430 PRINT
440 PRINT "DO YOU WISH TO REPEAT USING SAME"
450 PRINT "NETWORK (1=YES, 0=NO)";
460 INPUT B
470 IF B = 0 THEN 9999
480 GOTO 350
980 REM MINIMUM PATH SUBROUTINE ****************************
```

```
990 REM USE ALL NODES BUT LAST AS STARTING NODES
1000 FOR I = 1 TO N - 1
1010 REM INITIALIZE DISTANCES, LIST OF REACHED NODES
1020 FOR J = I TO N
1030 D(I,J) = M9
1040 U(J) = 0
1050 NEXT J
1060 REM STARTING NODE DISTANCE. REACHED
1070 D(I,I) = 0
1080 U(I) = 1
1090 REM DETERMINE DISTANCES TO REMAINING NODES
1100 FOR J = 1 TO N - I
1110 REM SET MIN DISTANCE AT INFINITY
1120 D1 = M9
1130 REM SEARCH THROUGH ALL LINKS
1140 FOR K = 1 TO L
1150 REM GET NODES, CHECK IF ONLY ONE REACHED
1160 I1 = Q(K)
1170 I2 = R(K)
1180 IF U(I1) + U(I2) <> 1 THEN 1320
1190 REM GET REACHED NODE INTO I1, OTHER INTO I2
1200 IF U(I1) = 1 THEN 1250
1210 I3 = I1
1220 I1 = I2
1230 I2 = I3
1240 REM GET DISTANCE, SUB IF LESS THAN CURRENT
1250 D2 = D(I,I1) + S(K)
1260 IF D2 >= D(I,I2) THEN 1290
1270 D(I,I2) = D2
1280 REM IF DISTANCE SMALLEST THIS ROUND, KEEP NODE
1290 IF D2 > D1 THEN 1320
1300 D1 = D2
1310 I4 = I2
1320 NEXT K
1330 REM CHECK IF NO LINK FOUND
1340 IF D1 < M9 THEN 1380
1350 PRINT "NETWORK NOT CONNECTED"
1360 GOTO 9999
1370 REM MARK MINIMUM DISTANCE NODE REACHED
1380 U(I4) = 1
1390 D(I4,I) = D(I,I4)
1400 NEXT J
1410 NEXT I
1420 FOR I = 1 TO N
1430 FOR J = 1 TO N
1440 D(I,J) = D(I,J) * W(I)
1450 NEXT J
1460 NEXT I
1470 RETURN
1480 REM VERTEX SUBSTITUTION ALLOCATION SUBROUTINE ********
1490 REM INITIALIZE FOR STARTING NODE SET
1500 FOR I = 1 TO N
1510 U(I) = 0
```

```
1520 NEXT I
1530 FOR J = 1 TO M
1540 U(A(J)) = 1
1550 NEXT J
1560 GOSUB 2000
1570 D1 = D2
1580 REM BEGIN ITERATION LOOP; SET NO SWAP VARIABLE
1590 S1 = 0
1600 REM GO THROUGH SWAP CANDIDATE NODES
1610 FOR I = 1 TO N
1620 IF U(I) = 1 THEN 1820
1630 REM INITIALIZE VARIABLE FOR SWAPPED NODE
1640 S2 = 0
1650 REM GO THROUGH FACILITY NODES
1660 FOR J = 1 TO M
1670 REM DETERMINE DISTANCE AND TEST
1680 S3 = A(J)
1690 A(J) = I
1700 GOSUB 2000
1710 A(J) = S3
1720 IF D2 >= D1 THEN 1750
1730 D1 = D2
1740 S2 = J
1750 NEXT J
1760 REM SWAP CANDIDATE NODE IF DISTANCE LOWERED
1770 IF S2 = 0 THEN 1820
1780 U(A(S2)) = 0
1790 A(S2) = I
1800 U(I) = 1
1810 S1 = 1
1820 NEXT I
1830 REM CHECK IF SWAP THIS ROUND
1840 IF S1 = 1 THEN 1590
1850 REM FINISH--FIND CLOSEST NODES AND WEIGHTS
1860 W1 = 0
1870 FOR I = 1 TO N
1880 W1 = W1 + W(I)
1890 D2 = M9
1900 FOR J = 1 TO M
1910 IF D(I,A(J)) >= D2 THEN 1940
1920 D2 = D(I,A(J))
1930 C(I) = A(J)
1940 NEXT J
1950 NEXT I
1960 D2 = D1 / W1
1970 RETURN
1990 REM SUBROUTINE TO COMPUTE DIST FROM FACILITY SET ******
2000 D2 = 0
2010 FOR I1 = 1 TO N
2020 D3 = M9
2030 FOR J1 = 1 TO M
2040 IF D(I1,A(J1)) >= D3 THEN 2060
2050 D3 = D(I1,A(J1))
```

```
2060 NEXT J1
2070 D2 = D2 + D3
2080 NEXT I1
2090 RETURN
3990 REM NETWORK INPUT SUBROUTINE ************************
4000 PRINT
4010 PRINT "NUMBER OF NODES IN NETWORK"
4020 PRINT "(MAXIMUM 50)";
4030 INPUT N
4040 PRINT
4050 PRINT "ENTER DEMAND WEIGHTS FOR EACH NODE"
4060 PRINT "(ZERO IF NO DEMAND)";
4070 FOR I = 1 TO N
4080 PRINT TAB(5); "NODE"; I;
4090 INPUT W(I)
4100 NEXT I
4110 PRINT
4120 PRINT "NUMBER OF LINKS IN NETWORK"
4130 PRINT "(MAXIMUM 150)";
4140 INPUT L
4150 FOR K = 1 TO L
4160 PRINT
4170 PRINT "ENTER DATA FOR LINK"; K
4180 PRINT TAB(5); "ORIGIN NODE";
4190 INPUT Q(K)
4200 PRINT TAB(5); "DESTINATION NODE";
4210 INPUT R(K)
4220 PRINT TAB(5); "LENGTH OF LINK";
4230 INPUT S(K)
4240 NEXT K
4250 RETURN
4490 REM FACILITY PROBLEM SPECIFICATION SUBROUTINE *********
4500 PRINT
4510 PRINT
4520 PRINT "NUMBER OF FACILITIES TO BE LOCATED"
4530 PRINT "(MAXIMUM 10)";
4540 INPUT M
4550 PRINT
4560 PRINT "STARTING LOCATIONS OF FACILITIES"
4570 PRINT "(ENTER NODE NUMBERS)"
4580 FOR J = 1 TO M
4590 PRINT TAB(5); "FACILITY"; J;
4600 INPUT A(J)
4610 NEXT J
4620 RETURN
6990 REM NETWORK OUTPUT ROUTINE **************************
7000 PRINT
7010 PRINT
7020 PRINT "NODES IN NETWORK"
7030 F0 = L1 - 5
7040 F1 = INT(N/F0 + .99)
7050 FOR F2 = 1 TO F1
7060 PRINT
```

```
7070 PRINT "NODE NO."; TAB(11); "DEMAND"
7080 F3 = (F2 - 1) * F0 + 1
7090 F4 = F3 + F0 - 1
7100 IF F4 <= N THEN 7120
7110 F4 = N
7120 FOR I = F3 TO F4
7130 PRINT I; TAB(11); W(I)
7140 NEXT I
7150 GOSUB 9900
7160 NEXT F2
7170 PRINT
7180 PRINT
7190 PRINT "LINKS IN NETWORK"
7200 F0 = L1 - 6
7210 F1 = INT(L/F0 + .99)
7220 FOR F2 = 1 TO F1
7230 PRINT
7240 PRINT "LINK"; TAB(11); "ORIGIN"; TAB(21);
7250 PRINT "DEST"; TAB(31); "LENGTH"
7260 PRINT "NUMBER"; TAB(11); "NODE"; TAB(21); "NODE"
7270 F3 = (F2 - 1) * F0 + 1
7280 F4 = F3 + F0 - 1
7290 IF F4 <= L THEN 7310
7300 F4 = L
7310 FOR I = F3 TO F4
7320 PRINT I; TAB(11); Q(I); TAB(21); R(I); TAB(31); S(I)
7330 NEXT I
7340 GOSUB 9900
7350 NEXT F2
7360 RETURN
7490 REM RESULTS OUTPUT SUBROUTINE *************************
7500 PRINT
7510 PRINT
7520 PRINT "FACILITY LOCATIONS"
7530 PRINT
7540 PRINT "FACILITY"; TAB(13); "NODE"
7550 FOR I = 1 TO M
7560 PRINT I; TAB(13); A(I)
7570 NEXT I
7580 PRINT
7590 PRINT "TOTAL DISTANCE ="; D1
7600 PRINT "AVERAGE DISTANCE ="; D2
7610 GOSUB 9900
7620 PRINT
7630 PRINT
7640 PRINT "ASSIGNMENT OF DEMAND POINTS"
7650 PRINT "TO NEAREST FACILITIES"
7660 F0 = L1 - 7
7670 F1 = INT(N/F0 + .99)
7680 FOR F2 = 1 TO F1
7690 PRINT
7700 PRINT "DEMAND"; TAB(13); "FACILITY";
7710 PRINT TAB(27); "DISTANCE"
```

```
7720 PRINT "NODE"; TAB(13); "NODE"
7730 F3 = (F2 - 1) * F0 + 1
7740 F4 = F3 + F0 - 1
7750 IF F4 <= N THEN 7770
7760 F4 = N
7770 FOR I = F3 TO F4
7780 PRINT I; TAB(13); C(I); TAB(27); D(I,C(I))/W(I)
7790 NEXT I
7800 GOSUB 9900
7810 NEXT F2
7820 RETURN
9890 REM PAUSE OUTPUT SUBROUTINE ***************************
9900 PRINT
9910 PRINT "CONTINUE";
9920 INPUT A$
9930 RETURN
9999 END
```

Chapter 11

Using Microcomputers
in Urban Planning

The BASIC programs for urban analysis presented in this book represent only one way microcomputers can be used in urban planning. The standard microcomputer software sold for general business applications has a wealth of possible uses in planning offices. More specialized software—some developed expressly for planners—will further increase the range of applications. With additional experience and new developments, the use of microcomputers in urban planning will continue to grow and new applications will continue to emerge.

Using Standard Microcomputer Software

For many planners, the initial applications of microcomputers will involve the use of the standard programs designed for business applications. Electronic spreadsheet programs, database management systems, business graphics packages, and project management software are all readily available. Such software offers many opportunities for increasing productivity and enhancing the quality of the work performed by planners in many areas.[1]

Planners will find perhaps the broadest range of immediate applications for electronic spreadsheet programs such as VisiCalc (the original), Multiplan, and Lotus 1-2-3, to name only a few. Electronic spreadsheet programs provide for the analysis of problems arrayed in tabular form. The spreadsheet is a large table with rows and columns. Any portion of the spreadsheet can be displayed on the computer screen. The user enters information into the cells of the table. This information may be text (for labels), numerical values, or formulas that refer to the values in other cells. When a formula is entered—such as the sum of a column of numbers—the value is calculated and displayed.

The real power of electronic spreadsheet programs arises from the opportunity provided to experiment and consider alternatives. Change any value in the table, and the spreadsheet is automatically recalculated and the results of the new analysis are displayed. The user is given the ability to ask what would happen if a change were made, make that change, and find out.

Many planning analyses can readily be carried out using electronic spreadsheet programs. Any budget preparation problem is a natural. Benefit–cost analyses can be done in the spreadsheet format, and any value—including the discount rate—can be altered to determine the impact of the change on the result. The cost–revenue calculations involved in fiscal impact analysis can be carried out with an electronic spreadsheet, and once again, the effects of any changes in a proposed development can be immediately ascertained. For many problems, these programs provide planners with the capability of examining many more alternatives than have previously been possible. The range of applications of electronic spreadsheet programs in planning is limited only by planners' imaginations. For many planners, electronic spreadsheets are likely to be the first type of commercial software used on microcomputers and the spreadsheet programs will become familiar tools that will continue to be useful.[2]

Much of the work of planning requires the manipulation of significant quantities of information. The largest planning problems will still require the capabilities of the large mainframe computers or minicomputers. For more modest data management problems, however, planners should be considering microcomputers. Commercially available database management software provides the key to such applications.

Database software provides for the specification of the fields of information to be stored for each record in the database. The information is entered and stored in files on a disk. Searches can be made for specific information that is required. Reports can be generated presenting the information from a database in a variety of ways.

Planning applications can involve the storage and reporting of information ranging from data for geographic areas, to information on requests for zoning changes, to data on the status of improvement projects. Nearly any data management software will allow planners to look up or update specific information and produce a variety of reports from any of these files. The more sophisticated relational database management systems go further, allowing information from different files to be used together. For example, in a relational database containing the types of information described above, a planner might be able to examine the characteristics of those census tracts in which specified requests for zoning changes were located. Relational database management systems provide the *potential* for combining the information used in planning in new and useful ways. Realization of this potential, however, will require the development of considerable experience and expertise.[3]

The large quantities of information handled by planners can often be more effectively presented in the form of charts and graphs. Most planners probably employ such graphs on occasion, but the time and expense associated with the preparation of such illustrations by draftsmen undoubtedly limits their use. Many microcomputers have graphics capabilities. Software is available—often called business graphics software—for automatically producing bar and line graphs, pie charts, and other representations of numerical information. The graphs can be displayed on the screen and can be output on paper using both printers and plotters.

Business graphics will find numerous planning applications. The presentation of information to outside audiences, in meetings or via reports, is greatly enhanced with graphics. Some hand-prepared graphs are already being used by many planners in these situations. Business graphics programs on microcomputers will allow more frequent and effective use, even when last-minute changes are required. Microcomputer business graphics software also allows the generation of charts and graphs as part of the day-to-day analysis and decisionmaking process within a planning agency. The ease with which the graphs can be produced makes it possible for the planner to use these to study trends, examine distributions, and otherwise develop a better understanding of the problem being addressed.

A newer form of general business software with great potential for planners automates the process of project scheduling and management. These programs provide for the entry of the many tasks (and their interdependencies) that make up complex projects. The programs can conduct critical path or PERT analyses and can produce the appropriate charts and reports. In addition to carrying out the rather complex calculations required by the scheduling techniques, the programs provide flexibility in generating and using the project schedules. Durations of tasks can be altered and resources can be reallocated. Because the information is stored in the computer, changes can be made easily to experiment while planning the project and to accommodate the changes that occur during project implementation. Planners involved with complex projects having many interdependent tasks should find such software to be very useful, allowing the utilization of the more sophisticated scheduling methods that may previously have been impractical.

Emerging Software Trends for Planning

While the general-purpose business software will be useful for many tasks, other planning problems will require more specialized software. Microcomputer software is being developed especially to meet such needs, ranging from transportation systems modeling to geographical data management to computer-aided design. As the potential of microcomputers for planning is appreciated, more of this specialized software for other planning applications is likely to emerge.

The large-scale simulation of travel behavior for transportation planning was one of the earliest applications of computers in planning. Developing and running these transportation systems models initially required the capabilities of large mainframe computers. For larger areas, the speed and storage capacities of the large computers will still be needed to deal with the massive amounts of data and the huge volumes of computations. For smaller areas, however, microcomputers already have the power required for transportation systems modeling. Software for the standard transportation planning models is now available for microcomputers. This brings the ability to do state-of-the-art transportation planning to many planners in agencies lacking access to large mainframe computers. Agencies that formerly turned to outside consultants for transportation planning can now do the work themselves and can have the models available for use on a continuing basis.

Other planning models—such as models to predict air pollution, for example—that were formerly available to planners only on mainframe computers will undoubtedly be developed for microcomputers as well. Especially as the power of microcomputers continues to increase, more planners will gain access to the most sophisticated analytical tools, available for use on relatively inexpensive desktop computers.

Urban and regional planning makes extensive use of geographically based data. Planners have been active in pursuing the use of computers for the manipulation of such information. Once again, this has been a task requiring the capabilities of larger computers. Now the first generation of software is being developed for geographical database management on microcomputers. While large databases will still require the processing speeds and storage capacities of larger computers, microcomputers will make the automated storage and manipulation of geographically based information available to many planning agencies with more modest needs. The software will allow not only the manipulation of the information but the automated generation of special-purpose maps for a variety of purposes.

Planners involved in design will soon be exploring the use of computer-aided design systems on microcomputers. Most current computer-aided design systems, already widely used in architectural and engineering offices, have been based on minicomputers and cost tens or hundreds of thousands of dollars. Far less expensive computer-aided design systems are now becoming available using microcomputers. They lack some of the capabilities of the more expensive systems, of course, but they could prove useful for some of the design activities carried out by planners. As in all of the areas mentioned, the capabilities of the microcomputer systems will rapidly be improving, further enhancing their utility to planners for computer-aided design.

Expanding Microcomputer Applications in Planning

Developments in microcomputer hardware and software are coming so rapidly that the potential for applications in planning is increasing continuously. In addition to new types of software for more varieties of planning applications, the very organization of information acquisition and use in planning will be altered. Microcomputers will play a role in information distribution and the use of large-computer databases, in the automation of planning offices, and even in communication with members of the public.

With appropriate communications software and a device called a modem, microcomputers can be used to access remote computer systems over the telephone lines. Census or other data stored on large computers can be distributed in this manner, for example. The microcomputer is used to communicate with the large system, and the desired data are "downloaded" to the microcomputer and stored there. Planners can then use the microcomputer for the analysis of this information.

Already, bibliographic and legal information, economic statistics, and census data in some areas are available on large computer systems providing for remote access. The volume of information available in this fashion will be increasing rapidly. Such systems will be of growing importance for information acquisition and distribution. The microcomputer becomes the key to obtaining this information and retaining it—on the microcomputer—for further use.

Microcomputers will play a major role in revolutionizing the functioning of planning offices. The automated office of the future will provide every person with a workstation—either a terminal attached to a multiuser computer system or a personal computer. Using a local-area network, all of the computers will be linked to each other, to centralized disk files, and to various peripheral devices such as printers and plotters. People will be able to share databases and work on different sections of the same document. Information will be sent from one user to another via electronic mail. The traditional flow of paper documents will be reduced or even eliminated. The time-wasting tasks of copying information from one form or report to another can be dispensed with. Office automation will play a major role in increasing productivity in planning offices.

Microcomputers will even come to play an important role in communications by planners with the public. Microcomputers are becoming increasingly easy to use. More members of the general public are becoming familiar with these machines. Microcomputers will become useful tools for disseminating information to and providing for the feedback of information from members of the public. Initial applications might involve the use of a microcomputer at public meetings to display information and to immediately present analyses of the consequences of any suggested changes in a plan. Computers might be made available to members of the public coming into the planning office. They could enter questions and obtain information on their own, without requiring staff assistance.

As the possibilities of using microcomputers for public interaction are explored, more interesting uses will be developed. Interactive simulations illustrating the consequences of planning alternatives could play an important role in public education. Data and software (and the computers as well?) might be provided to community groups for use in their own analysis and planning activities. Planning agencies might even establish electronic "bulletin boards" that members of the public could access with their own microcomputers. Such systems could provide information to the public and give people the opportunity to respond to the work of the planners.

The use of microcomputers in planning is only beginning. Planners need to initiate the learning process that must follow. Simple applications, useful implementations of the familiar planning models for urban analysis, offer one place to start.

Notes

[1] The author has written an introduction to such applications of microcomputers in government. See Ottensmann, J. R., *Using Personal Computers in Public Agencies* (New York: Wiley Interscience, John Wiley & Sons, Inc., 1985).

[2] For further information on spreadsheet applications in planning, see Ottensmann, J. R., "Analyzing Planning Alternatives Using Electronic Spreadsheets," *Journal of Planning Education and Research*, Vol. 4, No. 1 (August 1984), 33–42.

[3] For a good introduction to database management systems, see Date, C. J., *Database: A Primer* (Reading, Mass.: Addison-Wesley Publishing Company, 1983).

Character Graphics Routines

The interactive nature of microcomputers and the programs presented in this volume allow easy experimentation with the models and data. For at least some of the programs, the display of the output in graphic form can enhance the user's understanding of the results and lead to more effective use of the models. For example, plots of the data and projected trend lines could illustrate the patterns in the Trend Projection Models program. Population pyramids could indicate changing distributions in the Cohort-Survival Model program. Results from the Facility Location on a Plane Model program could be made clearer with maps of demand points and facility locations.

Graphics displays of data are becoming increasingly popular in microcomputer software. Unfortunately, differences among computers and versions of BASIC make it impossible to develop the highest-quality graphics software that would be usable on all (or even a wide variety) of systems. Some microcomputer versions of BASIC (and most large-system versions) provide no graphics capabilities whatsoever. Among those systems with graphics capabilities, differences are found in both the display characteristics and in the methods of generating these graphics displays in BASIC.

Nevertheless, the addition of graphics display capabilities to at least some of the programs was seen as an important objective. Crude graphic displays can be generated in virtually any version of BASIC by printing the standard alphanumeric characters in appropriate patterns. Routines to create such character graphics displays can be written in the limited subset of BASIC employed throughout this book. Such routines will be usable on virtually any system. Three character graphics routines are presented in this appendix to display output from the Trend Models program, the Population Cohort-Survival Model program, and the Facility Location on a Plane Model program. More refined high-resolution graphics routines will not be usable on all systems, but they have been written so that they may be adapted easily to many of the systems with the appropriate capabilities. Three high-resolution graphics routines for the same programs are presented in Appendix B.

All of the character graphics and high-resolution graphics routines present graphics output to the user on the video display following the printing out of results from the models. They are written as subroutines designed to be called from the main routines of the appropriate programs. The starting points of the subroutines have been selected so as to fit within the structure of the host programs. The listings of the graphics subroutines include the GOSUB statements (and, in one case, a DIMension statement) that must be inserted into the main routine for the proper functioning of the graphics option. All that is required to add the graphics capabilities to one of the programs is to add the statements in the listing of the graphics routine to the appropriate host program. Operation and presentation of the graphics displays then becomes automatic, with the information always displayed after the corresponding output has been printed.

The first of the three character graphics routines is the Trend Character Graphics subroutine for use with the Trend Projection Models program. Both the actual data values and the projected values are plotted on the vertical axis, against time on the horizontal axis. This plot allows the user to see both the trend of the actual data and the trend represented by the projected values computed using the model chosen for projection.

The character graphics display is automatically scaled so that the range of the values is expanded to cover the entire plotting area. Maximum and minimum values of the population (or other values being projected) and the time (years) are printed outside of the vertical and horizontal axes. Individual points are plotted on the graph with the letter D representing an actual data value and P representing a value projected by the model. When both an actual and a projected value would be displayed at the same position, a B (for both) is printed.

In order for the graph to be displayed on the entire screen, to provide the greatest detail, the user must specify the size the the display. This is accomplished when entering the program by assigning the appropriate values in lines 5020 and 5040. For example, $L1 = 24$ in line 5020 indicates that 24 lines on the video display are to be used in presenting the graph, and $K1 = 80$ in line 5040 causes 80 columns to be used. Smaller displays can be accommodated by adjusting these values accordingly.

The routine operates by first determining the minimum and maximum values to be plotted. The actual printing of the display must take place line by line. For each line, the range of values on the vertical axis falling on that line is determined. All of the actual and projected values are checked to see which, if any, fall in that range, and information on those that do is stored in the array *Y*. Then, for each horizontal position (year), the appropriate character (*D, P, B*, or nothing) is printed.

The Trend Character Graphics example shows what the graphics display will look like. The graph is printed immediately following the presentation of the model results. The example shown is for the sample problem for the Trend Projection Models program in Chapter 2. This is the plot of the actual data values and the values projected using the modified exponential model the first time through the original example.

The Cohort Character Graphics subroutine is next. It displays the population distributions in the standard form of population pyramids. This is to be used with the Cohort-Survival Model program. Each time the population values are printed out for any year, the shape of the distributions of both males and females by age is shown with bars for each cohort. Changes in the distribution over time, such as large cohorts working their way through the population while aging, can be readily identified with such displays.

The population pyramids are presented in the standard format, with male population indicated by bars extending left from a centerline and female population indicated by bars extending to the right. The use of *M*'s and *F*'s to plot the bars emphasizes this. Cohorts are arranged in order from the oldest at the top to the youngest at the bottom. Populations are automatically scaled so that the bar for the largest cohort fills the space available. This maximum cohort size is indicated as the range on the axis.

Forty columns are fully adequate for attractive population pyramids, so the routine is fixed to use this space. Narrower displays cannot utilize the routine without reprogramming. The routine assumes a 24 line display to handle the maximum of 18 cohorts for five-year intervals. Displays with fewer lines will result in the top lines of the plot scrolling off the screen with the maximum number of cohorts. (The same, of course, will happen with the tables of data.)

The graphics routine first determines the size of the largest cohort for scaling. The display is printed line by line beginning with the oldest cohort. Relative sizes of the male and female cohorts and thus the numbers of characters to be printed are calculated. The routine tabs over to the starting point for the *M*'s, prints these, prints an *I* for the centerline, and finally prints the appropriate number of *F*'s.

The Cohort Character Graphics example shows how the population pyramids will appear. These are printed immediately following the output of the population figures for any year. This example would be the first one generated for the sample problem for the Cohort- Survival Model program in Chapter 3. Thus, it represents the distribution of the initial starting population for 1980. As projections are made for subsequent years, similar population pyramids would be displayed.

Last comes the Facility Location on a Plane Character Graphics subroutine for operation with that program. The locations are plotted for both the demand points and the best facility locations as determined by the model. Of course the plot is helpful just for visualizing the solution. Perhaps even more important, however, would be the use of the plot for determining alternate starting points for the model. In locating multiple facilities, the algorithm will often produce solutions that are not optimal. By examining a solution that has been plotted, a user may be better able to identify starting locations that may lead to different (and perhaps better) solutions.

Demand points and facility locations are plotted in a space delineated by horizontal and vertical axes. Demand points are indicated with a D, facility locations with an F, and a B (for both) is used to indicate a facility located more or less at the same location as a demand point. Automatic scaling is used so that the points cover the entire plot area. This means that distances will generally not be the same along the vertical and horizontal axes, so one dimension may be stretched or squeezed relative to the other. This procedure does, however, give the maximum spread to the points. Given wide differences in horizontal to vertical spacing ratios on various machines, constant absolute spacing would be impossible without the input of values of which many users will not be aware.

As with the Trend Character Graphics subroutine, the numbers of lines and columns must be specified to allow plotting using the entire screen. The information is provided when entering the program by making the proper assignments of values to variables. In line 8000, $L1 = 24$ is used to indicate a display of 24 lines, and in line 8020, $K1 = 80$ would be used for an 80-column display. These can be adjusted as appropriate, including even the use of larger values if results are to be printed on paper rather than displayed on a screen. One additional note: The listing includes a DIMension statement on line 195 that is to be inserted into the main routine. This is needed to provide space for an array Z to contain the information to be plotted on one line. Dimensioning Z for 80 characters handles plots of up to 80 columns; wider plots would require a larger array.

The routine must first find the maximum and minimum values for both axes. Then, as in all of the character graphics routines, the plot must be generated one line at a time. All points are checked to determine whether their vertical coordinate falls within the interval currently being plotted. If so, the routine must determine in what horizontal interval that coordinate lies to determine the plotting position. An entry is made in the array Z corresponding to the column location at which the point is to be plotted. After going through all points and completing the filling of Z for each line, the routine then prints the appropriate characters at each position across the line as specified in Z.

The example problem for the Facility Location on a Plane Model program in Chapter 9 provides the data for the sample character graphics output produced by this subroutine. The problem included seven demand points and the location of two facilities. The plot shows the locations. One facility is located in the lower-right quadrant and is designated by the *F*. It serves the surrounding demand points (the *D*'s) plus the point in the upper-right corner. Near the upper-left corner, the *B* (for both) indicates the location of the other facility at one of the demand points. In addition to this demand point, the facility serves the point to the right and the demand point in the far lower-left corner.

TREND CHARACTER GRAPHICS EXAMPLE

D-DATA VALUES   P-PREDICTED VALUES   B-BOTH

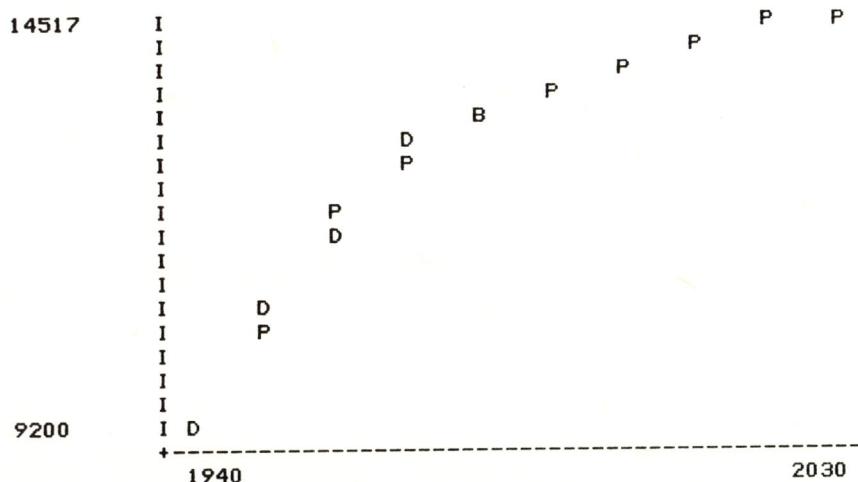

```
14517    I                                                      P     P
         I
         I                                                  P
         I                                            P
         I                                     P
         I                              B
         I                        D
         I                        P
         I
         I                  P
         I                  D
         I
         I
         I           D
         I           P
         I
         I
         I
9200     I D
         +--------------------------------------------------
           1940                                          2030
```

COHORT CHARACTER GRAPHICS EXAMPLE

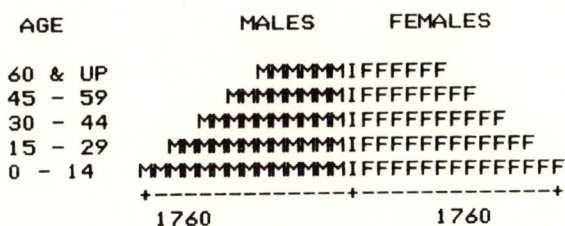

```
   AGE              MALES      FEMALES

60 & UP          MMMMMMIFFFFFF
45 - 59          MMMMMMMIFFFFFFFF
30 - 44          MMMMMMMMMIFFFFFFFFFF
15 - 29          MMMMMMMMMMMIFFFFFFFFFFFF
0 - 14           MMMMMMMMMMMMMIFFFFFFFFFFFFFF
                 +-------------+-------------+
                  1760           1760
```

```
FACILITY LOCATION ON A PLANE CHARACTER GRAPHICS
EXAMPLE

D-DEMAND POINT    F-FACILITY    B-BOTH
27        I                                              D
          I
          I                  D
          I
          I    B
          I
          I
          I
          I
          I                        D
          I
          I                           F
          I
          I
          I
          I              D              D
          I
 3        ID
          +---------------------------------------------
           3                               33
```

TREND CHARACTER GRAPHICS SUBROUTINE LISTING

```
550 GOSUB 5000
4890 REM TREND CHARACTER GRAPHICS SUBROUTINE **************
4900 REM VARIABLES
4910 REM     M1 - MIN VALUE
4920 REM     M2 - MAX VALUE
4930 REM     M3 - VERTICAL INTERVAL
4940 REM     L1 - LINES IN DISPLAY
4950 REM     L2 - PLOT LINES
4960 REM     K1 - COLUMNS IN DISPLAY
4970 REM     K2 - PLOT COLUMNS
4980 REM     K3 - HORIZONTAL INTERVAL
4990 REM     Y(I) - PLOT LINE VALUES
5000 GOSUB 9900
5010 REM SET L1 EQUAL TO LINES IN DISPLAY
5020 L1 = 24
5030 REM SET K1 EQUAL TO COLUMNS IN DISPLAY
5040 K1 = 80
5050 REM DETERMINE MIN AND MAX VALUES
5060 M1 = D(1)
5070 M2 = D(1)
5080 FOR I = 2 TO N
5090 IF D(I) >= M1 THEN 5110
5100 M1 = D(I)
5110 IF D(I) <= M1 THEN 5130
5120 M2 = D(I)
5130 NEXT I
5140 FOR I = T TO N + S
5150 IF P(I) >= M1 THEN 5170
5160 M1 = P(I)
5170 IF P(I) <= M2 THEN 5190
5180 M2 = P(I)
5190 NEXT I
5200 REM DETERMINE PLOTTING PARAMETERS
5210 L2 = L1 - 6
5220 M3 = (M2 - M1) / L2
5230 K2 = K1 - 15
5240 K3 = INT(K2 / (N + S - 1))
5250 PRINT
5260 PRINT
5270 PRINT "D-DATA VALUES  P-PREDICTED VALUES   B-BOTH"
5280 PRINT
5290 REM BEGIN LINE-BY-LINE PLOTTING
5300 FOR I = 1 TO L2
5310 FOR J = 1 TO N + S
5320 Y(J) = 0
5330 NEXT J
5340 REM DETERMINE LINE MIN AND MAX
5350 M4 = M2 - M3 * (I - 1)
5360 M5 = M2 - M3 * I
5370 IF I < L2 THEN 5400
```

```
5380 M5 = M5 - 1
5390 REM DETERMINE VALUES TO BE PLOTTED
5400 FOR J = 1 TO N
5410 IF D(J) > M4 THEN 5440
5420 IF D(J) <= M5 THEN 5440
5430 Y(J) = 1
5440 NEXT J
5450 FOR J = T TO N + S
5460 IF P(J) > M4 THEN 5490
5470 IF P(J) <= M5 THEN 5490
5480 Y(J) = Y(J) + 2
5490 NEXT J
5500 REM PRINT LINE
5510 IF I <> 1 THEN 5530
5520 PRINT M2;
5530 IF I <> L2 THEN 5550
5540 PRINT M1;
5550 PRINT TAB(12); "I";
5560 T1 = 14
5570 FOR J = 1 TO N + S
5580 IF Y(J) <> 1 THEN 5600
5590 PRINT TAB(T1); "D";
5600 IF Y(J) <> 2 THEN 5620
5610 PRINT TAB(T1); "P";
5620 IF Y(J) <> 3 THEN 5640
5630 PRINT TAB(T1); "B";
5640 T1 = T1 + K3
5650 NEXT J
5660 PRINT
5670 NEXT I
5680 REM FINISH BOTTOM
5690 PRINT TAB(12); "+";
5700 FOR I = 1 TO (N+S-1)*K3 + 3
5710 PRINT "-";
5720 NEXT I
5730 PRINT
5740 PRINT TAB(13); L;
5750 PRINT TAB((N+S-1)*K3+10); L+M*(N+S-1)
5760 RETURN
```

COHORT CHARACTER GRAPHICS SUBROUTINE LISTING

```
415 GOSUB 3000
2950 REM COHORT CHARACTER GRAPHICS SUBROUTINE **************
2960 REM VARIABLES
2970 REM     F1 - FEMALE CHARACTERS TO PLOT
2980 REM     M1 - MALE CHARACTERS TO PLOT
2990 REM      M - MAXIMUM POPULATION IN COHORT
3000 GOSUB 9900
3010 REM DETERMINE MAXIMUM POPULATION IN COHORT
3020 M = 0
3030 FOR I = 1 TO N
3040 FOR J = 1 TO 2
3050 IF Q(I,J) < M THEN 3070
3060 M = Q(I,J)
3070 NEXT J
3080 NEXT I
3100 REM PRINT GRAPH
3110 PRINT
3120 PRINT
3130 PRINT TAB(3); "AGE"; TAB(18); "MALES"; TAB(28);
3140 PRINT "FEMALES"
3150 PRINT
3160 FOR I = N TO 1 STEP -1
3170 IF I <> N THEN 3200
3180 PRINT (N - 1) * W; "& UP";
3190 GOTO 3210
3200 PRINT (I - 1) * W; "-"; I * W - 1;
3210 M1 = INT(14*Q(I,1)/M + .5)
3220 F1 = INT(14*Q(I,2)/M + .5)
3230 PRINT TAB(11 + (14 - M1));
3240 FOR J = 1 TO M1
3250 PRINT "M";
3260 NEXT J
3270 PRINT "I";
3280 FOR J = 1 TO F1
3290 PRINT "F";
3300 NEXT J
3310 PRINT
3315 NEXT I
3320 PRINT TAB(11);
3330 PRINT "+-------------+-------------+"
3340 PRINT TAB(11); M; TAB(30); M
3350 RETURN
```

FACILITY CHARACTER GRAPHICS SUBROUTINE LISTING

```
195 DIM Z(80)
405 GOSUB 8000
7860 REM FACILITY LOCATION ON A PLANE *********************
7870 REM CHARACTER GRAPHICS SUBROUTINE
7880 REM VARIABLES
7890 REM     V1 - VERTICAL MINIMUM
7900 REM     V2 - VERTICAL MAXIMUM
7910 REM     V3 - VERTICAL INTERVAL
7920 REM     H1 - HORIZONTAL MINIMUM
7930 REM     H2 - HORIZONTAL MAXIMUM
7940 REM     H3 - HORIZONTAL INTERVAL
7950 REM     L1 - LINES IN DISPLAY
7960 REM     L2 - PLOT LINES
7970 REM     K1 - COLUMNS IN DISPLAY
7980 REM     K2 - PLOT COLUMNS
7990 REM SET L1 EQUAL TO LINES IN DISPLAY
8000 L1 = 24
8010 REM SET K1 EQUAL TO COLUMNS IN DISPLAY
8020 K1 = 80
8030 L2 = L1 - 6
8040 K2 = K1 - 13
8050 REM FIND MINIMA, MAXIMA, INTERVALS
8060 V1 = Y(1)
8070 V2 = Y(1)
8080 H1 = X(1)
8090 H2 = X(1)
8100 FOR I = 2 TO N
8110 IF Y(I) >= V1 THEN 8130
8120 V1 = Y(I)
8130 IF Y(I) <= V2 THEN 8150
8140 V2 = Y(I)
8150 IF X(I) >= H1 THEN 8170
8160 H1 = X(I)
8170 IF X(I) <= H2 THEN 8190
8180 H2 = X(I)
8190 NEXT I
8200 V3 = (V2 - V1) / L2
8210 H3 = (H2 - H1) / K2
8220 PRINT
8230 PRINT
8240 PRINT "D-DEMAND POINT   F-FACILITY   B-BOTH"
8250 PRINT
8260 FOR I = 1 TO L2
8270 FOR J = 1 TO K2
8280 Z(J) = 0
8290 NEXT J
8300 REM DETERMINE LINE MIN AND MAX
8310 V4 = V2 - V3 * (I - 1)
8320 V5 = V2 - V3 * I
8330 IF I <> 1 THEN 8350
```

```
8340 V4 = V4 + 1
8350 IF I <> L2 THEN 8380
8360 V5 = V5 - 1
8370 REM DETERMINE VALUES TO BE PLOTTED
8380 FOR J = 1 TO N
8390 IF Y(J) > V4 THEN 8480
8400 IF Y(J) <= V5 THEN 8480
8410 FOR K = 1 TO K2 - 1
8420 H4 = H1 + K * H3
8430 IF X(J) > H4 THEN 8460
8440 Z(K) = 1
8450 GOTO 8480
8460 NEXT K
8470 Z(K2) = 1
8480 NEXT J
8490 FOR J = 1 TO M
8500 IF Q(J) > V4 THEN 8590
8510 IF Q(J) <= V5 THEN 8590
8520 FOR K = 1 TO K2 - 1
8530 H4 = H1 + K * H3
8540 IF P(J) > H4 THEN 8570
8550 Z(K) = Z(K) + 2
8560 GOTO 8590
8570 NEXT K
8580 Z(K2) = Z(K2) + 2
8590 NEXT J
8600 REM PRINT LINE
8610 IF I <> 1 THEN 8630
8620 PRINT V2;
8630 IF I <> L2 THEN 8650
8640 PRINT V1;
8650 PRINT TAB(12); "I";
8660 FOR K = 1 TO K2
8670 IF Z(K) <> 0 THEN 8690
8680 PRINT " ";
8690 IF Z(K) <> 1 THEN 8710
8700 PRINT "D";
8710 IF Z(K) <> 2 THEN 8730
8720 PRINT "F";
8730 IF Z(K) <> 3 THEN 8750
8740 PRINT "B";
8750 NEXT K
8760 PRINT
8770 NEXT I
8780 REM FINISH BOTTOM
8790 PRINT TAB(12); "+";
8800 FOR K = 1 TO K2
8810 PRINT "-";
8820 NEXT K
8830 PRINT
8840 PRINT TAB(12); H1; TAB(K2+2); H2
8850 GOSUB 9900
8860 RETURN
```

High-Resolution Graphics Routines

Many microcomputers include the capabilities for generating quite detailed graphics displays. Instead of being limited to the printing of letters or other characters, such high-resolution displays allow graphics to be generated using the individual picture elements (pixels) otherwise used to create characters. With such high-resolution graphics, each of the pixels can be turned on or off (or set to different colors) to produce the more detailed images. Such capabilities are ideal for producing attractive graphics displays of results from some of the programs in this book.

Unfortunately, nothing is standardized in microcomputer high-resolution graphics. Displays vary in their resolution—the numbers of dots or pixels horizontally and vertically. Options on colors differ. Assuming that BASIC supports the use of the high-resolution graphics, the required statements can be completely different from one system to the next. Thus, it is impossible to develop high-resolution graphics routines that can be used directly and without change on a significant number of different systems.

Any display of high-resolution graphics from BASIC must involve a common set of operations, however. The screen must be set up to begin the graphics display. Lines must be plotted between pairs of points on the screen denoted by horizontal and vertical coordinates. Finally, provisions must be made to continue with the display of text after the user has finished examining the graphics display. If these functions are appropriately isolated and identified, it is possible to develop high-resolution graphics routines that can be readily adapted to run on a variety of microcomputers having BASIC support for high-resolution graphics.

The three high-resolution graphics routines presented in this appendix have been developed in a manner intended for adaptation to different systems. When the routines are implemented, the user must specify the ranges of the horizontal and vertical coordinates for the display. Appropriate statements must be included to both initiate and terminate the graphics display. The statement for plotting a line from one point to another must also be provided.

The routines are liberally commented with instructions specifying the adaptations that are required. These remarks further include the actual statements required for use on both the IBM Personal Computer and the Apple II (and II+ and IIe), two of the most widely used microcomputers with high-resolutions graphics and the appropriate support in BASIC. The actual statements included in the listings are those for the IBM Personal Computer, so the routines are directly usable on IBM PC's with the color/graphics display adapter with no modifications. The routines have been tested both on an IBM PC and on an Apple II+.

No labels or other text are included on the actual graphics displays. The differences in the printing of text in high-resolution graphics are so great that no procedures could possibly be adaptable to systems as different as the IBM PC and the Apple II. Instead, a screen of introductory text is provided prior to displaying the graph. Since the purpose of the graphics displays is to provide a sense of the relationships in the results, such lack of labels on the graphics should not be a major problem.

All three of the graphics routines follow a similar structure in providing for the adaptations to different systems. The following description, focusing on the Trend High-Resolution Graphics subroutine, will be equally applicable to the other two subroutines. The first item of adaptation involves setting the coordinates of the screen window in which the image is to be plotted. This is handled in lines 4960 to 5050. The routine assumes that points on the screen are referred to by a coordinate system with the origin in the upper left-hand corner. This corner will have the lowest coordinates, generally (0, 0). The horizontal and vertical coordinates increase to the right and down, with the coordinates of the lower right-hand corner at the maximum, which depends on the resolution of the graphics display. Adaptation of the routine involves setting the minimum and maximum coordinates of the area in which the information is to be plotted, which must fall within the range determined by the resolution of the screen. $H8$ and $H9$ are the minimum and maximum horizontal coordinates, respectively, and $V8$ and $V9$ are the minimum and maximum vertical coordinates. On the IBM PC, the horizontal coordinates must lie within the range 0 to 319 for graphics mode 1 (with color) and within the range from 0 to 639 for graphics mode 2 (highest-resolution monochrome). The vertical coordinate range is 0 to 199, but if the 25th line is being used for BASIC function key prompts, the range is reduced to 0 to 191. On the Apple II, the high resolution graphics coordinates range from 0 to 279 horizontally and from 0 to 191 vertically (assuming the four-line text window is not being used).

The coordinate range specified for the plot window does not have to encompass the entire high-resolution graphics display. A plot window for the Apple II could, for example, be specified with the ranges $H8 = 140$, $H9 = 297$, $V8 = 0$, $V9 = 96$. This would result in a plot restricted to the upper-right quadrant of the screen. The plot window might be restricted to only a portion of the display to allow space for text to be added or to change the aspect ratio between the horizontal and vertical. The display for the population pyramid produced by the Cohort High-Resolution Graphics subroutine will actually look better to most users if it is plotted in a window somewhat narrower than the entire screen.

After the introductory text has been printed, the next task requiring adaptation involves the invocation of the graphics mode. In the Trend High-Resolution Graphics Subroutine, this is addressed in lines 5200 to 5240. Many systems separate the graphics display mode from the normal text display mode, and special BASIC statements are required to switch to the graphics mode. On the IBM PC, this is the SCREEN statement: SCREEN 1 invokes the medium-resolution mode with color, while SCREEN 2 invokes the highest-resolution monochrome mode. In Applesoft BASIC on the Apple II family, the statement HGR2 invokes the high-resolution graphics mode without the text window at the bottom. All of these statements clear the display along with the mode change. In a system without separate text and graphics modes, that does not require a mode change for graphics, the appropriate statement will be required to clear the screen for the graphics display. If any system with separate modes does not clear the screen upon switching modes, a clear screen statement would also be required.

For microcomputers with color graphics capabilities, one or more additional statements could be added here for color selection. In addition, if various elements in the graphics display are to be plotted in different colors, additional color statements could be added throughout the subroutine. The versions presented here utilize the default values arising from the invocation of the graphics mode in the simplest form.

The actual plotting of the graphics display is done by the drawing of straight lines from one point designated by the horizontal coordinate $H1$ and the vertical coordinate $V1$ to a second point with the coordinates $H2$, $V2$. Most versions of BASIC supporting high-resolution graphics will have a special statement for drawing such a line. This plotting of lines occurs at numerous locations in the subroutines. To avoid the need for adaptations throughout the routines, the following procedure is employed: Each time a line is to be drawn, the coordinates of the endpoints are stored in the variables $H1$, $V1$, $H2$, and $V2$. Then a call is made to a subroutine at the end of the listing, to line 6020 in the Trend High-Resolution Graphics subroutine. This subroutine contains the statement required to plot a line between the coordinate pairs $H1$, $V1$ and $H2$, $V2$. Thus, only this single statement needs to be adapted to conform to the requirements of the system being used. The IBM PC requires the LINE statement, in the form

```
LINE (H1,V1)-(H2,V2)
```

For Applesoft BASIC, the statement should be

```
HPLOT H1,V1 TO H2,V2
```

For any system, it is only necessary to determine the statement required to draw a straight line between two points and then enter that statement for the coordinates $H1$, $V1$ and $H2$, $V2$.

The final step in the process of adaptation involves sensing when the user has finished examining the graphics display and then returning to normal text operation to continue the program. This is handled by the termination section in lines 5860 to 5970 of the Trend High-Resolution Graphics subroutine. The text preceding the graphics display instructs the user to press Return to continue after the graph has been plotted. On the IBM PC, the INKEY$ statement can be used to detect a keypress without disturbing the display. The following loop repeats until it detects any keypress (including, but not limited to, Return):

```
5900 A$ = INKEY$
5910 IF A$ = "" THEN 5900
```

When any key is pressed, the user wishes to continue and control passes to the next statement. Applesoft BASIC lacks the INKEY$ statement, but printing is directed to the separate, hidden text page and does not appear on the graphics display. Instead of the two-statement loop above, the single statement INPUT A$ will suffice. This prints the prompting question mark on the text page. Pressing Return assigns the null string to A$ and allows the program to continue. Adaptations to other systems will require knowledge about how to detect the pressing of the Return key without interfering with the graphics display.

Finally, the system must be given instructions to return to the text mode for continued operation of the other parts of the host program. For the IBM PC, the statement SCREEN 0 clears the screen and shifts back to text display. The number of characters per line, however, is dependent on the graphics mode exited and is only 40 characters per line when returning from the medium-resolution color graphics mode. The additional statement WIDTH 80 will force an 80-column display, assuming that is desired. In Applesoft BASIC, the simple statement TEXT is all that is required to shift back. For some systems, a statement to clear the screen will be required or desirable. This is especially true on systems without separate text and graphics modes, where the clear screen statement is needed to clear the plotted image from the screen before proceeding.

These are the only changes required to adapt any of the graphics subroutines to different microcomputers and versions of BASIC. Anyone having general familiarity with the procedures for doing graphics from BASIC on a particular system—anyone able to write a very simple graphics program in BASIC—should be capable of making these adaptations easily. The remaining sections of these routines, the sections that do the actual work of creating the graphics displays, are written in the standard minimal BASIC and should require no adaptation.

The high-resolution graphics subroutines present the same information at the same points in the operation of their host programs as their character graphics counterparts. The only difference is that the information is presented in two parts. First, text information describing the graph is printed. Then, when the user chooses to continue, the actual high-resolution graphics display is plotted on the screen. Pressing Return then allows for the continuation of the program in the usual fashion.

The first of the three high-resolution graphics routines works with the Trend Projection Models program. As in the character graphics routine, the actual data values and the projected values are plotted on the vertical axis, against time on the horizontal axis. The display is automatically scaled so that the range of the values occupies the entire plotting area, which is indicated by a box drawn on the screen. The projected values are plotted with a line connecting the points. The actual data values are indicated by crosses. This allows the user to readily see the errors in projection—the deviations between the projected and actual values.

After the printing of the initial message and the initialization of the graphics, the Trend High-Resolution Graphics subroutine determines the minimum and maximum among the actual and projected data values. The box is then drawn on the screen. Lines are plotted from one projected point to the next, and crosses are plotted at the locations of the actual data values. The remainder of the subroutine then handles the termination process.

The Trend High-Resolution Graphics example illustrates the appearance of a typical display. The text message and graph are printed immediately following the presentation of the model results. The example is for the sample problem for the Trend Projection Models program in Chapter 2. Shown is the plot of the results obtained the first time through the original example, with the values projected using the modified exponential model.

The Cohort High-Resolution Graphics subroutine displays population pyramids of the population distributions generated by the Cohort-Survival Model program. The relative sizes of the male cohorts are indicated by bars to the left of the centerline, female cohorts by bars to the right. The oldest cohort is at the top, the youngest at the bottom. These population pyramids are displayed each time new population values are printed.

The population pyramid is scaled automatically to fill the plot window specified by the coordinates in the first part of the subroutine. If the entire display is used, the population pyramids will be relatively wider—more squat—than those traditionally presented. If a taller, narrower display is desired, the horizontal size of the plot window—specified by the values assigned to $H8$ and $H9$ in lines 3000 and 3010—should be reduced.

After the initial sections of the routine, computation begins by determining the largest cohort for scaling. Then the bars for the population pyramid are plotted, first for the male cohorts, then for the female cohorts. The center-line is drawn between the male and female plotting, also returning the co-ordinate location to the starting point at the bottom center of the plot window. The termination process is the same as in the other high-resolution routines.

The Cohort High-Resolution Graphics example shows the first population pyramid that would be printed for the Cohort-Survival Model example in Chapter 3. This represents the distribution of the initial starting population for 1980. As projections are generated for the following periods, appropriate population pyramids would be displayed in the same fashion.

The Facility Location on a Plane High-Resolution Graphics subroutine plots maps of the demand point locations connected to the closest facilities by straight lines. This display is useful for visualizing the assignment of the demand points to the facilities, illustrating the form of the solution generated. The area of the plot is enclosed within a box. Coordinates are scaled automatically so the area occupied by the points fills the display window.

The routines must determine the minimum and maximum demand point coordinates for the scaling of the display. The box outlining the display is plotted. Lines are then drawn from each demand point to the closest facility. The standard termination procedures conclude the routine.

The Facility Location on a Plane High-Resolution Graphics example is a plot of the results from the example in Chapter 9. The clusters of demand points served by the two facilities can be immediately identified. Ideas for alternative solutions and facility starting points may be discerned from such displays.

The graphics displays generated by these subroutines appear on the computer's video display. Users with software for graphics screen dumps and an appropriate printer could use these to generate printed, hard-copy output of the displays. Some readers may be interested in the procedures used to produce the printed high-resolution graphics output reproduced in this book. A C. Itoh Prowriter 8510 dot matrix printer was used to print the output. The original size of the printed graphs was a maximum of six inches wide and four inches high, a resolution of 480 dots horizontally and 288 dots vertically in the standard graphics mode of the printer. A bit-mapped copy of the image was generated in RAM, using an additional subroutine which was called to plot lines by setting appropriate bits from zero to one. Once the high-resolution graphics subroutines completed the plotting, a second subroutine was called to print this bit-mapped image in graphics mode to the printer.

TREND HIGH-RESOLUTION GRAPHICS EXAMPLE

PLOT OF VALUES VERSUS TIME

PREDICTED VALUES PLOTTED AS LINE
ACTUAL DATA VALUES PLOTTED AS CROSSES

AFTER GRAPH HAS BEEN PLOTTED
PRESS RETURN TO CONTINUE

CONTINUE?

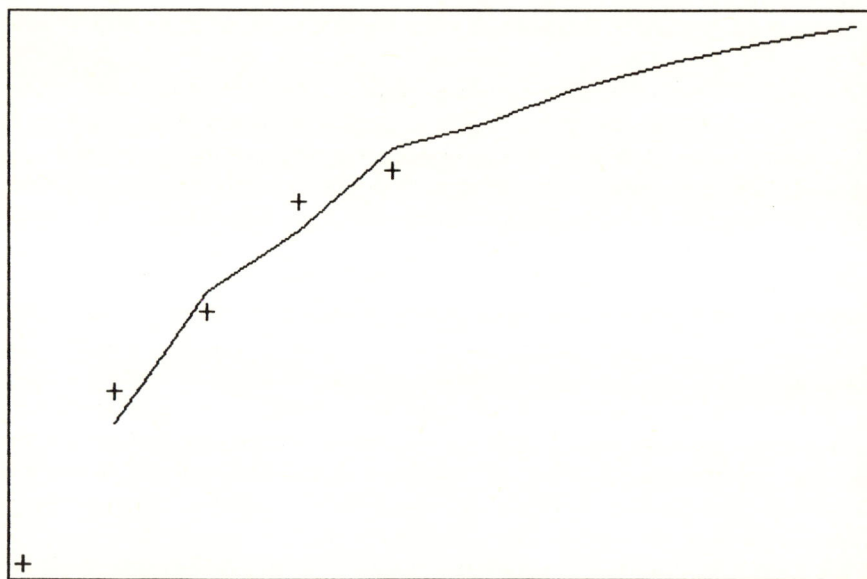

COHORT HIGH-RESOLUTION GRAPHICS EXAMPLE

POPULATION TREE

MALES ON LEFT, FEMALES ON RIGHT
OLDER COHORTS AT TOP, YOUNGER AT BOTTOM

AFTER GRAPH HAS BEEN PLOTTED
PRESS RETURN TO CONTINUE

CONTINUE?

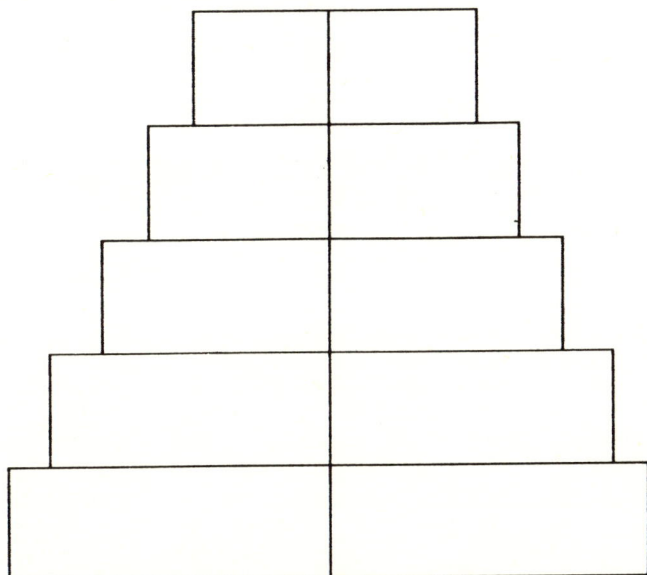

```
FACILITY LOCATION ON A PLANE HIGH-RESOLUTION
GRAPHICS EXAMPLE

PLOT OF DEMAND POINTS CONNECTED
TO FACILITY LOCATIONS

AFTER GRAPH HAS BEEN PLOTTED
PRESS RETURN TO CONTINUE

CONTINUE?
```

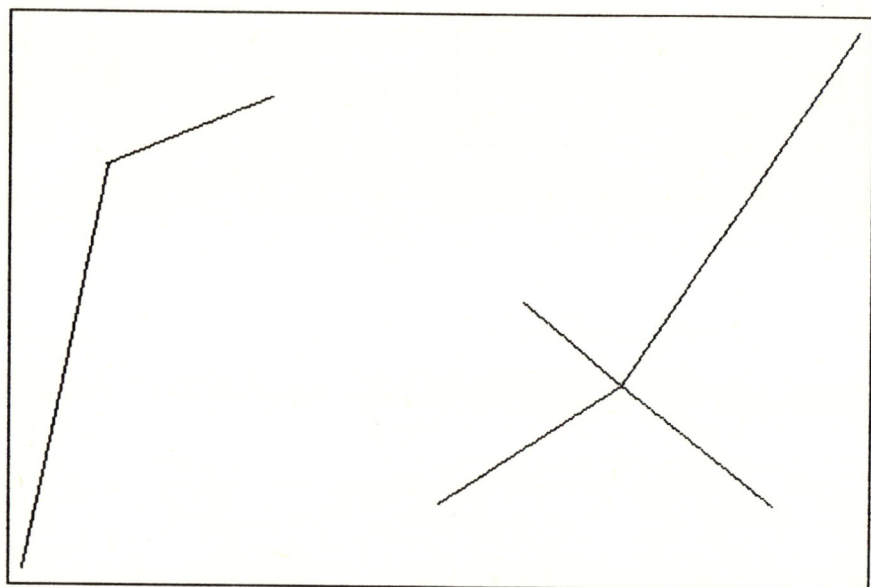

TREND HIGH-RESOLUTION GRAPHICS SUBROUTINE LISTING

```
550 GOSUB 5000
4900 REM TREND HIGH-RESOLUTION GRAPHICS SUBROUTINE *********
4910 REM VARIABLES
4920 REM      H1,V1,H2,V2 - PLOT COORDINATES
4930 REM      H8,V8,H9,V9 - SCREEN MIN AND MAX
4940 REM      V5,V6 - DATA MIN AND MAX
4950 REM      M1 - MARGIN AND CROSS SIZE
4960 REM SET SCREEN WINDOW FOR DISPLAY
4970 REM HORIZ RANGE WITHIN 0-319 OR 0-639 ON IBM PC
4980 REM HORIZ RANGE WITHIN 0-279 ON APPLE
5000 H8 = 0
5010 H9 = 319
5020 REM VERT RANGE WITHIN 0-199 ON IBM PC
5030 REM VERT RANGE WITHIN 0-191 ON APPLE
5040 V8 = 0
5050 V9 = 191
5060 REM SET MARGIN INSIDE BOX AND CROSS SIZE
5070 M1 = 8
5080 REM PRINT INTRODUCTORY SCREEN
5090 GOSUB 9900
5100 PRINT
5110 PRINT
5120 PRINT "PLOT OF VALUES VERSUS TIME"
5130 PRINT
5140 PRINT "PREDICTED VALUES PLOTTED AS LINE"
5150 PRINT "ACTUAL DATA VALUES PLOTTED AS CROSSES"
5160 PRINT
5170 PRINT "AFTER GRAPH HAS BEEN PLOTTED"
5180 PRINT "PRESS RETURN TO CONTINUE"
5190 GOSUB 9900
5200 REM INVOKE GRAPHICS MODE
5210 REM SCREEN 1 OR SCREEN 2 STATEMENT ON IBM PC
5220 REM HGR2 STATEMENT ON APPLE
5230 REM COLOR STATEMENT TO CHOOSE COLORS OPTIONAL
5240 SCREEN 1
5250 REM DETERMINE MIN AND MAX VALUES
5260 V5 = D(1)
5270 V6 = D(1)
5280 FOR I = 2 TO N
5290 IF D(I) >= V5 THEN 5310
5300 V5 = D(I)
5310 IF D(I) <= V6 THEN 5330
5320 V6 = D(I)
5330 NEXT I
5340 FOR I = T TO N + S
5350 IF P(I) >= V5 THEN 5370
5360 V5 = P(I)
5370 IF P(I) <= V6 THEN 5390
5380 V6 = P(I)
5390 NEXT I
```

```
5400 REM PLOT BOX IN WINDOW
5410 H1 = H8
5420 V1 = V8
5430 H2 = H9
5440 V2 = V8
5450 GOSUB 6020
5460 H2 = H8
5470 V2 = V9
5480 GOSUB 6020
5490 H1 = H9
5500 V1 = V9
5510 GOSUB 6020
5520 H2 = H9
5530 V2 = V8
5540 GOSUB 6020
5550 REM SET PLOT WINDOW WITHIN BOX
5560 H8 = H8 + M1
5570 V8 = V8 + M1
5580 H9 = H9 - M1
5590 V9 = V9 - M1
5600 M1 = M1 / 2
5610 REM PLOT PREDICTED VALUES LINE
5620 H1 = INT(((T-1)/(N+S-1))*(H9-H8) + H8 + .5)
5630 V1 = INT(((V6-P(T))/(V6-V5))*(V9-V8) + V8 + .5)
5640 FOR I = T + 1 TO N + S
5650 H2 = INT(((I-1)/(N+S-1))*(H9-H8) + H8 + .5)
5660 V2 = INT(((V6-P(I))/(V6-V5))*(V9-V8) + V8 + .5)
5670 GOSUB 6020
5680 H1 = H2
5690 V1 = V2
5700 NEXT I
5710 REM PLOT DATA VALUE CROSSES
5720 FOR I = 1 TO N
5730 H3 = INT(((I-1)/(N+S-1))*(H9-H8) + H8 + .5)
5740 V3 = INT(((V6-D(I))/(V6-V5))*(V9-V8) + H8 + .5)
5750 H1 = H3 - M1
5760 V1 = V3
5770 H2 = H3 + M1
5780 V2 = V3
5790 GOSUB 6020
5800 H1 = H3
5810 V1 = V3 - M1
5820 H2 = H3
5830 V2 = V3 + M1
5840 GOSUB 6020
5850 NEXT I
5860 REM TERMINATION ROUTINE
5870 REM DETERMINE WITH RETURN KEY IS PRESSED
5880 REM ON IBM PC USE INKEY$ TO KEEP ANYTHING
5890 REM FROM APPEARING ON SCREEN
5900 A$ = INKEY$
5910 IF A$ = "" THEN 5900
5920 REM ON APPLE USE INPUT STATEMENT
```

```
5930 REM INPUT A$
5940 REM RETURN TO TEXT MODE
5950 REM SCREEN 0, WIDTH 80 STATEMENTS ON IBM PC
5960 REM TEXT STATEMENT ON APPLE
5970 SCREEN 0 : WIDTH 80
5980 RETURN
5990 REM SUBROUTINE TO PLOT LINE FROM H1,V1 TO H2,V2
6000 REM LINE (H1,V1)-(H2,V2) ON IBM PC
6010 REM HPLOT H1,V1 TO H2,V2 ON APPLE
6020 LINE (H1,V1)-(H2,V2)
6030 RETURN
```

COHORT HIGH-RESOLUTION GRAPHICS SUBROUTINE LISTING

```
415 GOSUB 3000
2870 REM COHORT HIGH-RESOLUTION GRAPHICS SUBROUTINE ********
2880 REM VARIABLES
2890 REM      H1,V1,H2,V2 - PLOT COORDINATES
2900 REM      H8,V8,H9,V9 - SCREEN MIN AND MAX
2910 REM      H5 - HORIZONTAL MIDPOINT
2920 REM      V5 - VERTICAL STEP
2930 REM      H6 - MAXIMUM HORIZONTAL BAR
2940 REM      Q1 - MAXIMUM POPULATION
2950 REM SET SCREEN WINDOWN FOR DISPLAY
2960 REM FOR BEST APPEARANCES, WIDTH SHOULD BE
2970 REM LESS THAN HEIGHT
2980 REM HORIZ RANGE WITHIN 0-319 OR 0-639 ON IBM PC
2990 REM HORIZ RANGE WITHIN 0-279 ON APPLE
3000 H8 = 60
3010 H9 = 259
3020 REM VERT RANGE WITHIN 0-199 ON IBM PC
3030 REM VERT RANGE WITHIN 0-191 ON APPLE
3040 V8 = 0
3050 V9 = 191
3060 REM PRINT INTRODUCTORY SCREEN
3070 GOSUB 9900
3080 PRINT
3090 PRINT
3100 PRINT "POPULATION TREE"
3110 PRINT
3120 PRINT "MALES ON LEFT, FEMALES ON RIGHT"
3130 PRINT "OLDER COHORTS AT TOP, YOUNGER AT BOTTOM"
3140 PRINT
3150 PRINT "AFTER GRAPH HAS BEEN PLOTTED"
3160 PRINT "PRESS RETURN TO CONTINUE"
3170 GOSUB 9900
3180 REM INVOKE GRAPHICS MODE
3190 REM SCREEN 1 OR 2 STATEMENT ON IBM PC
3200 REM HGR2 STATEMENT ON APPLE
3210 REM COLOR STATEMENT TO CHOOSE COLORS OPTIONAL
3220 SCREEN 1
3230 REM DETERMINE MAX POPULATION
3240 Q1 = 0
3250 FOR I = 1 TO N
3260 FOR J = 1 TO 2
3270 IF Q(I,J) <= Q1 THEN 3290
3280 Q1 = Q(I,J)
3290 NEXT J
3300 NEXT I
3310 REM DETERMINE PLOT PARAMETERS
3320 V5 = INT((V9 - V8) / N)
3330 H5 = INT((H9 - H8) / 2 + H8)
3340 H6 = H5 - H8 - 1
3350 REM PLOT MALE COHORTS
```

```
3360 H1 = H5
3370 V1 = V9
3380 FOR I = 1 TO N
3390 H2 = INT(H5 - (Q(I,1)/Q1)*H6 + .5)
3400 V2 = V1
3410 GOSUB 3820
3420 H1 = H2
3430 V1 = V1 - V5
3440 GOSUB 3820
3450 H2 = H5
3460 V2 = V1
3470 GOSUB 3820
3480 H1 = H2
3490 NEXT I
3500 REM PLOT CENTER LINE
3510 H1 = H5
3520 V1 = V9
3530 GOSUB 3820
3540 REM PLOT FEMALE COHORTS
3550 FOR I = 1 TO N
3560 H2 = INT(H5 + (Q(I,2)/Q1)*H6 + .5)
3570 V2 = V1
3580 GOSUB 3820
3590 H1 = H2
3600 V1 = V1 - V5
3610 GOSUB 3820
3620 H2 = H5
3630 V2 = V1
3640 GOSUB 3820
3650 H1 = H2
3660 NEXT I
3670 REM DETERMINE WHEN RETURN KEY IS PRESSED
3680 REM ON IBM PC USE INKEY$ TO KEEP ANYTHING
3690 REM FROM APPEARING ON SCREEN
3700 A$ = INKEY$
3710 IF A4 = "" THEN 3700
3720 REM ON APPLE USE INPUT STATEMENT
3730 REM INPUT A$
3740 REM RETURN SCREEN TO TEXT MODE
3750 REM SCREEN 0, WIDTH 80 STATEMENTS ON IBM PC
3760 REM TEXT STATEMENT ON APPLE
3770 SCREEN 0 : WIDTH 80
3780 RETURN
3790 REM SUBROUTINE TO PLOT LINE FROM H1,V1 TO H2,V2
3800 REM LINE (H1,V1)-(H2,V2) ON IBM PC
3810 REM HPLOT H1,V1 TO H2,V2 ON APPLE
3820 LINE (H1,V1)-(H2,V2)
3830 RETURN
```

**FACILITY LOCATION ON A PLANE HIGH-RESOLUTION
GRAPHICS SUBROUTINE LISTING**

```
405 GOSUB 8000
7900 REM FACILITY LOCATION ON A PLANE **********************
7910 REM HIGH-RESOLUTION GRAPHICS SUBROUTINE
7920 REM VARIABLES
7930 REM     H1,V1,H2,V2 - PLOT LINE COORDINATES
7940 REM     H8,V8,H9,V9 - SCREEN MIN AND MAX
7950 REM     H5,V5,H6,V6 - DATA MIN AND MAX
7960 REM     M1 - DOT MARGIN INSIDE BOX
7970 REM SET SCREEN WINDOW FOR DISPLAY
7980 REM HORIZ RANGE WITHIN 0-319 OR 0-639 ON IBM PC
7990 REM HORIZ RANGE WITHIN 0-279 ON APPLE
8000 H8 = 0
8010 H9 = 319
8020 REM VERT RANGE WITHIN 0-199 ON IBM PC
8030 REM VERT RANGE WITHIN 0-191 ON APPLE
8040 V8 = 0
8050 V9 = 191
8060 REM SET MARGIN INSIDE BOX
8070 M1 = 8
8080 REM PRINT INTRODUCTORY SCREEN
8090 PRINT
8100 PRINT
8110 PRINT "PLOT OF DEMAND POINTS CONNECTED"
8120 PRINT "TO FACILITY LOCATIONS"
8130 PRINT
8140 PRINT "AFTER GRAPH HAS BEEN PLOTTED"
8150 PRINT "PRESS RETURN TO CONTINUE"
8160 GOSUB 9900
8170 REM INVOKE GRAPHICS MODE
8180 REM SCREEN 1 OR 2 STATEMENT ON IBM PC
8190 REM HGR2 STATEMENT ON APPLE
8200 REM COLOR STATEMENT TO CHOOSE COLOR OPTIONAL
8210 SCREEN 1
8220 REM DETERMINE MIN AND MAX COORDINATES
8230 H5 = X(1)
8240 H6 = X(1)
8250 V5 = Y(1)
8260 V6 = Y(1)
8270 FOR I = 2 TO N
8280 IF X(I) >= H5 THEN 8300
8290 H5 = X(I)
8300 IF X(I) <= H6 THEN 8320
8310 H6 = X(I)
8320 IF Y(I) >= V5 THEN 8340
8330 V5 = Y(I)
8340 IF Y(I) <= V6 THEN 8360
8350 V6 = Y(I)
8360 NEXT I
8370 REM PLOT BOX IN WINDOW
```

```
8380 H1 = H8
8390 V1 = V8
8400 H2 = H9
8410 V2 = V8
8420 GOSUB 8810
8430 H2 = H8
8440 V2 = V9
8450 GOSUB 8810
8460 H1 = H9
8470 V1 = V9
8480 GOSUB 8810
8490 H2 = H9
8500 V2 = V8
8510 GOSUB 8810
8520 REM SET PLOT WINDOW WITHIN BOX
8530 H8 = H8 + M1
8540 V8 = V8 + M1
8550 H9 = H9 - M1
8560 V9 = V9 - M1
8570 REM PLOT OF ACTUAL GRAPH
8580 FOR I = 1 TO N
8590 H1 = INT(((X(I)-H5)/(H6-H5))*(H9-H8) + H8 + .5)
8600 V1 = INT(((V6-Y(I))/(V6-V5))*(V9-V8) + V8 + .5)
8610 H2 = INT(((P(A(I))-H5)/(H6-H5))*(H9-H8) + H8 + .5)
8620 V2 = INT(((V6-Q(A(I)))/(V6-V5))*(V9-V8) + V8 + .5)
8630 GOSUB 8810
8640 NEXT I
8650 REM TERMINATION ROUTINE
8660 REM DETERMINE WHEN RETURN KEY IS PRESSED
8670 REM ON IBM PC USE INKEY$ TO KEEP ANYTHING
8680 REM FROM APPEARING ON SCREEN
8690 A$ = INKEY$
8700 IF A$ = "" THEN 8690
8710 REM ON APPLE USE INPUT STATEMENT
8720 REM INPUT A$
8730 REM RETURN TO TEXT MODE
8740 REM SCREEN 0, WIDTH 80 STATEMENTS ON IBM PC
8750 REM TEXT STATEMENT ON APPLE
8760 SCREEN 0 : WIDTH 80
8770 RETURN
8780 REM SUBROUTINE TO PLOT LINE FROM H1,V1 TO H2,V2
8790 REM LINE (H1,V1)-(H2,V2) ON IBM PC
8800 REM HPLOT H1,V1 TO H2,V2 ON APPLE
8810 LINE (H1,V1)-(H2,V2)
8820 RETURN
```

BASIC Program Standards
and Structure

As indicated in the first chapter, the programs in this book have been written in a very limited subset of BASIC. The purpose of these limitations is to produce programs that will work on most computers under most versions of BASIC. Furthermore, the programs make liberal use of subroutines and are structured in a standard fashion to make the programs easier to understand and modify. This appendix documents the BASIC language standards, describes the standard structure, and provides programming notes to those wishing to modify the programs or adapt them to unusual situations.

BASIC Language Standards

The limited subset of BASIC employed in this book follows common BASIC standards but includes only those features that will work with nearly all versions of the language.

Line numbers are limited to whole numbers in the range from 1 to 9999. Transfers of control from GOTO, IF ... THEN, and GOSUB statements can only be to executable statements, not REM or DIM statements. This is required by a few versions of BASIC and also allows REM statements to be deleted when entering programs. This explains why the REM statements at the head of subroutines begin on unusual line numbers: The GOSUB references the first executable statement in the subroutine.

Arithmetic constants can have the usual forms. They can be expressed as regular numbers, with or without a decimal point, or exponential notation can be used. Thus, 1E6 would be 1×10^6 or 1,000,000. The constant 1E20 is the largest value employed. String constants are enclosed in double quotes, for example, "ABC".

Simple numeric variables are designated by a single letter or by the combination of a letter and a digit. Examples would be A and B1. Subscripted variables are denoted by a single letter and may have one or two dimensions. Array sizes must be specified using positive integer constants in the DIM statements; variables are not used. Subscripts are assumed to start at one; the zero elements of arrays, if present, are not used. No assumption is made that variables are initialized to zero. String variables are designated by a letter plus the dollar sign, such as A$, and are used only for input in the continuation subroutine.

Arithmetic expressions are formed by combining variables, constants, functions, and the arithmetic operators. These operators, in order of precedence, are

- ^   exponentiation
- /   division
- *   multiplication
- −   subtraction
- +   addition

Multiplication and division are at the same level, as are addition and subtraction. Evaluation at the same level is from left to right. Parentheses can be used to alter the order of evaluation. The operation of exponentiation is assumed to correctly handle exponentiation of negative values for integer exponents, that is, negative numbers can be squared.

Relational expressions are used only in IF statements. They are formed by combining two arithmetic expressions with one of the following relational operators:

- =   equal
- <   less than
- >   greater than
- <=   less than or equal to
- >=   greater than or equal to
- <>   not equal

No logical operators are used.

The following statements are used, in these forms:

variable = expression
DIM subscripted variable (positive integer) [,...]
END
FOR variable = expression TO expr [STEP expr]
GOSUB line number
GOTO line number
IF relational expression THEN line number

INPUT <u>variable</u>
NEXT <u>variable</u>
PRINT <u>expression</u> [; <u>expression</u> ...]
REM <u>comment</u>
RETURN

The first statement, the assignment statement, optionally allows the use of LET, but this is not used here. Only the simplest form of the IF statement is used, with branching to the line number if the relational expression is true. PRINT statements use semicolons as separators (and hanging semicolons as terminators when needed). TAB functions may be used in the PRINT statements. END is always the final statement in the program and is the point for the normal termination of the program.
Only six functions are used in the programs:

ABS(<u>expression</u>)	absolute value
EXP(<u>expression</u>)	exponential
INT(<u>expression</u>)	integer portion (truncation)
LOG(<u>expression</u>)	natural logarithm
SQR(<u>expression</u>)	square root
TAB(<u>expression</u>)	move to column indicated, in PRINT statement

The spacing of printed output is controlled using semicolons and the TAB function in PRINT statements. Numeric values are assumed to be printed with leading and trailing blanks to provide separation from adjacent fields. Use of the TAB function assumes the first column is numbered one, though existence of a zero column will not cause problems. In printing numeric values that can assume arbitrary values, print fields 14 columns wide are provided, with the assumption made that these can handle any value to be printed. In general, printed output is limited to a maximum of 40 columns per line. Several programs allow the option of wider tables by assigning an appropriate value to the variable F in the initialization section. An 80-column display can handle five fields, so $F = 5$ can be assigned. Other numbers of columns can also be specified, as desired.

The programs assume video display screens with at least 24 lines. The printing of output is paused accordingly to keep output from scrolling off the top of the screen. Systems with screens displaying fewer lines of text will have output scrolling off the screen for the larger problems.

Program Structure

All of the programs in this book have been organized in a similar fashion. This common structure has been designed to make the programs easier to follow and understand and to simplify the process of modifying the programs for custom applications.

The main routine comes first, always beginning at line 10 with the program identification. The variables used in the program are defined, arrays are dimensioned, and any special constants used in the program are assigned to variables. Overall control of the program is handled by the main routine, which presents the user with options and directs the flow of the program accordingly. All of the major functions—input, computation, and output—are carried out by subroutines called from the main routine. Normal termination occurs with a branch to the last statement, END, at line 9999.

Three distinct types of subroutines are used in every program for data input, model computation, and output. All subroutines begin with their first executable statement (at which they are always called) on line numbers that are even multiples of 500. The various types of subroutines are always located as follows:

1000 – 3500	Model computation subroutines
4000 – 6500	Data input subroutines
7000 – 9500	Output subroutines

The model computation subroutines implement the algorithms required by the planning models. Only computations are performed; these subroutines do no input or output. The data input subroutines obtain the data interactively from the user (via INPUT statements). The entire process of data input is handled by these subroutines, except for the entry of program options and isolated values in the main routines. The only printing by the input subroutines is of the prompts required for the data entry. The output subroutines handle all of the printing of data to the screen. These routines print out the information that has been entered as well as the results from the model computations.

In some instances, subroutines in one section will call another subroutine in the same section to handle a procedure that is used repeatedly. Subroutines never make calls to other subroutines of different types, in different sections.

Every program includes a subroutine at line 9900 which is called to pause the printing of output to the display to prevent text from scrolling off the top of the screen. This routine simply prints the prompt CONTINUE and then includes an INPUT statement to a string variable A$. Any response to this—including a simple Return on most systems—continues operation. A RETURN statement directs operation back to the calling location, allowing the continued printing of output.

Programming Notes

This final section provides some observations that may be helpful in implementing the programs on various microcomputers and versions of BASIC and in modifying the programs to work in different ways. It is impossible to cover all versions of BASIC and all desired modifications. This brief section can only provide a few ideas for some of the most common concerns.

All of the input and output in these programs takes place through the standard user input and output devices. Except for those with printing terminals, occasionally still used with timesharing systems, all of the information will be printed to the video display. The most frequently desired modification will be a means for generating hard-copy output from a printer. Methods for directing output to the printer vary widely in different versions of BASIC, so it was impossible to include this feature in the standard programs. Some systems use special statements to redirect output from the screen to the printer (or to produce output to both), some require a different statement be used (such as the Microsoft BASIC LPRINT). It may even be necessary (on some timesharing systems), to direct the output to a disk file for later printing.

The program structure facilitates the making of modifications to obtain printed output, since all output is produced by the subroutines beginning at line 7000 and above. These subroutines print not only the results but the data entered by the user, thus providing a complete record of the problem and its solution. Appropriate printed output can be obtained by modifying these subroutines to print to the printer. The remainder of the program operations will still occur in their usual fashion on the video display. All PRINT statements in these subroutines could be changed to LPRINT statements or to PRINT # statements to print to a file (the file will probably require a previous OPEN statement). If output redirection statements are used, the statement to direct output to the printer can be added as the first line of each output subroutine and the statement to direct output back to the video display can be added at the end, before the RETURN. The choice of procedure will depend on the facilities available in a particular version of BASIC.

When the output is being printed, there is no need to pause the output using the continuation subroutine at line 9900. Calls to this subroutine could be deleted from the output subroutines. Alternately, the pause output subroutine itself could be disabled by changing line 9900 to RETURN, yielding a null, do-nothing subroutine.

Some microcomputers include screen printing capabilities invoked from the keyboard. Such a feature could, of course, be used to produce hard-copy output. As the programs currently stand, however, all of the output following one pause may not necessarily scroll off the screen before the next pause. Repeated screen prints would thus have some information repeated and would generally be messy. This problem can be readily solved, however, by inserting statements to clear the screen at appropriate points throughout the programs. This would also make the display more attractive even when screen printing is not used. Clear-screen statements have different formats and some versions of BASIC lack them entirely, so they could not be included in the programs as presented.

The interactive entry of data from the keyboard may not always be the ideal procedure. This procedure is cumbersome and error- prone with large volumes of data. The data may already be in machine-readable form. The same data may be needed for repeated use in numerous operating sessions. Thus, it may be desirable to modify the programs for other forms of data input. Generally, this will involve reading data from disk files, although READ and DATA statements could also be used. All of the data input is handled by the subroutines in the range from 4000 to 6500. It should not be difficult to determine by examining these routines the functions performed—which data are entered into which variables—since the user prompts are part of the routines. Modification then involves the writing of replacement code to read the data from a file into the appropriate variables. Since the program prints out the data entered, a check is always available on the performance of the alternate data entry routines.

While there are variations, the programs generally include data input subroutines both for the entry of the initial data (which is usually the most voluminous) and for the specification of a set of computations (which often may be repeated). The Facility Location on a Plane Model program provides a simple example. The first data entry subroutine obtains the coordinates and weights for all of the demand points, which are then used for all analyses. The other data entry subroutine obtains the number of facilities to be located and their starting locations. In modifying data input routines, one is most likely to read the initial data (in this example, the information on demand points) from an external file. The problem-specification data entry (the facilities to be located) would continue to be entered interactively using the original subroutine(s).

The Cohort-Survival Model program poses special issues, because it is possible to return to any of the data input subroutines to change (enter new) information. Obviously, if a subroutine were modified to read the data from a file on the disk, one could not return to enter new data. Awareness of the problem should make it possible to establish appropriate procedures.

The maximum sizes of the problems that can be handled by these programs is limited by the dimensioning of the arrays. These values were selected to limit the problems to a size so that information printed in tables did not scroll off the top of a 24-line video display. Exceptions are the two facility location programs that will automatically break longer tables into segments for display. To use the programs for larger problems, the values in the DIMension statements need to be increased. The only limit is available memory. Except for the facility location programs, output will then scroll off the screen. The user has three options: quick use of a pause output command (if available) from the keyboard; rewriting output routines to print results in segments (as in the last two programs); or reliance on hard-copy output (which totally avoids the problem). Since larger problems produce greater volumes of information, printed output may be the most appropriate—and easiest—solution.

In using the programs for such large problems, the interactive data input provided for in the programs is likely to become unwieldy. Reading the data from disk files will be far more satisfactory, suggesting the modification discussed earlier.

The programs have been written in the limited subset of BASIC so that they might run, without modification, on nearly any system. Nevertheless, variations in BASIC are so great that some problems still might be encountered, causing minor difficulties in operation or even complete failure of the programs on some systems. Those problems known to the author are discussed here, and suggestions are offered for dealing with them.

Obviously the very limited, "tiny" BASIC's common in the early days of microcomputers cannot handle these programs. Integer BASIC's lacking floating-point processing capabilities cannot carry out the computations required. Nor can versions of BASIC with severe limits on the handling of arrays—such as the original TRS-80 Level I BASIC—run these programs. Presumably no one understanding these simple BASIC's would even attempt to use these programs on such systems. They are now becoming less common in any case.

Any BASIC lacking required statements, functions, or operations would present problems. Of the otherwise full-featured floating-point BASIC's known to the author, Atari BASIC presents a problem due to the absence of the TAB function. Using such a BASIC would require the rewriting of virtually all of the PRINT statements, substituting spaces for TAB functions and would still be less than completely satisfactory. A version of Microsoft BASIC is available for Atari computers, however, that will handle these programs without problems.

Lack of sufficient memory could be a problem on some systems with limited RAM. Using Microsoft BASIC-80 under the CP/M operating system, the programs themselves require anywhere from 4.7K to 8.7K of RAM. To execute, the space needed for the programs plus variable storage ranges from 5.4K to 18.5K, though only two exceed 10.8K—the Double-Constrained Gravity Model and the Facility Location on a Network Model programs. Requirements can vary widely from system to system depending on the manner in which both program statements and variables are stored.

The need for RAM can be easily reduced in two ways: First, the REMark statements can be deleted from the programs. Since REMark statement line numbers are never the targets of program jumps—from GOTO's, GOSUB's, or IF . . . THEN's—this will cause no problems. Furthermore, the sizes of the arrays can be reduced by lowering the values in the DIMension statements. This will, of course, decrease the program capacity but will allow operation with less memory.

Other problems may not affect the ability of the programs to operate on various systems but may create minor problems during that operation. The programs assume that all numeric values are printed with one or more leading and trailing blanks that will separate the numbers from adjacent text. Some versions of BASIC— most notably Applesoft BASIC—do not insert these spaces on output. Thus, a print statement such as PRINT "ORIGIN"; I would run the string and number together without a space: ORIGIN1. This problem is not fatal, just aesthetically unsatisfying. The difficulty can be readily solved by inserting spaces into the strings adjoining the numeric output.

Another assumption made was that all numeric output would fit within 14-column print fields. Versions of BASIC with greater precision—such as CBASIC—can print longer numeric values. This is especially likely for repeating decimals from division, such as $10/3 = 3.3333333333....$. When longer numeric values are printed, all of the following output on that line will be misplaced. The correct values will be printed out, but they will be out of position. Correction requires either the expansion of the print fields beyond 14 columns to accommodate the longest values that can be printed or the addition of appropriate rounding routines to keep all output within the appropriate limits.

One final, minor problem was encountered with CBASIC that might also exist in some other versions of BASIC. The programs use the exponentiation operator (^) for squaring values. CBASIC allows exponentiation only of positive numbers (even for integer exponents) and reports a run-time error for each attempt to square a negative number. It does automatically take the absolute value of the number and then does the exponentiation, producing the correct results. The only real problem is that the output becomes littered with the error messages. The problem is readily solved either by using the absolute value function in the program or by squaring the number by multiplication by itself.

Index